Love and Justice

LOVE
AND
JUSTICE

Selections from the Shorter Writings
of
REINHOLD NIEBUHR

Edited by D. B. ROBERTSON

Westminster/John Knox Press
Louisville, Kentucky

This book is printed on acid-free paper that meets the American National Stan-dards Institute Z39.48 standard. ∞

Published by Westminster/John Knox Press
Louisville, Kentucky

PRINTED IN THE UNITED STATES OF AMERICA

9 8 7 6 5 4 3 2 1

Library of Congress Cataloging-in-Publication Data

Niebuhr, Reinhold, 1892–1971.
  Love and justice : selections from the shorter writings of
Reinhold Niebuhr / edited by D. B. Robertson.
       p.   cm. — (Library of theological ethics)
  Previously published: Philadelphia : Westminster Press, 1957.
  Includes index.
  ISBN 0-664-25322-9 (alk. paper)

  1. Christianity and justice. 2. Church and social problems.
3. Church and the world. I. Title. II. Series.
BR115.J8N54 1992
241′.622—dc20   92-3167

CONTENTS

LIBRARY OF THEOLOGICAL ETHICS
General Editors' Introduction

The field of theological ethics possesses in its literature an abundant inheritance concerning religious convictions and the moral life, critical issues, methods, and moral problems. The Library of Theological Ethics is designed to present a selection of important texts that would otherwise be unavailable for scholarly purposes and classroom use. The series will engage the question of what it means to think theologically and ethically. It is offered in the conviction that sustained dialogue with our predecessors serves the interests of responsible contemporary reflection. Our more immediate aim in offering it, however, is to enable scholars and teachers to make more extensive use of classic texts as they train new generations of theologians, ethicists, and ministers.

The volumes included in the Library will comprise a variety of types. Some will make available English-language texts and translations that have fallen out of print; others will present new translations of texts previously unavailable in English. Still others will offer anthologies or collections of significant statements about problems and themes of special importance. We hope that each volume will encourage contemporary theological ethicists to remain in conversation with the rich and diverse heritage of their discipline.

Robin W. Lovin
Douglas F. Ottati
William Schweiker

PREFACE

THE IMPORTANCE OF THE PROBLEM OF LOVE AND justice in Reinhold Niebuhr's thought is well known. It is in general the problem of the relationship between the Christian faith and the ethical life of men as individuals and as groups. In his books Dr. Niebuhr has explored the many angles, subtleties, heights, and depths of the problems of man and society. Where he actually stands on given social issues, and where he sees the points of contact between Christian love and the multiple ramifications of justice — these factors are best seen in his occasional writings.

Some changes in Niebuhr's thinking in social ethics will be evident over the period covered by these articles, though it has not been a primary purpose in the choice of the selections to show the various stages in the development of his social ethic. The major purpose has been to select articles that illustrate the richness and variety of his analyses of love and justice, to show the points at which he insists that positive decisions and actions are possible, even imperative, for the Christian, and to underline his characteristic approach to typical ethical problems. Even though there has been change and development in his thought and change of emphasis at some points, there has also been a rather notable consistency of approach, particularly since the late 1930's.

This volume brings together a group of selected essays on some of the many issues that have engaged Dr. Niebuhr's attention over a period of more than twenty-five years. The articles in Part I are intended to give some introduction to his views on love and justice and may be particularly useful to those not very familiar with his other writings. At the beginning of Parts II and III, and a few of the subdivisions, one or so of the more general essays dealing with particular subjects is included. Otherwise the articles are organized in chronological order within the various sections. Part IV, devoted solely to the pacifist issue, includes a goodly number of articles in chronological order. While there is considerable repetition of argument here, it was thought that the importance of this issue in Niebuhr's social ethic warranted rather full coverage.

The magazine articles are presented exactly as they were originally printed. The only exceptions are occasional changes in punctuation and word usage made by The Westminster Press copyeditors in accordance with their style rules.

I should like to express my thanks to the editors of the following journals for permission to print articles which they have carried: *The American Scholar, The Atlantic Monthly, The Christian Century, The Messenger, The Nation, The New Leader, The Progressive, Religion in Life,* and *Theology.* To Dr. Niebuhr thanks are due for his willingness to permit the use of articles from *Radical Religion, Christianity and Society, The World Tomorrow,* and *Christianity and Crisis.*

D. B. Robertson

INTRODUCTION

"THE STRUGGLE FOR JUSTICE IS AS PROFOUND A REV-elation of the possibilities of historical existence as the quest for truth. In some respects it is even more revealing because it engages all human vitalities and powers more obviously than the intellectual quest." (*The Nature and Destiny of Man*, II, p. 244.) This statement suggests a (if not *the*) primary area of emphasis in Reinhold Niebuhr's thought. The relationship between love and justice has been the major problem for Niebuhr in his elaboration of a social ethic, and he makes a special point of explaining why it must be a "social ethic." The point is important ". . . in the sense that it [an ethic] must give guidance not only in terms of the ultimate possibilities of life, for which sacrificial and forgiving love is the norm, but must also come to terms with the problem of establishing tolerable harmonies of life on all levels of community." ("The Problem of a Protestant Social Ethic," *Union Seminary Quarterly Review*, November, 1959, pp. 1–2.) In assessing his life and thought in his latest book, Niebuhr reaffirms the point in these words: "I might define this conviction [that a realist conception of human nature should be made the servant of an ethic of progressive justice] as the guiding principle throughout my mature life of the relation of religious responsibility to political affairs." (*Man's Nature and His Communities*, pp. 24–25.) As John Bennett says, "There is no more fruitful analysis in all his ethical writings than his discussion of this problem." (The Library of Living Theology, II, p. 58.) The richness of Niebuhr's understanding and discussion of human motivation and group relationships appears not only in the direct and specific treatment of the subject of love and justice, it comes also in his analysis of issues related to peace and justice, order and justice, power and

9

justice, law and justice, equality and justice, rights and justice, security and justice, prudence and justice, and in other combinations. So, also, as this collection makes clear, is the meaning of love a persistent theme in relationship to justice, to law, to prudence, etc. The importance of the problem for Niebuhr is amply illustrated in most of his writings; however, the centrality and the persistence of the great theme is more obvious in the great mass of articles he has published in dozens of magazines and papers through the years.*

CHRISTIAN LOVE

Love is the "basic law of life." Love on the human side is an expression of man's distinguishing characteristic: his freedom. In fact, "Love is the only final structure of freedom" (No. 5, this volume). Niebuhr has consistently used the word "love" in his ethical analyses to mean *agape*, the "immortal Love, forever full, forever flowing free." It is the out-going, unmeasured love of Christ on the cross. Niebuhr disagrees with Anders Nygren (*Agape and Eros,* Westminster, 1953), however, in making the contrast between *agape* and the doctrines of love (*eros*) in classical thought too absolute. He notes that Jesus Himself ". . . does not regard the contrast between natural human love and the divine *agape* as absolute." (*The Nature and Destiny of Man,* II, n. 16, p. 84.)

Niebuhr's view of the relationship between love and justice was suggested in one of his early formulations by the paradoxical phrase

---

* For those unfamiliar with Niebuhr's thought, a good introduction to aspects of his discussion of love and justice, as well as to his thought as a whole, is to be found in Volume II of The Library of Living Theology (*Reinhold Niebuhr, His Religious, Social, and Political Thought,* edited by C. W. Kegley and R. W. Bretall, Macmillan, 1956). Of special value for the subject covered here are the pieces by John Bennett and Paul Ramsey. I am particularly indebted to Dr. Bennett's essay. The relationship of love and justice to "natural law" doctrines is discussed in many places in Dr. Niebuhr's works. In addition to the article included in this collection (No. 5), longer treatments are to be found in Chapter 10 of *Christian Realism and Political Problems, The Nature and Destiny of Man,* I, Chapter 10, and "The Problem of a Protestant Social Ethic," *Union Seminary Quarterly Review,* November, 1959. Recent expressions of a more positive appreciation of aspects of the Roman Catholic natural law tradition are to be found in Dr. Niebuhr's Preface to Maurice Cranston's *What Are Human Rights?* (Basic Books, 1963), in a chapter entitled "The Development of a Social Ethic in the Ecumenical Movement," in R. M. Mackie and C. C. West, editors, *The Sufficiency of God* (Westminster, 1963), and in Dr. Niebuhr's book *Man's Nature and His Communities,* Introduction.

"impossible possibility." (*An Interpretation of Christian Ethics*, Chapter 4, entitled "The Relevance of an Impossible Ethical Ideal.") To say that love is an "impossible possibility" is Niebuhr's way of asserting the ever-present relevance of love in human affairs, while at the same time pointing to its difficulties. Love is relevant in terms of judgment upon all that we do, even our very best. It is also relevant (possible) in terms of motive. It is possible in varying degrees to approximate love in human life, particularly if the corruption of self-righteousness can be avoided in the process.

At the same time, Niebuhr intends to underline by these words the impossibility of love as a wholly adequate social ethic. Love is the final or highest possibility in man's relationship to man; it is the peak of the fulfillment of man's nature as a social being. But down in the valleys of human experience "the common currency of the moral life is constituted by the 'nicely calculated less and more' of the relatively good and the relatively evil." (*Ibid.,* p 103.)

The expression of love in human relationships, then, is not, as Niebuhr often insists, a "simple possibility." Man does not for the most part love disinterestedly, because he is both finite and sinful. Christ on the cross reveals love in its perfect form and symbol. Here is revealed at the same time God's love and history's meaningfulness, as well as man's capacity for lovelessness and destructiveness. The Christian ethic cannot be simply love, for men live in history, and "perfect love" in history has not fared well. According to Niebuhr, it is this failure to understand the social dimensions of *agape* that has been the source of confusion in modern discussions of ethics.

Niebuhr's reputation as a theologian is to a considerable degree related to his elaboration of the "Biblical understanding" of man and history and his polemics against what he has seen as the liberal and utopian corruption of this understanding. He has explored the fallacies and weaknesses of both secular liberalism and the "sentimental version" of the Christian faith wherein the doctrine of love is transformed into an overly simplified moralism in which we "ought to love everybody"; wholly eliminate strife from social life, or act as though it did not exist; and "be like Jesus." Judaism and Catholicism have escaped most of the limitations of a pure "love ethic," the weakness of both sectarianism and much of liberal Protestantism. This extreme love ethic Niebuhr characterized in a sermon recently at Union Theological Seminary as appropriate for "mystics, monastics, martyrs, and mothers!" On the other hand, it should be noted immediately that he has opposed as "equally absurd" the position of the "realists" and the orthodox Christians who qualify too rigidly, or destroy the relevance of the love ideal by dwelling too exclusively upon the implications of "depravity." But the brunt of Niebuhr's attack, especially after the early 1930's, has been borne by the "liberals" and "utopians." The liberal code, Niebuhr believed at one point, could be summarized in six major propositions:

1. That injustice is caused by ignorance and will yield to education and greater intelligence.
2. That civilization is becoming gradually more moral and that it is a sin to challenge either the inevitability or the efficacy of gradualness.
3. That the character of individuals rather than social systems and arrangements is the guarantee of justice in society.
4. That appeals to love, justice, good will, and brotherhood are bound to be efficacious in the end. If they have not been so to date we must have more appeals to love, justice, good will, and brotherhood.
5. That goodness makes for happiness and that the increasing knowledge of this fact will overcome human selfishness and greed.
6. That wars are stupid and can therefore only be caused by people who are more stupid than those who recognize the stupidity of war. ("The Blindness of Liberalism," *Radical Religion,* Autumn, 1936.)

These propositions were expanded and elaborated in later writings; but such convictions, Niebuhr argued, have been the enemy of clarity and of effectiveness in social ethics.

Words similar to these often appear in Niebuhr's works: "I find it impossible to envisage a society of pure love as long as man is man" ("Must We Do Nothing," *Christian Century,* March 30, 1932). Mutual love is possible in varying degrees in many types of human relationships, particularly where the relationships are personal. But "pure love" cannot be a possible foundation for an adequate social ethic because of man's sin, which an adequate ethic must take into account. "Every definition of justice presupposes sin as a given reality. It is only because life is in conflict with life, because of sinful self-interest, that we are required carefully to define schemes of justice which prevent one life from taking advantage of another." (No. 5.) A responsible approach to social problems requires a sensitive and intelligent regard for man's tendency to think more highly of himself and his cause than he ought. A responsible approach to social problems also concerns itself with the structures of justice which may help to temper the dangers of excessive concentrations of power. Love can never, even in the most intimate groups, be a perfect alternative to the "pushing and shoving" which characterize the struggle for justice. The political structures and pressures are perpetually necessary.

A note should be entered here about what Niebuhr has lately referred to as "...a rather unpardonable pedagogical error in *The Nature and Destiny of Man.*" (*Man's Nature and His Communities*, p. 23.) His theology prompted him "to define the persistence and universality of man's self-regard as 'original sin,'" and while Niebuhr believes this designation to be historically and symbolically correct, he sees the "error" in trying "to challenge modern optimism with the theological doctrine which was anathema to modern culture." (*Ibid.*) His use of this traditional symbol allowed his critics, therefore, to picture him "as a regressive religious authoritarian, caught in the toils of an ancient legend." (*Ibid.*, p. 24.) Even more important, he thinks, is that his use of traditional symbols led many "realists," who (including many political philosophers) agreed generally with his views in the Gifford Lectures, to go to considerable lengths to explain that their agreement did not include his theological presuppositions. He therefore intends to correct this error by discussing the "same human nature" by the use of "more sober symbols." Dr. Niebuhr concludes the point, however, by saying that he still thinks that "the 'London Times Literary Supplement' was substantially correct when it wrote some years ago: 'The doctrine of original sin is the only empirically verifiable doctrine of the Christian faith.'" (*Ibid.*, p. 24.)

JUSTICE

Justice, Niebuhr says, is an "approximation of brotherhood under conditions of sin" (*The Nature and Destiny of Man*, II, p. 254). Justice is also characterized as action in which "God causeth the wrath of man to praise him." Niebuhr has on occasion referred to justice as the plumbing between the ground and the superstructure (love). Sometimes he calls it "second-rate Christianity," of which, he emphasizes, we need a great deal. It is again described in terms of some viable balance of power, though a mere balance of power is not enough. "Imaginative justice" is nearest to love, but even prudence springs finally from it. "A genuine charity is the father of prudence," Niebuhr wrote, in an article discussing racial conflict (No. 31), "for genuine love does not propose abstract schemes of justice that leave the human factor out of account." The "desire for justice is one form of love," he writes elsewhere, not perhaps the highest form but one that cannot be despised." ("The Problem of a Protestant Social Ethic," *Union Seminary Quarterly Review,* November, 1959, p. 4.)

The "regulative principle" of justice, in Niebuhr's discussion, is clearly equality, or "it is the best nexus between love and justice." "Equality as a pinnacle of the ideal of justice implicitly points toward love as the final norm of justice" (*The Nature and Destiny of Man,* II, p. 254). The fact that the principle of equality is perpetually recurring in varieties of social theory is enough to refute the consistently pessimistic view of human nature. It proves that man not only has some capacity to act in other than his own interest, but neither in his theorizing does he "simply use social theory to rationalize [his] own interest." (*Ibid.*)

The ideal of equality is a valuable and necessary standard to hold over social inequalities and power disparities of all kinds, from those in family relations to those in international relations. Absolute equality is not a meaningful social goal. This is true because there are certain inevitable inequalities associated with function in society and because actual social institutions or historical circumstances make the abstract ideal meaningless when it is used in an "all or nothing" sense. One must recognize the moral obligation to choose between very relative degrees of justice in practice, though no vested interest should take any comfort from this point.

Of the traditional values associated with the "natural law" doctrines of the West—justice, equality, order, etc.—Niebuhr has given most of his attention in his writings to the first two, though not typically in a context of natural law thinking. Order, however, he recognizes as a necessary value in the partnership, for ultimately without its consistent, if relative, presence all other values are jeopardized. The present revolutionary zeal of Chinese Communism carries with it, amongst other things, the peril of chaos for many parts of the world where unjust order (tyranny) has prevailed. This fact, says Niebuhr, should be a vivid reminder to us of the perpetual problem of political order and at the same time should underscore the special difficulties faced today in balancing justice and order without falling into worldwide nuclear destruction. Because of the revolutionary elements in our world and concomitantly the problem of establishing a viable order in many of the newer nations, we are reminded that "communities, both parochial and international, are bound to place order first in their hierarchy of values. But justice comes as a quick second in the political hierarchy, because unsatisfied desires are bound to challenge every order, whatever may be its prestige, power, or force." ("Some Things I Have Learned," *Saturday Review,* Nov. 6, 1965.)

Niebuhr credits John Milton with establishing "liberty" as a partner to "equality" as one of the regulative principles of justice. It was Milton, he says, who "established the true relation of Protestant individualism to an open society." (*Man's Nature and His Communities,* p. 26.) Actually, as Niebuhr himself acknowledges elsewhere (*ibid.,* pp. 24–25; and for example, in *Pious and Secular America,* pp. 68 ff., and in "The Problem of a Protestant Social Ethic," *Union Seminary Quarterly Review,* November, 1959, p. 5), Milton was by no means the sole architect here. The lesser-known radicals in Cromwell's army—left-wing Calvinists and sectarian perfectionists included—not only wrote but acted on the principle or principles—including the notion of a duty of resistance to tyranny, and an obvious passion for liberty and justice. This combination Niebuhr says in fact, "is the only form of Protestant social ethic which I find congenial to present perplexities." (*Ibid.*) Niebuhr sees, perhaps more so after his years of work with the ecumenical movement, the necessity, in the amalgam of the "open society," to recognize the part played by ". . . those aspects of truth in the political policy of the English Reformation, particularly of the Elizabethan settlement, so clearly elaborated in Hooker's *Laws of Ecclesiastical Polity.*" (Mackie and West, *op. cit.,* p. 119.)

A distinguishing element in Niebuhr's contribution to the discussion of social ethics is the "moral man and immoral society" theme running through his writings. The thesis he elaborated in his book by this title (in 1932) was already suggested in some of his writings, and it has not been a passing phase of his thought. The thesis is that "a sharp distinction must be drawn between the moral and social behavior of individuals and of social groups, national, racial, and economic; and that this distinction justifies and necessitates political policies which a purely individualistic ethic must always find embarrassing" (*Moral Man and Immoral Society,* p. xi). Niebuhr argued that one of the greatest points of confusion in contemporary ethical discussions was the belief that what the individual conscience perceives, and what the individual is able to achieve singly, can be simply regarded as a possibility for social groups. This view lacks the realism about man, especially in social groups, required by an adequate ethic. The will to power, he believes, is to some degree a threat to the best of human relationships. The larger the group, the more complicated the problem. "The full evil of human finitude and sin is most vividly revealed in conflicts between national communities." (*An Interpretation of Christian Ethics*, p. 125.) But evil is evident on all levels of life. It was the necessity to deal with this problem that led Niebuhr to state the point too sharply—more sharply, in fact, than his own position called for. A young friend recently suggested that in the light of the facts, and Niebuhr's more consistent realism as applied to individuals as well as to groups, a better title may have been *The Not So Moral Man in His Less Moral Communities* (*Man's Nature and His Communities*, p. 22.).

LOVE, JUSTICE, AND "NATURAL LAW"

In contrast to the traditions which have developed social ethical systems on the basis of "natural law," Niebuhr has argued that "it is not possible to state a universally valid concept of justice from any particular sociological locus in history." (No. 5.) Those who have attempted to do it too exclusively by way of natural law arguments have inevitably incorporated culturally conditioned or contingent factors into presumed absolute and universal concepts. Thus the Roman Catholic view has harbored feudal elements, and eighteenth-century natural law had bourgeois accents. Provisional definitions are necessary, but it must be recognized, Niebuhr emphasizes, that these definitions are provisional— not absolute or fixed. Otherwise, along with other weaknesses of such systems, the unique and the possible in each new situation will be missed.

More recently Niebuhr has expressed an appreciation of the natural law tradition in its contribution to a contemporary social ethic. Initially, apparently, it was through engagements with Anglican spokesmen in the Ecumenical Movement that the "creative" possibilities in natural law for Protestantism began to be appreciated. This emphasis Niebuhr sees as creative for two reasons: One, "because it typifies the quest for the most authoritative general norm." In the second place, "natural law conceptions invariably emphasize justice, rather than order, as the basic norm of political and economic life." (Mackie and West, *op. cit.*, pp. 121–122; 125.) This ethic, again perhaps the greatest contribution of the ecumenical movement, is still "pragmatic" and relative in the sense that it recognizes that the unpredictability of historical events makes "fixed norms dangerous." On the other hand, pragmatism alone degenerates into opportunism, so that "modern Christian pragmatism" is saved from opportunism "by certain definite principles.... These principles have to do with the relation of freedom and equality in the determination of justice." ("The Problem of a Protestant Social Ethic," *Union Seminary Quarterly Review,* November, 1959, p. 9.)

As for the Roman church and its doctrines of natural law, Niebuhr notes that his increasing admiration has "had the same socially pragmatic prompting" as his long-time appreciation of Judaism. As against some forms of Protestantism, he now has "a new appreciation of the fact that a great religious tradition, emancipated from the organic collectivism of the Middle Ages, has been able creatively to help modern technical cultures of the West to solve the moral problems of industrial collectivism." (*Man's Nature and His Communities,* p. 19.) Beyond that, Catholic universalism and its characteristic sense of justice have provided the base for creativity in the civil-rights movement, sadly lacking in so much of Protestantism. (*Ibid.,* p. 20.)

Niebuhr makes clear, though, that he has not qualified his criticism of moral theories based on natural law, "drawn from a metaphysical base," because they are too rigid. He has also been critical of the certainty, especially claimed by spokesmen of the Roman church in the past, about the content of natural law ethics. The condemnation of contraception is an example Niebuhr has frequently used, though of course this whole question is being seriously reexamined by the church today.

It would, in any case, be a mistake to assume on the basis of his publicly expressed appreciation of the tradition that Niebuhr has embraced natural law doctrines as such (or, as one writer put it, because of the teleological element in Niebuhr's thought, he is "a natural law thinker despite himself." (Lindbeck, G. A., *Notre Dame Natural Law Forum,* 1959, p. 149.)) For, to refute legal positivism, or a pure "love ethic" as adequate bases for a social ethic on the one hand, is not to flee to an ethic of principles or of natural law on the other, if by the latter is meant something built into the universe and that man draws upon by deduction for his guidance in moral decisions and social ethics.

"Ideals," "natural laws," "middle axioms," or "common moral standards" may reflect the "moral aspirations" of an age or a culture. They may reflect, as against moral relativism, what it means to be genuinely human. These standards therefore cannot be seen as arbitrary simply because they are culturally conditioned. (Preface to Cranston, *op. cit.*) Principles of justice "transcend the positive enactments of historic states"; they are not so specifically spelled out and defined as positive law, but they are more "specific than the law of love." These principles of justice, says Niebuhr, "are generated in the customs and mores of communities; and they may rise to universal norms which seem to have their source not in particular communities but in the common experience of mankind." (*Christian Realism and Political Problems*, p. 148.)

Obviously Niebuhr never worked out a very systematic epistemology; nor has he spelled out an order of casuistry. These would run counter to his understanding of man and society and of God's ways of working in history. The relationship of love to justice is complex and dynamic. But Niebuhr has come more and more to believe that to take seriously and responsibly the two Great Commandments means being open to "the truth," from whatever source it may come. If there is no neat system of casuistry to be found in his writings, the following statement may be taken as a sort of Niebuhrian pre-casuistry or way of describing the essential ingredients for a social ethic:

> Naturally an adequate Christian social ethic must avail itself of non-Biblical instruments of calculation, chiefly a rational calculation of competing rights and interests and an empirical analysis of the structures of nature, the configurations of history and the complexities of a given situation in which decisions must be made. Since the third century the Christian Church has availed itself of classical and other philosophies and disciplines for this task. Radical Reformation thought, including Barth's Neo-Reformation theology, has sought to dispense with all non-Biblical sources of judgment. But the result is bound to create caprice in the field of ethical judgment. . . . A vital Christian faith must undertake a constant commerce with the culture of its day, borrowing and rejecting according to its best judgment. ("The Problem of a Protestant Social Ethic," *Union Seminary Quarterly Review*, November, 1959, p. 11.)

The "Gloomy Dean" (so-called because of his pre-World War II predictions) is reported to have said later, "Things turned out worse than I thought." Niebuhr is not known to have made such a statement. However, his presumed "pessimism," or "defeatism," (related somehow to what he has called his "pedagogical error") attacked particularly since the publication of *Moral Man and Immoral Society,* has turned out not to be overdrawn. Certainly today there is no need for Dr. Niebuhr or his friends to bother with an attempt at an "apologia" on the point. His own life and work are witness enough to belie the appellation. At a point when history supported little optimism, Niebuhr could remind his fellow Christians and countrymen that:

> The Christian faith cannot be defeatist. It sees men's sin and the tragedies of life. It knows the depths of human degradation; and the long hard road to the City of God. But also it sees men in the strength of God rising to the need and the struggle, confident, victorious in spirit. ("The Crisis Deepens," *Christianity and Crisis,* May 5, 1941.)

A Note on a Few Particular Issues

Dr. Niebuhr has continued his searching thought and writing in the decade since the latest of these articles were written. Book-length writings on national and international problems have been published. Many occasional pieces have also appeared. A few notes on some of the particular issues may serve to bring up to date Dr. Niebuhr's current positions. The Niebuhr sources are both written and partially from Dr. Niebuhr himself directly.

The Race Issue

Niebuhr's concern for justice as a young pastor in Detroit included not only the Ford workers but also the scandalous treatment of the Negro. He was appointed chairman of the mayor's first interracial commission. In retrospect he does not evaluate the commission's efforts very highly. After going to Union Theological Seminary in New York in 1928, he continued his work with groups, some of the work involving more direct social action than was the case in Detroit; but, of course, it was pale in comparison to the dimensions of the "revolution" of the past decade.

There are apparently many who are uninformed about Dr. Niebuhr's precise views on the question of "civil disobedience" as a strategy in the struggle for social justice. The fact is that as early as 1932 he put in writing (*Moral Man and Immoral Society,* pp. 252–254) the suggestion that the Negro in America could never free himself from the accumulated injustices by simply depending on the "love and goodness" of the white man's heart. He specifically suggests that Gandhi's methods be used to force the hand of the white populace, suggesting boycotts and even the non-payment of taxes when necessary. The general point made was that "non-violent coercion and resistance . . . is a type of coercion which offers the largest opportunities for a harmonious relationship with the moral and rational factors in social life. It does not destroy the process of a moral and rational adjustment of interest completely during the course of resistance." (*Ibid.,* p. 251.) However, this qualification is entered: for all of the advantages of non-violent methods, "they must be pragmatically considered in the light of circumstances." (p. 252.)

In terms of his own personal involvement in social action, the simple fact is that in the last decade and more since racial injustice has been most hotly engaged, Dr. Niebuhr's health has not permitted him to be involved at all in social action. Otherwise, he says, he would most certainly have been involved in some particular cases where civil disobedience was clearly present, and he would have taken his chances of getting arrested and tried in court along with the group.

As for the current situation, Dr. Niebuhr believes, as he believed in 1932, that resistance and coercion by the Negro must be employed in the achievement of justice, and while he is no pacifist, he believes that Martin Luther King's position is right. King's "sentimentality" Niebuhr discusses critically, but he still believes that Martin Luther King is "the most creative Protestant, white or black." Those who advocate the use of violence and talk of "the right of self defense" may be logical, and it takes little imagination to understand their angry frustration. "But they are terrible political leaders for a racial minority of only ten per cent. Any violence by the Negro is bound to prompt excessive violence against them." In advocating this policy and social strategy for achieving Negro rights, Dr. Niebuhr is not, of course, reverting to the old "go slow" argument. He believes that "The brutalities of tyranny, whether in Nazi Germany or in South Africa or in Mississippi, are more wounding in human self-esteem than any conflict." (*Man's Nature and His Communities,* pp. 86–87.)

Niebuhr saw already in Detroit the ineptness of almost all of the white Protestant churches in dealing with social injustice. One of the "heresies" he sought to refute was the belief of many Christians that "religious faith is the guarantor of virtue." This was especially evident to him in relationship to the race issue. Niebuhr draws an analogy between the Cromwellian revolution in England in the seventeenth century and the current revolt of the Negro, in the United States and elsewhere. Fortunately, he believes, the Negro church plays "somewhat the same role in the present struggle as did the Puritan sects in Cromwellian England." This is an important role, for a great percentage of the Negro churches have managed to maintain a degree of vitality which is absent from many white churches. "They [the Negroes] also profit from the convergence of religious inspiration and the interests of their members, which is characteristic of all religiously inspired revolutions." ("The Quality of Our Lives," *Christian Century,* May 11, 1960, p. 569.)

International Relations

Because Dr. Niebuhr was the scourge of pacifists before World War II, and because he supported the Allied war effort in the defeat of the Nazis, many appear to be surprised today to find him critical of Administration foreign policy. He has been particularly critical of the Vietnam policy of the Johnson Administration. Some have wondered if he has become a pacifist again! Some find a peculiar contradiction in his present criticism of American democracy's action against "communist tyranny," when previously he had been a chief advocate of resistance to tyranny. There is misunderstanding on both counts.

Pacifism was long ago given up for good as a sound basis for a social ethic. Niebuhr does not regard himself even as one of the "new-type" or "nuclear pacifists."

As for his criticism of Administration foreign policy, particularly in Vietnam, there is nothing in his social ethic or his way of thinking which ever suggested any uncritical acceptance of the policy and practice of any government or institution. The Government's defense of our involvement in Vietnam is fallacious—in terms of our claim simply to be defending a "nation's right to self-determination," and our official parallelism between the struggle against Hitler and the struggle against North Vietnam. Our motives are not so pure as we pretend, and so most of the world rightly does not take us at our word. And, Ho Chi Minh is no Hitler racist; but Ho also seeks "self-determination." ("Vietnam and the Imperial Conflict," one of Niebuhr's longer discussions of the various aspects of the involvement, is published in the *New Leader,* June 6, 1966.)

A final note on Dr. Niebuhr's thinking about the United Nations and World Government. During and after the War Dr. Niebuhr explored the great variety of proposals for organizing the world in order to preserve the peace. (See Nos. 43-47.) One persistent note in his discussions was that genuine world government must await the development of some substructure of community. He attempted to temper the arguments of the cynics. Even more persistent was the warning about expecting too much from the United Nations, assuming the two (now three) great power blocs and their contending interests. Writing about the Congo, Dr. Niebuhr pointed out to those who may have had some lingering hopes that the U.N. would sooner or later become a world government that, as of that date, the Congo was proof, if it had not been evident before, that there is no world government ("The U.N.: An End to Illusions" *New Leader,* Feb. 27, 1961). One saw there not the actions of a world united but rather a battleground for contending interests.

One finds, then, in Reinhold Niebuhr's writings, not only an unusual insight into political and social facts—in terms of the theme of love and justice; there is always the elaboration of ideal possibilities, the harsh and unlovely facts of the case, and the search for any redeeming element in the situation.

PART
I

---

*General Essays
on Love and Justice*

1. THE SPIRIT OF JUSTICE

IN THE CHRISTIAN FAITH THE FINAL LAW IN WHICH all other law is fulfilled is the law of love. But this law does not abrogate the laws of justice, except as love rises above justice to exceed its demands. The ordinary affairs of the community, the structures of politics and economics, must be governed by the spirit of justice and by specific and detailed definitions of rights and duties.

American Christianity tends to be irrelevant to the problems of justice because it persists in presenting the law of love as a simple solution for every communal problem. It is significant that the " social gospel," which sought to overcome the excessive individualism of the Christian faith in America, never escaped this sentimentality and irrelevance because it also preached the same ethic that it pretended to criticize. It insisted that Christians should practice the law of love not only in personal relations but in the collective relations of mankind. In these relations love as an ecstatic impulse of self-giving is practically impossible. Nations, classes, and races do not love one another. They may have a high sense of obligation to one another. They must express this sense of obligation in the desire to give each one his due.

The effort to substitute the law of love for the spirit of justice instead of recognizing love as the fulfillment and highest form of the spirit of justice, is derived from the failure to measure the power and persistence of self-interest. It is because self-interest is not easily overcome in even the life of the " redeemed " that most of the harmonies of life are not the perfect harmonies of fully co-ordinated wills but the tolerable harmonies of balanced interests and mutually

Christianity and Society, Summer, 1950.

recognized claims. Even in the family, in which the spirit of love may prevail more than in any other human institution, the careful calculation of rights is an important element in the harmony of the whole, though it must be observed that rights are so complexly intertwined in intimate relations that the calculations of justice lead to friction if love is not constantly infused into them.

Christians pride themselves upon an ethic that exceeds the requirements of law. But it is significant that Jews, schooled in their legalistic tradition and also the inheritors of the prophetic spirit, are on the whole more adept in the field of justice than Christians. They might well say to Christians what Cosimo de' Medici said to Catholics in the Renaissance: " You have built your ladders into the heavens. We will not seek so high nor sink so low." Christian businessmen are more frequently characterized by a spirit of philanthropy than by a spirit of justice in assessing the claims and counterclaims of economic groups. Love in the form of philanthropy is, in fact, on a lower level than a high form of justice. For philanthropy is given to those who make no claims against us, who do not challenge our goodness or disinterestedness. An act of philanthropy may thus be an expression of both power and moral complacency. An act of justice on the other hand requires the humble recognition that the claim that another makes against us may be legitimate.

The pronouncements of church bodies and the preachments of the pulpit still tend to smell of sentimentality in our day because the law of love is presented without reference to the power of the law of self-love. " All coercion," wrote a Christian businessman recently, " is foreign to the Christian life because we Christians know that only uncoerced goodness is real goodness." This does not take into account that we need a great deal of second-rate goodness to get along with one another. We have to have a taxation system that demands more of us than we are inclined to give voluntarily; and we must maintain a social security system that holds us responsible for the security of other families than our own beyond our natural inclination. We cannot preserve the health of the free world without American aid to other nations that must go far beyond the utmost limits of voluntary philanthropy.

2. JUSTICE AND LOVE

" A Christian," declared an eager young participant in a symposium on Christianity and politics, "always considers the common welfare before his own interest." This simple statement reveals a few of the weaknesses of moralistic Christianity in dealing with problems of justice. The statement contains at least two errors, or perhaps one error and one omission.

The first error consists in defining a Christian in terms which assume that consistent selflessness is possible. No Christian, even the most perfect, is able " always " to consider the common interest before his own. At least he is not able to do it without looking at the common interest with eyes colored by his own ambitions. If complete selflessness were a simple possibility, political justice could be quickly transmuted into perfect love; and all the frictions, tensions, partial co-operations, and overt and covert conflicts could be eliminated. If complete selflessness without an admixture of egoism were possible, many now irrelevant sermons and church resolutions would become relevant. Unfortunately there is no such possibility for individual men; and perfect disinterestedness for groups and nations is even more impossible.

The other error is one of omission. To set self-interest and the general welfare in simple opposition is to ignore nine tenths of the ethical issues that confront the consciences of men. For these are concerned not so much with the problem of the self against the whole as with problems of the self in its relation to various types of " general welfare." " What do you mean by common interest? " retorted a shrewd businessman in the symposium referred to. Does it mean the family or the nation? If I have to choose between " my family " and " my nation," is the Christian choice inevitably weighted in favor of the nation since it is the larger community? And if the choice is between " my " nation and another nation, must the preference always be for the other nation on the ground that concern for my own nation represents collective self-interest? Was the young pacifist idealist right who insisted that if we had less " selfish concern for our own civilization " we could resolve the tension between ourselves and Russia, presumably by giving moral preference to a communist civilization over our own?

Christianity and Society, Fall, 1950.

Such questions as these reveal why Christian moralism has made such meager contributions to the issues of justice in modern society. Justice requires discriminate judgments between conflicting claims. A Christian justice will be particularly critical of the claims of the self as against the claims of the other, but it will not dismiss them out of hand. Without this criticism all justice becomes corrupted into a refined form of self-seeking. But if the claims of the self (whether individual or collective) are not entertained, there is no justice at all. There is an ecstatic form of agape which defines the ultimate heroic possibilities of human existence (involving, of course, martyrdom) but not the common possibilities of tolerable harmony of life with life.

In so far as justice admits the claims of the self, it is something less than love. Yet it cannot exist without love and remain justice. For without the " grace " of love, justice always degenerates into something less than justice.

But if justice requires that the interests of the self be entertained, it also requires that they be resisted. Every realistic system of justice must assume the continued power of self-interest, particularly of collective self-interest. It must furthermore assume that this power will express itself illegitimately as well as legitimately. It must therefore be prepared to resist illegitimate self-interest, even among the best men and the most just nations. A simple Christian moralism counsels men to be unselfish. A profounder Christian faith must encourage men to create systems of justice which will save society and themselves from their own selfishness.

But justice arbitrates not merely between the self and the other, but between the competing claims upon the self by various " others." Justice seeks to determine what I owe my family as compared with my nation; or what I owe this segment as against that segment of a community. One of the strange moral anomalies of our times is that there are businessmen and men of affairs who have a more precise sense of justice in feeling their way through the endless relativities of human relations than professional teachers of morals. Practical experience has made them sensitive to the complex web of values and interests in which human decisions are reached, while the professional teachers of religion and morals deal with simple counters of black and white. This certainly is one of the reasons why the pulpit frequently seems so boring and irrelevant to the pew. At his worst the practical man of affairs is morally heedless and considers only his own interest, mistaking collective self-interest for selfless virtue. At his best he has been schooled in justice, while his teacher confuses the issue by moral distinctions which do not fit the complexities of life.

The realm of justice is also a realm of tragic choices, which are seldom envisaged in a type of idealism in which all choices are regarded as simple. Sometimes we must prefer a larger good to a smaller one, without the hope that the smaller one will be preserved in the larger one. Sometimes we must risk a terrible evil (such as an atomic war) in the hope of avoiding an imminent peril (such as subjugation to tyranny). Subsequent events may prove the risk to have been futile and the choice to have been wrong. If there is enough of a world left after such a wrong choice we will be taxed by the idealists for having made the wrong choice; and they will not know that they escaped an intolerable evil by our choice. Even now we are taxed with the decision to resist nazism, on the ground that the war against nazism has left us in a sad plight. The present peril of communism seems to justify an earlier capitulation to nazism. But since we are men and not God, we could neither anticipate all the evils that would flow from our decision to resist nazism, nor yet could we have capitulated to the immediate evil because another evil was foreshadowed.

The tragic character of our moral choices, the contradiction between various equal values of our devotion, and the incompleteness in all our moral striving, prove that " if in this life only we had hoped in Christ, we are of all men most miserable." No possible historic justice is sufferable without the Christian hope. But any illusion of a world of perfect love without these imperfect harmonies of justice must ultimately turn the dream of love into a nightmare of tyranny and injustice.

3. THE ETHIC OF JESUS AND THE SOCIAL PROBLEM

Since Walter Rauschenbusch aroused the American church to the urgency of the social problem and its relation to the ethical ideals of the gospel, it has been rather generally assumed that it is possible

Religion in Life, Spring, 1932.

to abstract an adequate social ethic for the reconstruction of society from the social teachings of Jesus. Dozens of books have been written to prove that Jesus' ideals of brotherhood represented an outline of the ideal society, that his law of service offered an alternative to the competitive impulse in modern society, that guidance for the adjustment of every political and economic problem could be found in his words, and that nothing but a little logic would serve to draw out the " social implications " of his teachings.

Most of this energy has been vainly spent and has served to create as much confusion as light. There is indeed a very rigorous ethical ideal in the gospel of Jesus, but there is no social ethic in the ordinary sense of the word in it, precisely because the ethical ideal is too rigorous and perfect to lend itself to application in the economic and political problems of our day. This does not mean that the ethic of Jesus has no light to give to a modern Christian who faces the perplexing economic and political issues of a technological civilization. It means only that confusion will be avoided if a rigorous distinction is made between a perfectionist and absolute ethic and the necessities of a social situation.

The ethic of Jesus was, to begin with, a personal ethic. It was not individual in the sense that he believed in individual perfection abstracted from a social situation. He saw that wealth tempted to covetousness and that poverty prompted the virtue of humility. He spoke of the Kingdom and not of salvation, and the Kingdom meant an ideal social relationship, even though he might emphasize that it proceeded from internal spiritual forces. His ethic was an ethic of love, and it therefore implied social relationships. But it was an individual ethic in the sense that his chief interest was in the quality of life of an individual. He regarded as a temptation the suggestion that he become a political leader or that he develop the political implications of the Messianic idea, and he resisted the effort to make him king. He was not particularly interested in the Jewish people's aspirations toward freedom from Rome, and skillfully evaded the effort to make him take sides in that political problem. He accepted monarchy on the one hand and slavery on the other, though he called attention to the difference between the ideal of his Kingdom, which measured greatness by service, and the kind of greatness which the " kings of the Gentiles " attained.

His lack of concern for social and political issues is, however, not as important from the perspective of this problem as the kind of ethical ideal which he actually developed. In terms of individual life his ethical ideal was one of complete disinterestedness, religiously motivated. No one was to seek his own. The man who asked him to persuade his brother to divide an inheritance with him was rudely rebuked. Evil was not to be resisted, the borrower was to be given more than he asked for without hope of return. A special premium was placed upon actions which could not be rewarded. In other words, the prudential motive was treated with utmost severity. There are, of course, words in the teachings of Jesus which are not as rigorous as this. He promised rewards. Some of these words belong to a humanist strain in his teachings in which he merely makes a shrewd analysis of the effect of certain actions. The severe judge will be judged severely. The proud man will be abased and the humble man exalted. Here the social rewards of social attitudes are recognized. Other offers of reward occur, but with one or two exceptions they can be placed in the category of ultimate rewards — " in the resurrection of the just," " treasures in heaven," favor with God. On the whole, they do not seriously qualify his main position that moral action must be motivated purely by obedience to God, emulation of God's attributes, and gratitude for the forgiving grace of God. An ulterior motive (desire for social approval, for instance) for a worthy action would destroy the virtue of the action and would result only in the attainment of the object of the ulterior motive — " verily, they have their reward."

Jesus did not deny that disinterested action would result in rewards; " all these things " would be added, and the man who forgot himself completely would find himself most truly. Here is the recognition of the basic ethical paradox that the highest result of an action can never be its desired result. It must be a by-product. If it is desired, the purity of the action is destroyed. If I love to be loved or to be socially approved, I will not be loved or approved in the same way as if my fellow men caught in me a glimpse of pure disinterestedness. Obviously the only way to achieve such pure disinterestedness is to have actions motivated purely by religious motives. But this very emphasis upon religious motives lifts the ethic of Jesus above the area of social ethics. We are asked to love our enemies, not because the social consequences of such love will be to make friends of the enemies, but because God loves with that kind of impartiality. We are demanded to forgive those who have wronged us, not because a forgiving spirit will prove redemptive in the lives of the fallen, but because God forgives our sins. Here we have an ethic, in other words, which we can neither disavow nor perfectly achieve. We cannot disavow it because it is a fact that the prudential motive destroys the purity of every ethical action. We have a right to view the social and personal consequences of an action in retrospect, but if we view it in prospect we have something less than the best. So powerful is the drive of self-interest in life, however, that this ideal is as difficult to achieve as it is to disavow. It remains, therefore, as an ideal which convicts every moral achievement of imperfection, but it is always a little beyond the realm of actual human history.

Though Jesus was as indifferent to the social consequences of pure disinterestedness as he was critical of concern for the personal consequences, it is not difficult to draw conclusions in regard to the social ideal implied by such disinterestedness. In practical terms it means a combination of anarchism and communism dominated by the spirit of love. Such perfect love as he demands would obviate the necessity of coercion on the one hand because men would refrain from transgressing upon their neighbor's rights, and on the other hand because such transgression would be accepted and forgiven if it did occur. That is anarchism, in other words. It would mean communism because the privileges of each would be potentially the privileges of all. Where love is perfect the distinctions between mine and thine disappear. The social ideal of Jesus is as perfect and as impossible of attainment as is his personal ideal. But again it is an ideal that cannot be renounced completely. Whatever justice men attain in the society in which they live is always an imperfect justice. The careful limitation and definition of rights which Stoicism gave to the world as a social ideal always develop into injustice in actual life because every person views rights not from an absolute but from a biased perspective. The result is a society in which the perspective of the strong dictates the conceptions of justice by which the total community operates and necessitates social conflict through the assertion of the rights of the weak before the injustice is corrected. Justice, in other words, that is only justice is less than justice. Only imaginative justice, that is, love that begins by espousing the rights of the other rather than self, can achieve a modicum of fairness.

Whether we view the ethical teachings of Jesus from the perspective of the individual or of society we discover an unattainable ideal, but a very useful one. It is an ideal never attained in history or in life, but one that gives us an absolute standard by which to judge both personal and social righteousness. It is a standard by comparison with which all human attainments fall short, and it may offer us the explanation of Jesus' words, " Why callest thou me good? no one is good save God." Perhaps it ought to be added that an attempt to follow this ideal in a world that is, particularly in its group relationships, hardly human and certainly not divine, will inevitably lead us to where it led Jesus, to the cross.

Valuable as this kind of perfectionism is, it certainly offers no basis for a social ethic that deals responsibly with a growing society. Those of us who believe in the complete reorganization of modern society are not wrong in using the ideal of Jesus as a vantage point from which to condemn the present social order, but I think we are in error when we try to draw from the teachings of Jesus any warrant for the social policies which we find necessary to attain to any modicum of justice. We may be right in believing that we are striving for a justice which approximates the Christian ideal more closely than the present social order, but we are wrong when we talk about achieving a " Christian social order." The Barthians are quite right, I think, in protesting against the easy identification of the Kingdom of God with every movement of social reform and social radicalism that has prevailed in American Christianity in particular and in liberal Protestantism in general. Those of us who dissociate ourselves from the easy optimism of modern liberalism and who believe that a just society is not going to be built by a little more education and a few more sermons on love have particular reason to reorient our thinking in this matter so that we will not come forward with a social ethic involving the use of force and coercion and political pressure of every kind and claim the authority of Jesus for it.

Our confusion is, of course, no worse than that of the conventional teachers of Christian ethics and theology who have a rather complacent attitude toward the present economic society and criticize us for violating the ethic of Jesus in our espousal of the class struggle, for instance. Our confusion is, in fact, not quite as bad as theirs. They have used every kind of exegetical device to prove that the teachings of Jesus are not incompatible with participation in nationalistic wars or, if they have been a little more clearheaded, they have found ethical justification for their actions by proving that the ethic of Jesus does not provide for the responsibilities of politics and economics, and therefore leaves them free to choose a political strategy that is most consonant with their conception of the moral good will which they believe Jesus to idealize. The critics of the former type have no ground to stand upon at all when they accuse radical Christians of violating the ethic of Jesus; for participation in a nonviolent strike action, to choose an obvious example, is certainly not more incompatible with the ethic of Jesus than participation in an international conflict. Critics of the latter type have cut the ground for criticism from under their own feet. They admit that any responsible relationship to political and economic affairs involves compromise, and they ought to have a difficult time proving that the assertion of national interest or the protection of national rights is more compatible with the perfectionist ideal of pure disinterestedness than the assertion of class interests and the protection of class rights.

But the confusion of our critics does not absolve us of the necessity of clear thought for ourselves. The struggle for social justice in the present economic order involves the assertion of rights, the rights of the disinherited, and the use of coercion. Both are incompatible with the pure love ethic found in the Gospels. How, then, do we justify the strategy of the " class struggle "? We simply cannot do so in purely Christian terms. There is in the absolute sense no such thing as " Christian socialism." We must justify ourselves by considerations of the social situation that we face and the human resources that are available for its solution. What we discover in the social situation is that human life in its group interests moves pretty much upon the basis of the economic interests of various groups. We realize that intelligence and spiritual and moral idealism may qualify economic interest, but they do not destroy it. Whatever may be possible for individuals, we see no possibility of a group voluntarily divesting itself of its special privileges in society. Nor do we see a possibility of pure disinterestedness and the spirit of forgiveness on the part of an underprivileged group shaming a dominant group into an attitude of social justice. Such a strategy might possibly work in intimate personal relationships but it does not work in the larger group relations. The Negro has been forgiving in his subordinate position in society for a long time, but he has not persuaded the white man to grant him larger privileges in society. Whatever place the industrial worker has won in society has been won by the assertion of his rights through his trade-union organizations. Even the most imaginative urban dwellers lack the imagination to envisage the needs of the farmer. The farmer has been forced to exert political pressure for the attainment of even such minimum justice as he is granted in the present economic organization of our country. No one who looks realistically at the social scene can fail to discover that economic, racial, and national groups stand on a moral level considerably lower than that of the most sensitive individuals. They are not easily persuaded to a voluntary sacrifice of privileges, and an attitude of pure nonresistance on the part of those who suffer from their exactions does not produce the spirit of repentance among them. Intelligence, which may create a spirit of justice among individuals by persuading them to grant to their fellows what they claim for themselves, is generally not acute enough to function in similar fashion in group relations. More frequently it does no more than to create rational sanctifications for special group interests. Only rarely does intellectual force rise high enough to create a perspective from which group prejudices and biases have been banished. The relations between groups are so indirect that the consequences of our actions in the life of another group are not easily discerned, and we therefore continue in unethical conduct without the restraint upon our conscience that intimate personal relations create. Very few white men have any conception of the havoc that is wrought in the souls and upon the bodies of Negroes by prevailing race prejudices; and there is not one American in a million who knows what our reparations policy means for starving workers of Germany. This unhappy group seems under the necessity of asserting its interests, not only against the rest of the world, but against the more comfortable middle classes of their own country.

The social struggle involves a violation of a pure ethic of love, not only in the assertion of rights, but in the inevitable use of coercion. Here again one need but state the obvious; but the obvious is usually not recognized by academic moralists. No society can exist without the use of coercion, though every intelligent society will try to reduce coercion to a minimum and rely upon the factor of mutual consent to give stability to its institutions. Yet it can never trust all of its citizens to accept necessary social arrangements voluntarily. It will use police force against recalcitrant and antisocial minorities, and it will use the threat of political force against a complacent and indifferent group of citizens which could never be relied upon to initiate adequate social policies upon its own accord. No government can wait upon voluntary action on the part of the privileged members of a community for an adequate inheritance or income tax. It will use political force created by the votes of the disinherited and less privileged to initiate and enforce taxation policies, designed to equalize privileges. Privileged groups may accept such legislation without violent revolt, but they will probably argue against its justice until the day of their death. An intelligent society will constantly strive toward the goal of a more equal justice by initiating a more rigorous policy just as soon as a previous and more tentative one has been accepted and absorbed into the social standards of the community. If this is not done by gradual process, with the unrealized goal of essential equality beckoning each generation to surpass the approximations of justice achieved in the past, the inequalities of the social order, always increasing through natural process, are bound to grow until an outraged sense of justice (probably spurred by actual physical want on the part of the least privileged members of a community) will produce a violent revolt. In such nations as Germany, for instance, it is really an open question whether any political measures can achieve the desired end of social justice quickly enough to prevent violent revolution.

The necessity of this kind of coercion, based upon the assertion of interest on the part of the less privileged, is such a clear lesson of history that one hesitates to belabor the point and would refrain from doing so were it not for the fact that half of the academic treatises on social ethics and Christian ethics were written as if no such necessity existed. In this respect secular moralists are frequently as naïve as religious ones. In the one case it is expected that a change in educational technique will eliminate the drive of self-interest which determines economic life and in the other case there is a naïve confidence in the possibility of changing human nature by religious conversion or religious inspiration. It is the thesis of the radical wing of Christian social theorists, whether in England, Germany, or America, that nothing accomplished by either education or religious suasion will be able to abolish the social struggle. We believe that such hopes are corrupted by the sentimentalities of the comfortable classes and are caused by their lack of understanding of the realities of an industrial civilization. In what sense, then, may we call ourselves Christian, or how do we hope to insinuate Christian and ethical values into the social struggle? The simplest answer is that we believe that the highest ethical and spiritual insight may mitigate the social struggle on the one hand and may transcend it on the other.

We believe that it makes some difference whether a privileged group makes a stubborn and uncompromising defense of its special privileges or whether it has some degree of social imagination and tries to view its privileges in the light of the total situation of a community. Education ought to create some of that social imagination, and in so far as it does, it will mitigate the class struggle or the social struggle between races. The religious contribution to the same end may consist of various elements. Real religion produces the spirit of humility and repentance. It destroys moral conceit. Moral conceit is precisely what makes privileged groups so stubborn in the defense of their privileges. The human animal is just moral enough to be unable to act immorally with vigor if he cannot find a moral justification for his actions. If the Christian church used the ethical ideal of Jesus, the ideal of pure disinterestedness, more rigorously, and if the modern pulpit made a more astute analysis of human motives in the light of this ideal, many of the rationalizations that now support the antisocial policies and attitudes of privileged and powerful people would be destroyed. At least they might be qualified. One of the most unfortunate facts about our contemporary moral situation is that the church has ceased to convict men of selfishness at the precise moment in history when human greed is more obvious and more dangerous than at any previous time. Nowhere has the liberal church played more false to its generation than in its optimistic and romantic interpretation of human nature, just when an industrial civilization revealed the drive of self-interest in all its antisocial power. The part of the Christian church that has tried to convict the generation of sin knows too little about the problems of modern life to convict men of their significant sins. Thus religion has on the whole produced moral complacency rather than the spirit of repentance. The number of men who are sufficiently sensitized by religion actually to renounce their privileges must always remain small. But it ought not to be impossible for the church to create enough contrition and consciousness of human selfishness to prompt men to a more willing acceptance of and less stubborn resistance against social policies that aim at the restriction of power and privilege. If we dealt realistically with the facts of human nature, we might be able to create an attitude of complacency toward increasing social restraint, based upon the realization that few, if any, of us are wise enough to restrain our expansive desires voluntarily in a degree sufficient for the needs of our highly interdependent society. If there were a better understanding of human nature in the church today, an understanding that we could acquire by the study of psychology and economics but which we might appropriate just as easily from the insights of great religion, there would be fewer Christian captains of industry who lived under the illusion that they were good enough and wise enough to hold irresponsible power and exercise it for the good of the community. They would know that the very possession of irresponsible power tempts to its selfish use and that the benevolent pretensions of despotism rest either on unconscious self-deception or conscious hypocrisy.

True religion could mitigate the cruelties of the social struggle by its creation of the spirit of love as well as the spirit of repentance. The love ideal which Jesus incarnates may be too pure to be realized in life, but it offers us nevertheless an ideal toward which the religious spirit may strive. All rational idealism creates a conflict between the mind and the impulses, as in Stoicism and Kantian morality. The mind conceives ideals of justice which it tries to force upon recalcitrant selfish impulses. Real religion transmutes the social impulses until they transcend the limits set them by nature (family, race, group, etc.) and include the whole human community. Real religious imagination is able, furthermore, to create an attitude of trust and faith toward human beings, in which the potentialities rather than the immediate realities are emphasized. Through such imagination the needs of the social foe are appreciated, his inadequacies are understood in the light of his situation, and his possibilities for higher and more moral action are recognized. Only the religious spirit which surveys the human scene from the perspective of its presuppositions about the character of life is thus able to disregard present facts and appeal to ultimate possibilities. The fact that in Jesus the spirit of love flowed out in emulation of God's love, without regard to social consequences, cannot blind the eye to the social consequences of a religiously inspired love. If modern religion were really producing it, it would mitigate the evils of the social struggle. It would, to emphasize the obvious once more, not abolish the social struggle, because it would not approximate perfection in sufficiently numerous instances. The fight for justice in society will always be a fight. But wherever the spirit of justice grows imaginative and is transmuted into love, a love in which the interests of the other are espoused, the struggle is transcended by just that much.

It is the fashion among many Christian idealists to criticize the political movements of the disinherited for the spirit of hatred which they generate. The church, so it is said, would espouse their cause much more readily if the spirit of love were manifest in it. What the church fails to realize is that its responsibility is chiefly for the moral and spiritual attitudes of the privileged rather than the disinherited; for it is the former who makes professions of Christian idealism. If the church wants to insinuate the spirit of love into the social struggle, it ought to begin with the privileged groups, not only because it has greater responsibility for them, but because those who hold entrenched positions in the social struggle are obviously under the greater obligation to be imaginative in gauging the needs and discounting the limitations of those who suffer from social injustice. The perfectionist ethic of Jesus allows for no such distinctions; for it demands that love be poured forth whether or not we suffer from injustice. But no one can avow such an ethic from the vantage point of privilege and security. If the portion of society that benefits from social inequality and which is endangered by a rising tide of social discontent attempts to counsel love, forgiveness, and patience to the discontented, it will convict itself of hypocrisy, except it is able first of all to reveal fruits of the Spirit, which it commends, in its own life. Even if it were to reveal some fruits, but too meager to justify a more trusting and a less vehement attitude on the part of the underprivileged, its moral ideals would be regarded as pretensions. The race situation in the South offers interesting commentary upon this point. The fine work which the interracial commission has done has failed to preserve the respect of the more eager young Negroes for it, because they feel that through its efforts of conciliation white men have yielded only inconsequential social advantages in order that they may hold to their major ones. The most perfect love may not ask for social justification, but any love within the capacity of ordinary men and groups does. The disinherited will have their spirits corrupted by hatred and their policies tinctured with violence except they are able to detect some genuinely ethical elements in the policies of the privileged and entrenched social groups. If the spirit of love is to qualify and mitigate the social struggle, the groups that profess to believe in the efficacy of love and who, at the same time, have favored positions in society are clearly under obligation to introduce this Christian element in society. They may be quite sure that any solid ethical achievement among them would result in practically immediate ethical reactions of trust and faith among those who are trying to advance socially. Only the faith and trust of the advancing group will not and ought not ever rise to the point where purely voluntary action toward equality is expected. A degree of ethical insight on the part of the whole community will not abolish the necessity of social conflict, but it may prevent violence and reduce the hatred that must inevitably arise when the disinherited are faced, not only with the stubborn greed of the powerful and comfortable social classes, but also with the protection of their privileges by the covert use of force and their hypocritical pretension of virtue.

A Christian ethical idealism that espouses the cause of proletarian groups and identifies itself with their political movements is, in short, as pure as any Christian movement that assumes a responsible attitude toward society. The compromises that it makes with the pure Christian ethic are inevitable compromises which everyone must make who deals with the social problem from the perspective of society rather than that of the individual. It might claim, in addition, to appropriate the Christian ethical ideal more closely than a type of thought that fears contamination in the social struggle. For the social struggle is a reality in society and we will be contaminated by it except we get out of society. The ascetic may possibly have a vantage point from which to criticize the ethical purity of Christian socialism or Christian radicalism. Those who stay in society have not. If our critics were less confused about the moral and social realities of modern society, they would know that neutrality in a social struggle between entrenched and advancing social classes really means alliance with the entrenched position. In the social struggle we are either on the side of privilege or need. No ethical perfectionism can save us from that choice.

4. WHEN WILL CHRISTIANS STOP FOOLING THEMSELVES?

The church has always felt the ministry of reconciliation to be one of its tasks. It has admonished men to " live at peace with all men as much as in you lieth." In orthodox Christianity it was assumed that no perfect justice could be achieved in society; and the reconciling love which it preached was therefore something that was to ease and qualify but not change the relative injustices of society. In the modern period the liberal church, rightly impatient with a conception of static justice, thought of its task as one that demanded the achievement of a more perfect justice. Since, however, it believed that the gospel law of love was a source of an effective social ethic, it insisted that this more perfect justice was to be achieved by admonishing those who have undue privileges to sacrifice them in the interest of those who have been defrauded.

The church's ministry of reconciliation was thus conceived in purely moral terms. It was to make selfish people unselfish, at least sufficiently unselfish to permit the creation of justice without conflict. Only a few years ago a leader of the social gospel movement wrote a book in which he deplored the " increasing temptation to solve the problem of justice by political means." In other words, he still held to the belief that pure moral suasion could solve every social problem.

WHERE IDEALISM CREATES ILLUSION

When it became obvious that problems of social justice are not solved in terms of pure moral suasion, but that the establishment of justice always involves a certain degree of pressure, of claims and counterclaims, of pushing and shoving, a portion of the church decided to allow for such pressure but to insist that it must never lead to violent conflict. The task of the Fellowship of Reconciliation, a radical Christian organization, has been conceived in essentially such terms. The Fellowship espoused the cause of the social underdogs in racial and economic conflict but drew the line at violent conflict.

Whether the task of reconciliation is conceived in terms of pure moral suasion or whether it recognizes the inevitabilities of conflict in society and only seeks to avoid violence in such conflicts, it is interesting that the consequence of such conceptions is to create moral idealists who imagine that they are changing the world by their moral ideals. In the first case the church has encouraged a whole horde of Christian idealists and philanthropists who express their Christian spirit in more or less generous philanthropies and in more or less thoroughgoing efforts at reform. Almost invariably these idealists come to believe that the problem of justice has been solved and that one need only wait for the day when other businessmen will be as unselfish as they are and when workers will acknowledge this idealism with grateful appreciation and stop their own pretentious efforts toward justice.

In the second case a slightly more realistic and more radical type of Christian idealism is achieved, but it can not escape moral confusion. Since it draws an absolute line between violence and non-violence in social struggles, it gives a moral advantage to all the good Christian people who have never used violence in their lives, who stand aghast at the counsels of violence heard in the ranks of the disinherited, and who thereby miss the fact that we are all involved in the violence of life. In other words, the church by its emphasis upon moral idealism tends to create hypocrites who underestimate their own selfishness and the persistence of selfishness in society.

Sometimes a healthy realism among laymen breaks through the illusions created by superficial moral preaching. I remember out of my own days of liberal preaching how a certain young businessman approached me after a sermon on the necessity of justice through love and nonviolence and told me that he had " fired " fifty men that week from a construction job on orders from the " head office." He said he didn't like to do it, but that he would have lost his job if he had failed to comply with orders. With a sly gleam of derision in his eye for my rather romantic pacifism, he declared that his conscience wasn't eased a bit by the fact that he had not hit any of the fifty dismissed men over the head.

It is just this kind of realism that the church has been failing to supply in the social struggle. It has preached too much moral idealism at the expense of religious realism. If one looks at life from a religious perspective, if one judges human actions in the light of the law of love and tests every action by the admonition " Thou shalt love thy neighbor as thyself," one soon discovers what a world of nature this human world is and how necessary it is and remains to establish basic justice in it by the contest of interest with interest. Moral idealists are incapable of recognizing that fact. They will live under the illusion that they can be so unselfish that they will be able to grant other people justice without any pressure on the part of the latter.

But any religious realist who has ever looked deeply into his heart and felt the scrutiny of a holy God upon his sin will not make such a mistake. He will say with Saint Paul: " I know nothing against myself, but I am not thereby justified. He who judges me is the

Lord." We can, of course, do a good deal to judge ourselves by our own highest standards. But our own highest standards are nevertheless very much our own and are conditioned by our own interests. The number of people who do not mix a considerable amount of will-to-power with their kindnesses and philanthropies is extremely small.

CHRISTIAN REALISM

The church would do more for the cause of reconciliation if, instead of producing moral idealists who think that they can establish justice, it would create religious and Christian realists who know that justice will require that some men shall contend against them. In the more privileged congregations this would mean the education of Christian laymen who understood the profound realities of the social struggle, and who would therefore not give themselves to the deception that they know what is good for their workingmen and that their philanthropies are a refutation of the worker's insistence on organization. This kind of Christian realism would understand the perennial necessity of political relationships in society, no matter how ethical ideals rise.

The wise minister will not apply this realism only to businessmen. There are probably few churches in America in which the janitor might not well be justified in demanding a larger share of the total wage bill of the congregation. This does not mean that the demand will be successful. It will probably not be, because janitors find difficulty in organizing and if they were organized they would find still greater difficulty in engaging in collective bargaining with hundreds of church boards. There is probably no community so ethical that its justice could not be improved by political as well as ethical relationships in it. Technical difficulties frequently make the introduction of political relationships impossible in certain communities. The members are therefore dependent solely upon the ethical insight of their superiors for the attainment of justice. This may be inevitable, but it does not prove that political relationships would not be abstractly desirable even though practical and technical difficulties spoil their efficacy in certain situations.

THE ROLE OF LOVE

Emphasis upon political and religious realism and Christian contrition does not mean that there should be or that there would be less moral idealism and a less genuine effort to understand the interest of the other person and to meet it by voluntary action. All justice established by pressure is in need of being elaborated by love; and there is no reason to suppose that people who know themselves to be selfish will be less anxious to try to approximate unselfishness than those who imagine that unselfishness is an easy attainment. In a final conflict only those who have learned the grace of humility can be loving, for in a conflict love requires forgiveness and forgiveness is possible only to those who know themselves to be sinners. Moral idealists never forgive their foes. They are too secure in their own virtue to do that. Men forgive their foes only when they feel themselves to be standing under God with them, and feel that under the divine scrutiny all " our righteousness is as filthy rags."

There are a large number of eager young radical preachers in American Protestant churches who are engaged in the business of trying to make proletarians out of their middle-class church members. It is a futile task from which these young radicals should have long since been dissuaded by whatever Marxian determinism they have learned. It is, in fact, a strange phenomenon to find Marxian Christian leaders insisting in one moment that social justice must be established by a class conflict and in the next trying to persuade one class to espouse the cause of another. It is always possible and necessary to persuade a few sensitive spirits to transcend class, race, or national interests completely in the cause of justice. But surely every common-sense realist, not to speak of religious realists, must know that masses of men, even when they are in Christian churches, move by interest. It is important that they should know that. It will mitigate the fury of their class interest, and thus a reconciling influence will be exerted upon the social struggle.

MINISTRY TO THE PRIVILEGED

The most important ministry of reconciliation on the part of the church must be to the privileged classes, not only because the church has the ear of these classes to a greater degree than that of the disinherited, but also because the privileged classes are most tempted to identify their particular interests with the eternal sanctities and with the peace and order of society. When privileged groups fighting for their rights claim to be fighting for God and all the angels, they become truly demonic, and nothing will exorcise these demons but the worship of the true God. If the church is to reduce the fury of the righteous man who does not know how unrighteous he is, it will have to be more than a socio-moral institution. It will have to be a religio-moral fellowship in which there is some sense of a holiness which transcends all human perfections and imperfections.

A ministry of reconciliation must, of course, affect both sides of a conflict. In the modern social struggle the demonic pretensions of the privileged community are met by similar pretensions on the part of the disinherited, who in one moment sneer at the religious sanctifications of injustice in the privileged community, and in the next moment engage in the religious divinization of their class as a messianic one. Marxian politics and economics are extremely realistic, but Marxian religion is a form of blindness. This blindness is dangerous not only to society but to the cause represented by the disinherited champions of justice. It tends to make them narrow, bigoted, and unable to enlist allies such as farmers and other poor people whom they desperately need in their struggle.

The Christian idealists who have allied themselves with the disinherited classes have tried to qualify this hatred by insisting that no violence be used in the social struggle. This advice is confusing. Violence is, of course, always dangerous both to society and to those who use it. It ought to be discouraged for pragmatic reasons, but not for religious ones. If the latter emphasis is attempted, the disinherited who are always suffering from the covert violence of the privileged will rightly regard the advice of religious idealists as being unconsciously prompted by middle-class idealism rather than by religious realism.

If the church has a ministry of reconciliation to the disinherited, it is to bring the deepest insights of the Christian religion to bear upon their situation. That does not mean to counsel them against violence, but to dissuade them from hatred, or rather to set their problem in such a perspective that hatred will be mitigated. The irreligious radical foolishly imagines that the sin of the capitalist is absolutely peculiar to the capitalist, and that the destruction of the latter will therefore remove sin from the world. The religious sentimentalist is going to eliminate sin from capitalism by converting all capitalists to love and good will. The religious radical knows that capitalism represents a particularly grievous form of social injustice which can probably not be eliminated without the destruction of capitalism itself. But he does not give himself to the romantic hope that a new society will not face the problem of human sin and will not have to seek to solve that problem on the three levels of politics, ethics, and religion.

Such convictions inevitably mitigate the fury and qualify the wrath with which the social enemy is met. If it should be thought that fury and wrath are necessary to insure the success of a militant cause, the answer is that on the most pragmatic grounds this is not true, for blind fury increases the size of the enemy's ranks. Lack of spiritual discrimination is tempting radicalism in every Western nation to sacrifice statesmanship for furious energy.

If the Christian church is not to be " blown up " by the political conflicts that threaten the Western world, it will have to add religious depth to its moral idealism. Pure morality divides people and does not unite them. Moral idealists can live with other people only if their ideals are identical with their own. Only religious realists can have respect, pity, and forgiveness for the foe whom they do not understand. If this kind of love and forgiveness within and above the inevitable battles of life seem unimportant, one may become convinced of their importance if one has suffered for a while from the fury of liberal moral idealists and of radical moral idealists who have little in common except what they share with all moral idealists, that is, complete lovelessness toward those who disagree with them.

5. CHRISTIAN FAITH AND NATURAL LAW

In his challenging article entitled " Theology Today," the Archbishop of York presents several questions which in his opinion require a fresh answer in the light of contemporary history. One of these questions is: " Is there a natural order which is from God, as Catholic tradition holds, or is there only natural disorder, the fruit of sin, from which Christ delivers us, as Continental Protestantism has held? " I should like to address myself to this question and sug-

Theology, February, 1940.

gest that the facts of human history are more complex than either the traditional Catholic or Protestant doctrines of natural order and natural law suggest.

According to Thomistic doctrine, the Fall robbed man of a *donum superadditum* but left him with a *pura naturalia,* which includes a capacity for natural justice. What is lost is a capacity for faith, hope, and love — that is, the ability to rise above the natural order and have communion with divine and supernatural order, to know God and, in fellowship with him, to be delivered of the fears, anxieties, and sins which result from this separation from God. The fallen man is thus essentially an incomplete man, who is completed by the infusion of sacramental grace, which restores practically, though not quite, all of the supernatural virtues which were lost in the Fall. The Fall does not seriously impair man's capacity for natural justice. Only this is an incomplete perfection, incapable of itself to rise to the heights of love.

According to Protestant theology, the Fall had much more serious consequences. It left man " totally corrupt " and " utterly leprous and unclean." The very reason which in Catholic thought is regarded as the instrument and basis of natural justice is believed in Protestant thought to be infected by the Fall and incapable of arriving at any true definition of justice. Calvin is slightly more equivocal about the effects of sin upon reason than Luther, and as a consequence Calvinism does not relegate the natural law and the whole problem of justice so completely to the background as does Lutheranism. Nevertheless, the theory of total depravity is only slightly qualified in Calvinism.

I should like to maintain that the real crux of the human situation is missed in both the Catholic and the Protestant version of the effect of sin upon man's capacity for justice. Something more than a brief paper would be required to prove such a thesis; I must content myself therefore with suggesting the argument in general outline.

The Biblical conception of man includes three primary terms: (a) he is made in the image of God, (b) he is a creature, and (c) he is a sinner. His basic sin is pride. If this pride is closely analyzed, it is discovered to be man's unwillingness to acknowledge his creatureliness. He is betrayed by his greatness to hide his weakness. He is tempted by his ability to gain his own security to deny his insecurity, and refuses to admit that he has no final security except in God. He is tempted by his knowledge to deny his ignorance. (This is the source of all " ideological taint " in human knowledge.) It is not that man in his weakness has finite perspectives that makes conflicts between varying perspectives so filled with fanatic fury in all human history; it is that man denies the finiteness of his perspectives that tempts him to such fanatic cruelty against those who hold convictions other than his own. The quintessence of sin is, in short, that man " changes the glory of the incorruptible God into the image of corruptible man." He always usurps God's place and claims to be the final judge of human actions.

The loss of man's original perfection therefore never leaves him with an untarnished though incomplete natural justice. All statements and definitions of justice are corrupted by even the most rational men through the fact that the definition is colored by interest. This is the truth in the Marxist theory of rationalization and in its assertion that all culture is corrupted by an ideological taint. The unfortunate fact about the Marxist theory is that it is used primarily as a weapon in social conflict. The enemy is charged with this dishonesty, but the Marxist himself claims to be free of it. This is, of course, merely to commit the final sin of self-righteousness and to imagine ourselves free of the sin which we discern in the enemy. The fact that we do not discern it in ourselves is a proof of our sin and not of our freedom from sin. Christ's parable of the mote and the beam is a perfect refutation of this illusion.

The fact remains, nevertheless, that reason is not capable of defining any standard of justice that is universally valid or acceptable. Thus Thomistic definitions of justice are filled with specific details which are drawn from the given realities of a feudal social order and may be regarded as " rationalizations " of a feudal aristocracy's dominant position in society. (The much-praised Catholic prohibition of usury could be maintained only as long as the dominant aristocratic class were borrowers rather than lenders of money. When the static wealth of the landowners yielded to the more dynamic wealth of the financiers and industrialists, the prohibition of usury vanished. Catholics hold Protestantism responsible for this development, but it is significant that the Catholic Church makes no effort to impose the prohibition of usury upon its own bourgeois members.)

Bourgeois idealists of the eighteenth century invented new natural law theories and invested them with bourgeois rather than feudal-aristocratic content. The natural law of the eighteenth century was supposed to be descriptive rather than prescriptive. It was, more exactly, a " law of nature " rather than a " law of reason." But its real significance lay in its specific content. The content of this law justified the bourgeois classes in their ideals, just as the older law justified the feudal aristocrats. In short, it is not possible to state a universally valid concept of justice from any particular sociological locus in history. Nor is it possible to avoid either making the effort or making pretenses of universality which human finiteness does not justify. This inevitable pretense is the revelation of " original sin " in history. Human history is consequently more tragic than Catholic theology assumes. It is not an incomplete world yearning for completion, and finding it in the incarnation. It is a tragic world, troubled not by finiteness so much as by " false eternals " and false absolutes, and expressing the pride of these false absolutes even in the highest reaches of its spirituality. It is not the incarnation as such that is the good news of the gospel, but rather the revelation of a just God who is also merciful; this is the true content of the incarnation. That is, it is the atonement that fills the incarnation with meaning.

But Catholic thought not only fails to do justice to the positive character of the sinful element in all human definitions and realizations of natural justice. It also fails to do justice to the relation of love to justice. In its conception, natural justice is good as far as it goes, but it must be completed by the supernatural virtue of love. The true situation is that anything short of love cannot be perfect justice. In fact, every definition of justice actually presupposes sin as a given reality. It is only because life is in conflict with life, because of sinful self-interest, that we are required carefully to define schemes of justice which prevent one life from taking advantage of another. Yet no scheme of justice can do full justice to all the variable factors which the freedom of man introduces into human history. Significantly, both eighteenth-century and medieval conceptions of natural law are ultimately derived from Stoic conceptions. And it is the very nature of Stoic philosophy that it is confused about the relation of nature to reason. This confusion is due to the fact that it does not fully understand the freedom of man. In all Greco-Roman rationalism, whether Platonic, Aristotelian, or Stoic, it is assumed that man's freedom is secured by his rational transcendence over nature. Since reason and freedom are identified, it is assumed that the freedom that man has over nature is held in check and disciplined by his reason. The real situation is that man transcends his own reason, which is to say that he is not bound in his actions by reason's coherences and systems. His freedom consists in a capacity for self-transcendence in infinite regression. There is therefore no limit in reason for either his creativity or his sin. There is no possibility of giving a rational definition of a just relation between man and man or nation and nation short of a complete love in which each life affirms the interests of the other. Every effort to give a definition of justice short of this perfect love invariably introduces contingent factors, conditions of time and place, into the definition.

Love is the only final structure of freedom. Human personality as a system of infinite potentialities makes it impossible to define absolutely what I owe to my fellow man, since nothing that he now is exhausts what he might be. Human personality as capacity for infinite self-transcendence makes it impossible from my own standpoint to rest content in any ordered relation with my fellow men. There is no such relation that I cannot transcend to imagine a better one in terms of the ideal of love. Provisional definitions of justice short of this perfect love are, of course, necessary. But they are much more provisional than any natural law theory, whether medieval or modern, realizes. The freedom of man is too great to make it possible to define any scheme of justice absolutely in terms of " necessary " standards.

According to Catholic theology, it is this structure of ultimate freedom that is lost in the Fall just as the accompanying virtue of love is lost. The real situation is that " original justice " in the sense of a mythical " perfection before the Fall " is never completely lost. It is not a reality in man but always a potentiality. It is always what he ought to be. It is the only goodness completely compatible with his own and his fellow man's freedom — that is, with their ultimate transcendence over all circumstances of nature. Man is neither as completely bereft of " original justice " nor as completely in possession of " natural justice " as the Catholic theory assumes.

Protestant theory, on the other hand, partly because of Luther's nominalistic errors, has no sense of an abiding structure at all. Luther's theory of total depravity is, in fact, more intimately related to his nominalism than is generally realized. Only in nominalistic terms, in which love is regarded as good by the fiat of God and not because it is actually the structure of freedom, can it be supposed that life could be completely at variance with itself. " Sin," said Saint Augustine quite truly, " cannot tear up nature by the roots."

Injustice has meaning only against a background of a sense of justice. What is more, it cannot maintain itself without at least a minimal content of justice. The "ideological taint" in all human truth could have no meaning except against the background of a truth that is not so tainted. Men always jump to the erroneous conclusion that because they can conceive of a truth and a justice that completely transcend their interests, they are therefore also able to realize such truth and such justice. Against this error of the optimists, Protestant pessimism affirms the equally absurd proposition that sin has completely destroyed all truth and justice.

Protestantism has been betrayed into this error partly by its literalism, by which it defines the Fall as a historic event and "perfection before the Fall" as a perfection existing in a historical epoch before the Fall. When Luther essays to define this perfection he indulges in all kinds of fantastic nonsense. The perfection before the Fall is always an ideal possibility before the act. It describes a dimension of human existence rather than a period of history. It is the vision of health which even a sick man has. It is the structure of the good without which there could be no evil. The anarchy of Europe is evil only because it operates against an ideal possibility and necessity of order in Europe. The blindness of the eye is evil only because the ideal possibility is sight.

Protestant pessimism has been rightfully accused by Catholic thinkers of leading to obscurantism in culture and to antinomianism in morals; and it would be difficult to estimate to what degree our present anarchy is due to Protestant errors. But Catholics forget that Protestant pessimism is but a corrupted form of a prophetic criticism which Christianity must make even against its own culture, and that the medieval culture was subject to such a criticism by reason of its inability to recognize to what degree Christianity as a culture and as an institution is involved not only in the finiteness of history but in the sin of history — that is, precisely in the effort to hide finiteness and to pretend a transcendent perfection which cannot be achieved in history.

It may be useful to apply to contemporary history the theory that all human life stands under an ideal possibility purer than the natural law, and that at the same time it is involved in sinful reality much more dubious than the natural justice that Catholic thought declares to be possible. I will choose one specific example, prompted by the Archbishop of York's splendid wireless address in October last in favor of a "negotiated" rather than an "imposed" peace. The Peace of Versailles was an imposed peace. Its territorial provisions were really more just than is sometimes supposed at the present moment. But among its provisions it contained the forced admission of guilt by the vanquished, a piece of psychological cruelty which reveals self-righteousness at its worst. (It is interesting how our worst sins are always derived from self-righteousness, which is what gives Christ's contest with the Pharisees such relevance.) Against such a peace his Grace, and with him many others, are now pleading for a negotiated peace. They rightly believe that only in such a peace can Europe find security.

Yet it must be recognized that there is no definition of natural justice that can give us a really adequate outline of a just peace. Justice cannot be established in the world by pure moral suasion. It is achieved only as some kind of decent equilibrium of power is established. And such an equilibrium is subject to a thousand contingencies of geography and history. We cannot make peace with Hitler now because his power dominates the Continent, and his idea of a just peace is one that leaves him in the security of that dominance. We believe, I think rightly, that a more just peace can be established if that dominance is broken. But in so far as the Hitlerian imperial will must be broken first, the new peace will be an imposed peace. We may hope that a chastened Germany will accept it and make it its own. But even if vindictive passions are checked, as they were not in 1918, the fact that Germany will be defeated will rob her of some ideal possibilities in Europe, which she might have had but for her defeat in the war.

Nor is it possible for us to be sure that our conception of peace in Europe, in even our most impartial moments, could do full justice to certain aspects of the European situation that might be seen from the German but not from our perspective. On the other hand, we must assume that even the most chastened Germany would not be willing, except as she is forced, to accept certain provisions for the freedom of Poland and Czechoslovakia and the freedom of small nations generally. The inclination of the strong to make themselves the sponsors of the weak, and to claim that they are doing this not for their own but for the general good, is not a German vice. The Germans have merely accentuated a common vice of history and one that influences every concrete realization of justice. The concretion of justice in specific historic instances always depends upon a certain equilibrium of forces, which prevents the organizing will of the strong from degenerating into tyranny. Without resistance even the best ruler, oligarchy, or hegemonous nation would be tempted to allow its creative function of organization to degenerate into tyranny. Furthermore, even the most resolute moral resistance against vindictive passion cannot prevent retributive justice from degenerating into vindictiveness, if the foe is so thoroughly defeated as to invite the type of egotism which expresses itself in vindictiveness. It is significant, moreover, that no " rational " standard of retributive justice can be defined. What is worked out in each particular instance is always some *ad hoc* compromise between vindictiveness on the one hand and forgiveness on the other. This is particularly true of international disputes in which there are no genuinely impartial courts of adjudication. (Neutral nations are interested in the particular balance of power that emerges out of each conflict.) The structure of justice that emerges from each overt conflict must therefore be established to a very considerable degree by the disputants in the conflict, more particularly by the victors.

Yet men are not completely blinded by self-interest or lost in this maze of historical relativity. What always remains with them is not some uncorrupted bit of reason, which gives them universally valid standards of justice. What remains with them is something higher — namely, the law of love, which they dimly recognize as the law of their being, as the structure of human freedom, and which, in Christian faith, Christ clarifies and redefines, which is why he is called the " second Adam." It is the weakness of Protestant pessimism that it denies the reality of this potential perfection and its relevance in the affairs of politics.

The effort of the Christian church in Britain at the present moment to stem the tide of vindictiveness, which it rightly anticipates as an inevitable danger after the war, is a truer expression of the Christian spirit than pacifist disavowals of war as such. It is not possible to disavow war absolutely without disavowing the task of establishing justice. For justice rests upon a decent equilibrium of power; and all balances of power involve tension; and tension involves covert conflict; and there will be moments in history when covert conflict becomes overt. But it is possible to transcend a conflict while standing in it. Forgiveness is such a possibility. But forgiveness to the foe is possible only if I know myself to be a sinner — that is, if I do not have some cheap or easy sense of moral transcendence over the sinful reality of claims and counterclaims which is the very stuff of history.

This does not mean that it would ever be possible to establish a justice based upon perfect forgiveness after a war. The sinfulness of human nature will relativize every ideal possibility. Vindictiveness (which is an egoistic corruption of justice) cannot be completely eliminated. But the quality of justice that can be achieved in a war will depend upon the degree to which a " Kingdom of God " perspective can be brought upon the situation. It is this higher imagination rather than some unspoiled rational definition of retributive justice that pulls justice out of the realm of vindictiveness.

Human nature is, in short, a realm of infinite possibilities of good and evil because of the character of human freedom. The love that is the law of its nature is a boundless self-giving. The sin that corrupts its life is a boundless assertion of the self. Between these two forces all kinds of *ad hoc* restraints may be elaborated and defined. We may call this natural law. But we had better realize how very tentative it is. Otherwise we shall merely sanction some traditional relation between myself and my fellow man as a " just " relation, and quiet the voice of conscience which speaks to me of higher possibilities. What is more, we may stabilize sin and make it institutional; for it will be discovered invariably that my definition of justice guarantees certain advantages to myself to which I have no absolute right, but with which I have been invested by the accidents of history and the contingencies of nature and which the " old Adam " in me is only too happy to transmute into absolute rights.

*Love and Justice
on the National Level*

A. American Politics

6. OUR FAITH AND CONCRETE POLITICAL DECISIONS

IN A PRESIDENTIAL YEAR THE AIR IS FULL OF POLITI-cal speculations and opinions. Christians, no less than other citizens, are called upon to make fateful political decisions which may determine the fate of the country and the world. One might well ask whether there is anything in their Christian commitment that will lead them to morally superior decisions. We in Christian Action assume that it is possible to express our faith in terms of our political responsibilities. However, probably none of us is as certain as we once were that the Christian faith can be identified with some neat ideological position or political program. It is significant that in this Presidential year Christians of all shades of belief will probably unite in rejecting nationalist-isolationist candidates and programs, while there will be less agreement on domestic problems. This is why a Taft candidacy will arouse an almost united opposition in the Christian community, while an Eisenhower candidacy will not.

This situation is symptomatic of the very problematic way in which Christian convictions are related to the political order. We should long since have known that there are no clear choices between good and evil in the realm of politics and economics. Our primary quarrel in Christian Action today is with those Christians who identify a pretty unqualified free enterprise doctrine with the Christian faith. We must admit, however, that people with our general shade of conviction once were inclined to challenge this libertarianism with equally questionable collectivist doctrines, which we regarded as radical alternatives to the morally complacent position. Meanwhile, Russian communism presented modern history with a complete corruption of the collectivist doctrine. This does not prove,

Christianity and Society, Summer, 1952.

as some contemporary conservatives would have it, that all political
control of economic processes must end in tyranny. But it does prove
that political control has its own perils, which may or may not be
greater than the perils of an uncontrolled economy. These alternate
perils are due to the fact that in the realm of politics and economics
we must harness and provisionally justify the forces of egoism and
of power even though they be ultimately hazardous either to freedom or to brotherhood. We cannot disavow the use of power because it is hazardous, but neither must we obscure the moral peril of
power. This is the reason why no political program can be simply
equated with the highest sanctities of life, and why our political decisions must be more circumspect than Christian decisions in America have been either on the right or on the left. Nothing is clearer
than that ideologically consistent political positions have on the
whole been refuted by history, while healthy nations have preserved
freedom and extended justice by various pragmatic policies which
borrowed from various strategies.

This does not mean that we must not and cannot make clear-cut
decisions on matters of principle. It is becoming apparent, for instance, that the question of national health insurance (usually referred to by its opponents as "socialized medicine ") will become an
increasingly important political issue. In deciding for or against it
we decide for or against certain broad political strategies. But we
ought not to decide for or against it on the basis that the policy is
abstractly in violation of " freedom," or that abstractly it enhances
state control. We ought to make our decision by asking such questions as these: Can a system of economic freedom in medicine guarantee minimal standards of health? Can a socialized scheme be
subjected to professional rather than political standards? Is there
protection in the scheme against inordinate and disproportionate
demands upon it? If the presuppositions of such questions are analyzed, it will be apparent that they are rooted in a Christian interpretation of the human situation, for on the one hand they recognize
the law of love as our norm, they assume our responsibility for our

neighbor's welfare. On the other hand, they recognize the persistence of self-love, including the indeterminate character of human desires, as a perennial factor in any human situation. A Christian faith
that recognizes both of these factors will be prevented from aggra-
vating the ideological conflict in modern society. It may even prevent political acrimony in a Presidential year.

7. CHRISTIAN FAITH AND POLITICAL CONTROVERSY

A Presidential election year once again brings into focus the problem of how Christians should relate their religious commitments to their political opinions and decisions. This is a problem of conscience for every individual Christian. It is also a practical problem for Christian congregations and communities. It arises as a problem for the church because the church is a community of faith which is not organized on the basis of common political convictions; yet its members do have political convictions and sometimes very contradictory ones. The more passionately they are held, the more they rise to the religious level and the more they tend to affront fellow Christians who hold different convictions. Sometimes the problem emerges, particularly with reference to different convictions between pastors and congregations. For, generally speaking, the congregations of American Protestantism are more conservative politically than their clerical leaders.

We can approach a solution of the problem of relating religious commitments to political decisions by excluding two wrong answers to the issue. The one wrong answer is to equate religious and political commitments and to regard every political decision as simply derived from our faith. This is a wrong answer because political issues deal with complex problems of justice, every solution for which contains morally ambiguous elements. All political positions are morally ambiguous because, in the realm of politics and economics, self-interest and power must be harnessed and beguiled rather than eliminated. In other words, forces which are morally dangerous must be used despite their peril. Politics always aims at some kind of a harmony or balance of interest, and such a harmony cannot be regarded as directly related to the final harmony of love of the Kingdom of God. All men are naturally inclined to obscure the morally ambiguous element in their political cause by investing it with religious sanctity. This is why religion is more frequently a source of confusion than of light in the political realm. The tendency to equate our political with our Christian convictions causes politics to generate idolatry.

The other wrong answer stands at the opposite extreme. It is to find no relevance at all between our faith and our political actions. This answer is wrong because it denies the seriousness of our political decisions and obscures our Christian responsibilities for the good order and justice of our civil community.

If we rule out these two extremes, we still face the primary question of how politics is to be related to faith. We can advance a little farther toward a solution of the problem if we recognize that political issues represent various grades and levels which range all the way from clear moral issues to problems of strategy and means.

It is obvious, for instance, that the Christian churches of America have, with a fair degree of consistency, espoused the idea of America's responsibility to a world community, and have resisted nationalist and isolationist politics in the name of the Christian faith. They have been right in doing so. But this broad moral purpose must be distinguished from problems of strategy. Various strategic devices will be advanced as the best ways of fulfilling our responsibilities. Such devices can never be invested with full religious sanctity. It would be impossible to claim, for instance, that the Christian faith requires that America give preference to either the European or the Asiatic field of strategy, or that we should defend the free world primarily by air, rather than by land, power.

In the same fashion the commandment " Thou shalt love thy neighbor as thyself " brings us under religious and moral compulsions to eliminate the violations of brotherhood in the field of race relations. But it can hardly compel us to choose between the efficacy of a state as against a Federal Fair Employment Practices Act. In such questions of strategy there are reasons for honest differences of opinion.

In actual life, however, no clear distinction between moral principles and strategy can be made. This is why Christian convictions that deal only with ultimate principle and exclude strategic issues tend to become wholly irrelevant. Yet the farther one moves from a principle that is clearly related to the love commandment to detailed applications in particular situations, the more hazardous the decision becomes, and the more impossible it is to compel others to a similar conviction by appeal to a common faith.

That is why it is important to distinguish between the responsibility of individual Christians and voluntary groups, and the responsibility of the church as a community of faith. Christians must make these hazardous political decisions with full recognition that others equally devoted to the common good may arrive at contrary conclusions. They will be less affronted and baffled by the different conclusions if they have some humble recognition of the taint of individual and collective self-interest which colors even our purest political and moral ideals. The different emphases, for instance, that the more and the less privileged members of a democratic community give to the value of freedom on the one hand and to the value of justice on the other (a difference that is at the very heart of politics in all free societies) should be recognized as flowing inevitably from the peculiar interests and ideologies of each group.

We are well aware that unity in a free society requires a high degree of what our secular friends define as tolerance. As Christians we are inclined to regard the attitude of tolerance as rooted in a religious humility, which recognizes the partial and fragmentary character of all human wisdom and the interested character of all human striving. Whenever religion obscures, rather than illumines, this human situation, it tends to aggravate political controversies and adds an element of pretension to the natural self-righteousness of men. On the other hand, a mere emphasis upon religious humility may empty the political struggle of seriousness by persuading men that all their causes are equally true or equally false. That is why it is important to emphasize our responsibility for hazardous political decisions at the same time that we seek to understand the reasons why different men of equal sincerity and wisdom arrive at contrary conclusions. We must not obscure the issue of justice which is hidden in every political question or pretend to be gods and not men, transcending the frailties of mortals. Ideally a democratic society is best preserved by a religious quality of life which regards our political as our other decisions of great importance, even while recognizing the incapacity of men to arrive at a purely rational, or purely moral, or purely Christian solution of any perplexing problem.

8. RATIONING AND DEMOCRACY

A leader of Christian thought and life, recently returned from a tour of the country, reported that there was an appalling confusion in the minds of church people on the question of liberty and democ-

Christianity and Society, Winter, 1942.

racy. These church people insisted on identifying rationing with fascism, as they had previously identified conscription with tyranny. This fact reveals to what degree democracy is based upon libertarian assumptions in both secular and religious circles in America. Democracy is supposed to be identical with freedom; and any restriction upon freedom is thought of as a denial of the democratic way of life. It was in that spirit that conscription was condemned as undemocratic. In the same spirit the pious housewife now regards rationing as a proof that we have sacrificed democracy.

Rationing is actually the best implementation of the spirit of equality. When, as in wartime, consumers' goods are scarce, it is impossible to maintain a free market. The scramble of competitive buyers would merely result in a special advantage to the rich over the poor. The privileged would be able to pay the higher prices for scarcer goods, and the poor would have to be content with leftovers. No semblance of justice can be maintained in wartime without price ceilings on the one hand and rationing on the other. Despite some mistakes, the Government has done rather well in both its price fixing and rationing programs. Its record is particularly good if we remember that it has had to deal with very ignorant opposition, not a little of which has been informed by supposedly Christian presuppositions.

It is a rather sad commentary on the state of Christian thought that men should identify the right to do as they please, without regard to the weal and woe of others, with " Christian liberty." It is high time that Christian libertarians learned something of the paradoxical relation between liberty and equality in the heart of democracy. Democracy does not mean absolute equality; for no society can live without differentiation of functions which qualify equality. Therefore a dogmatic equalitarianism inevitably results in a destruction of liberty, as the history of Stalinism proves. But on the other hand democracy does not mean absolute liberty either. For absolute liberty always turns out in the end to be the liberty of the strong to take advantage of the weak. Liberty can never stand alone. The problem of a democratic society is always to preserve the greatest amount of liberty compatible with the necessities of the community.

If the general public does not understand this relation, the invariable consequence is an actual loss of liberty. For any society is bound to preserve its unity in a time of crisis; and if it cannot count on the voluntary compliance with fixed rules of justice, it must increase the measure of coercion by which they are enforced. Ideally, a society composed of socially intelligent and responsible citizens achieves many standards of justice by methods that are neither purely voluntary nor purely coercive. They are not voluntary, because the standard is set by governmental authority. They are voluntary if the citizen recognizes the necessity of the restriction and complies with it gladly. If a society is informed by too libertarian conceptions of democracy, it actually destroys some of its liberties by this mistake. For it encourages defiance of necessary restrictions and forces the government to increase the measure of coercion required to maintain them.

9. THE REPUBLICAN VICTORY

A Presidential election, particularly one that reverses the trends of two decades, should be a good laboratory in which to test theories of how men come to terms with the problems of their community. The regnant theory of our culture is that man has the rational capacity to survey the needs of his community; and that if he is lacking in disinterested intelligence, the development of education will cure this defect. The realities, on the other hand, particularly those which we experienced recently, show that in all practical encounters of men with their fellow men, their reason is the servant of their interest and passion. A democratic society is, therefore, not so much the consequence of mind meeting mind as of interest balanced by interest.

Let us consider first the political balance that was overturned recently. It was established by Roosevelt two decades ago. It was based upon the discovery and conviction that the sovereign power of the state could and should be used to establish minimal standards of general welfare. In every election in twenty years it was necessary to wait until the suburban vote and the farm vote came in to balance the vote of the large cities if one wanted to be sure of the outcome. For the masses of the city said yes to this program and suburbs said no, and the farmers were ambivalent. The city said yes because its thousands were exposed to the inequalities and the hazards of technical society, and they believed in a state that would equalize the

Christianity and Crisis, November 24, 1952.

inequalities and mitigate the hazards of economic life. The people in the suburbs, on the other hand, said no. They had, either in terms of economic power or by their own skills and competence, the source of security within themselves. They therefore adhered to the principles of classical liberalism and regarded the interference of government as nefarious. The people of the farm were ambivalent. Their mode of work made them individualists. Yet they desired the help of the Government to support the prices of farm products, to achieve rural electrification, and to assure help on loans for the purchase of farms. Their ambivalence made their adhesion to the grand alliance constructed by Roosevelt insecure. They were expected to depart in 1948, but their departure delayed by four years contributed to the overthrow. Their choice was a rational step because disgust with corruption in government accentuated the farmer's original individualist fear of big government.

But the defection of the farmer was not sufficient to account for the radical overturn. The second reason for it was the personal popularity of the Republican candidate. This popularity exceeded the party sentiments of the voters, though it must be observed that his popularity measured against the rising popularity of the Democratic candidate, appreciated as a new and authentic voice in the counsels of the nation, was strongly influenced by party loyalties.

The third factor was the Korean War. The pains and frustrations of that war were a part of the price that America was forced to pay for its position of world leadership. Through the exigencies of history the Democratic Party was the symbol and the instrument of that responsibility. The Republican Party was deeply divided on the issues of foreign policy. The Republican candidate was drawn from the wing of the party that believed in accepting our responsibilities. Another wing, whether prompted by the irresponsibility of a party in opposition or by deep impulses in the American business community, held to isolationist convictions.

But now the Korean ordeal made our role of world leadership unpopular — or at least, one burden of that role very difficult to bear. Eisenhower reacted to the Korean problem in terms that would satisfy both the internationalist and the isolationist sentiments of his party. A more consistent approach would have been politically less successful. The gesture of a trip to Korea was a politically brilliant device for covering up the inconsistency. It did not arouse the interventionist to apprehensions about our abandonment of Korea, and it allowed anxious mothers to hope against hope that somehow or other the ordeal would be ended. The Democratic leadership made a mistake in not taking the sentiment in regard to Korea seriously enough. The frustration of a war that cannot simply be either won or ended is a very great problem for a youthful nation always accustomed to having its own way. Thus it was on foreign policy that the real shift of sentiment occurred. And a position slightly inconsistent, if not dishonest, was the force causing the overturn.

It must be appreciated that one of the real gains of a Republican victory is that it makes the party of the dominant business group of the nation thoroughly responsible for foreign policy. In its irresponsibility it was developing some dangerous tendencies toward hysteria. Against this gain we must, of course, count the increase of prestige of McCarthy due to the fact that his questionable methods may have contributed to the Republican victory.

In short, the election campaign, taken as a laboratory test, reveals political man as capable of rational analysis of our common fate and of moral estimates of his own and his neighbor's rights. But the rational and moral considerations are in every instance colored by interest and passion. The democratic process is, therefore, not so much a meeting of minds in which the truth prevails, as it is a contest of interests dominated by the fortuitous circumstance and not by rational argument. Democracy must be regarded, on the one hand, as a system of government which men's rational and moral capacities make possible, and on the other hand, as a system of checks and balances which the corruptions by interest and passion make necessary. For these corruptions as revealed in the campaign are precisely those which make life insufferable in a tyrannical regime and which are robbed of their virulence by the checks and balances of democracy.

The paramount question that faces modern technical civilization, which is how our economic affairs shall be regulated without unduly heightening the peril of governmental power, has not been rationally answered. But we can take satisfaction in the knowledge that, though there is no absolute answer to this question, it is answered practically when neither those who fear governmental power too much nor those who trust it too much gain preponderant or permanent power in the state. The truth emerges from the competition of interest and half-truths between these groups rather than by what they hold dear as truth. Thus democracy is a device by which God causes the "wrath of man to praise him," rather than a scheme for exploiting only the virtues of man.

10. DEMOCRACY AND THE PARTY SPIRIT

A few days before Lincoln's Birthday, President Eisenhower pleaded with both parties to avoid extremism in party conflict in view of the seriousness of the times. This did not prevent his own party followers from celebrating Lincoln's Birthday all over America by accusing the opposition of having been in "twenty years of treason."

Whether or not the President's advice is heeded may be more fateful for the health of our nation than the victory of either party, or of the policies that they may follow. The fact is that democracy requires not only the organization of political parties, but also a certain degree of mutual respect or at least tolerance. Whenever the followers of one political party persuade themselves that the future of the nation is not safe with the opposition in power, it becomes fairly certain that the nation's future is not safe, no matter which party rules. For such political acrimony endangers the nation's health more than any specific political policies.

The danger that democratic freedom may destroy the unity of the nation is in fact so great that our founding fathers never envisioned the organization of national parties as we know them. Madison was as fearful of the baneful effects of "faction" as was Washington. Madison argued, in fact, that one virtue of a federal community would be that it would prevent the organization of "factions." He was right in the sense that our political parties are loosely organized federations of local and regional political groups, which lack the ideological consistency of European political parties. But he would certainly have been surprised by the consistency of the national organization of each political group.

The fear of the founding fathers of national disruption through the organization of "factions," and the complete silence of the Constitution on political instrumentalities which are now the very stuff of the political process, put party government in the same category as constitutional monarchy in, say, Britain. They are both unintended instruments of democracy which contain more wisdom than anyone could have consciously intended.

Theoretically, the " rulers " should be subject to the constant scrutiny of the " people " and hold their office only by their suffrage. Practically, the " people " can make their decisions only when they are confronted with specific alternatives. Thus, modern democracies have evolved the organization of an alternative government which constantly challenges the party in power while it is in office, and tries to replace it in office at the end of the term. Our Electoral College, a vestigial remnant of the written Constitution made otiose by our unwritten constitution with its development of parties, is a reminder of the unintended place of parties in our system.

But the necessity of party government makes it all the more important to curb the excesses of the party spirit which our fathers feared so much. The unity of the national community must not be endangered by party strife. The respective parties are bound to contest elections as if the future of the nation depended upon their victory. But they must nevertheless have a reserve conviction that this is not true, that the nation will be safe in the keeping of either party. Parliamentary government is, in the phrase of the English historian Herbert Butterfield, a form of " limited war." Its success depends upon the constant willingness of the defeated minority to trust both itself and the nation to the victorious majority.

It is worth noting that stable democracies have developed a technique for limiting party conflict that might strike the visitor from Mars as very illogical. The technique requires that the election contest be fought with few restraints, generating emotions that sometimes divide families and friends. But, when the count is in, the defeated minority submits with what grace it is able to summon, and the party truce goes into effect for the general public — though the professional politicians are expected to carry on a guerrilla warfare. We are told that Latin-American observers are " shocked " by our custom requiring the loser to congratulate the victor and assure him of support. In Latin America, that gesture smacks of " insincerity." Actually, it is a ritualistic observance defining the difference between stable nations, in which the political struggle has limits, and those nations in which the struggle may be as bitter as it is " sincere " and where the minority is not reconciled to defeat.

The mutual trust between parties, which makes the limitation of party conflict possible, rests upon certain conditions. The party programs must not be too contradictory and a large segment of the population must not be irrevocably committed to either party. Above all, there must be a reserve of loyalty to the nation — and, what may be more important, to principles of justice and freedom — which transcends the party conflict. Whenever these common loyalties and standards of justice are subordinated to party advantage, the community is imperiled by threats of schism.

President Eisenhower's warning against party extremism is thus extremely relevant, for the parties not only must not be too far apart but must not be made to appear more contradictory in their objectives than they really are. Our experience in this matter is partly conditioned by European history.

In Europe, it could be taken for granted that a small number among the parties of the Right were either fascist-minded or tolerant of fascist ideas. An equally small number among the parties of the Left were sympathetic to, or tolerant of, communism. The " vital center " of democracy was held by neither Right nor Left but by both conservatives and liberals, who put the standards of justice above party advantage. This vital center was constantly threatened by the extremists of the Right, who tried to prove that the whole Left was involved with the communist conspiracy and that, in any case, fascism was justified as a weapon against communism; and by the leftist extremists, who tried to prove that every kind of conservatism was tantamount to fascism and that communism was justified as a weapon against the fascist danger. Both theories proved wrong. If they had been right, no democracy could have survived.

There was an ironic quality in history's refutation of these theories. For the two forms of extremism, each of which tried to justify itself as the most effective weapon against the other, were revealed to have identical consequences of tyranny and cruelty. This was the most indisputable proof of the thesis that democracy depends not so much upon particular policies as upon the fairness and justice with which the conflicts of interest are composed and basic rights preserved. This is the more true since the political debate in every modern technological nation centers on the question of how much or how little the Government shall interfere in the free play of economic forces. There can be no final solution of this problem. Approaches to it by Right and Left cannot be " objective," for they are prompted by the respective interests on the one hand of those classes which are powerful enough to have security and want liberty for the exercise of their power, and on the other hand of the less privileged classes, which prefer security to liberty, since they have no skill or power of their own to gain security amid the hazards of a technological society. The health of modern societies requires that this debate remain inconclusive.

The first threat to unity above and below party conflict came from the Left. The Marxist dogma of the class struggle oversimplified the complex class structure of technical civilization and obscured the mutualities of interest transcending the conflict of economic interests, which Madison recognized as the root of political controversy long before Marx. We know the baleful consequences of a consistent application of the Marxist doctrine in modern communism. Democratic socialism has only slowly extricated itself from the power of the dogma, though it is only fair to say that its practices have been, for a long time, more consistent with democratic mutuality than with the theory to which it payed lip service.

In modern democratic societies, particularly in our own, the danger of party extremism now comes from the Right rather than the Left. There are obvious historical reasons for this development, not related to the fortuitous presence of gifted and unscrupulous demagogues on the Right.

The fact that the Left was influenced by viewpoints and accepted credos which in their most consistent form resulted in the hated communist conspiracy, offered a great temptation to the Right to pretend to see the whole political spectrum left of center as involved in the conspiracy. In our nation, the temptation has been particularly great because the party in power during the period when the hated foe of today was an ally in the struggle against nazism, was of the Left. There was, therefore, a certain plausibility to the absurd charge that the New Deal was involved in " twenty years of treason." This charge seemed the more plausible because the climate of opinion in those two decades made it quite impossible to foresee the present demonic realities of Soviet politics. It is significant that those members of the present Administration who shared the responsibility of government in the Roosevelt era were as touched with illusions in regard to Russian realities and intentions as members of the Democratic Party. The charge of connivance with treason is particularly significant, for it is always the final weapon of the demagogue to accuse the political opponent of being in secret or open connivance with the enemy of the nation.

If these considerations do not convince the thoughtful observer that the contest between the President and the extremists of his party is more fateful for the health of our nation than the contest between the parties, a comparison between two contemporary democracies, Britain and France, may be convincing. The one enjoys a stability beyond that of any other nation. The other has been involved in social instability since the French Revolution.

The sources of British stability are many, but one of the most important surely is the limited character of the party conflict. The common sense of the whole national community enforces these limits. Thus Britain has survived both the assumption of power by a socialist party and its defeat by the Conservatives without an appreciable rent in the national unity. The socialist party was significantly not orthodox Marxist and refrained from challenging the whole national tradition. Unlike Continental parties, it therefore gained the suffrage of the whole national community. When it became apparent that the cherished policy of collectivization could not overcome the poverty of a war-impoverished nation and that the hiatus between dream and reality could not be overcome by more rigorous collectivization, the prestige of Labor declined and Churchill returned to power.

The Conservatives, on the other hand, did not lend themselves to the illusion that they could or should undo everything that Labor had done. They were schooled in an older and wiser tradition than our conservatism. They believed that the economic process must always be subordinated to political power and moral principle. There was an incident in the election after the war which brought Labor to power that shows that even a wise and magnanimous leader such as Mr. Churchill may be tempted to overstep the bounds of " limited war " in the heat of an election campaign. He prophesied that a Labor victory would usher in a " police state." But the satire of the potent cartoonist David Low refuted this extremism better than the opposition could have done. Mr. Low merely pictured Clement Attlee trying to look like Stalin. Everybody laughed the analogy out of court. The difference between an ostensible socialist party and an ostensible conservative party is significantly less than the difference between the two American parties which have elaborated two facets of the old liberalism.

By contrast the French instability obviously derives from the heat of the party conflict. Who remembers the creeds of the various

French parties? What remains memorable is the acrimony between the parties, no matter what their policies. Incidentally, the fact that this party conflict takes place in a multiple-party system, as contrasted with the two-party system which distinguishes Anglo-Saxon democracies, is instructive.

Theoretically, two parties might be expected to divide the nation more consistently than a profusion of parties. But this is another case in which experience refutes theories. Mr. Churchill, in a memorable speech, attributed the two-party system to the indirect influence of the rectangular, rather than circular, architecture of the House of Commons. If this should be true, architecture would have had a most grateful influence upon the health of nations. Fortunately, the two-party system proved powerful enough to transcend its architectural cradle. For we inherited it from the British, though we built our Congressional chambers after the pattern of the Continent.

The French party struggle certainly contributed to the French defeat by Hitler. For the French Right, including military leaders such as General Weygand, were so obsessed with the domestic peril from the Left that they were ineffective against a foreign foe, and in some cases overtly preferred capitulation to a victory that would have given the domestic competitor prestige. The indignities to French honor during the Vichy period are well known. In the present instance, communism actually has a power on the French Left which it does not enjoy in any other modern nation. But even when the Left is rigorously anticommunist, it imperils the security of the nation by neutralist illusions which have their source in the acrimony of the domestic political situation.

In the temper of our political life, we are probably equidistant from the standards of Britain on the one hand, and France on the other. Our political health is correspondingly less robust than that of Britain but more robust than France. That circumstance makes the tension between the President and his party so fateful for our future. Eisenhower obviously is a man of the middle ground in terms of his temper. This remains true despite his unfortunate definition of his campaign as a "crusade," for the word connotes unlimited, rather than limited, conflict. In addition to temper, the President is deeply committed by conviction and previous experience to the foreign policy course that the previous Administration elaborated. He is also surprisingly loyal to the domestic policy of controlling economic life at least to the extent of avoiding undue fluctuations of "boom or bust." This is surprising in view of the temper of his campaign. The contest between the President and the extremists in his party is, therefore, a contest between those who would narrow and those who would widen the distance between the parties.

When President Eisenhower stood resolutely against the Bricker Amendment and the isolationist nationalism that it expressed and symbolized, it seemed for a time that the issue had been finally joined and we would soon know whether the one or the other type of Republicanism would be victorious. But an old pattern repeated itself, and an equivocal one. The President did not act until it was too late to rescue an inept Secretary of the Army from at least the appearance of capitulation to Senator McCarthy and thus increased the status of this demagogue at home and his caricature of American life abroad.

This incident, together with his failure to enforce anything more than an outward compliance to his rule of moderation even upon members of his own staff, raises the question whether the party in power may not have elaborated, either by design or inadvertence, a method of working both sides of the street. If this works, the President will remain an unsullied symbol of moderation and wisdom, who will appeal to the dominant mood of the nation, while the "bully boys" will "rough up" the opposition without real hindrance and will appeal to that part of the electorate which speaks of a "Republican revolution" and desires to set the clock back on both domestic and foreign policy. If this policy should succeed, it would make confusion worse confounded in our nation and make our future ominous.

11. CATHOLICISM AND ANARCHISM IN SPAIN

The Catholic Church is fighting for a " Christian civilization " in Spain. Its claims would seem to be amply justified if one remembers that the stoutest protagonists of the constitutional government in Spain are anarchists. These anarchists are not only opposed to religion, as the communists are, but they are opposed to the very idea of government. Their power in Spain is a curious survival of a political ideology that was once a specter to haunt the " good people " of nineteenth century Europe. Anarchism scared the bourgeoisie a hundred years ago even more than communism scares them now. One finds significant remnants of these fears in the inclination of modern plutocrats to lump anarchism and communism in one lump, though the theories of Proudhon and Bakunin have little in common with those of Marx. Marx in fact directed the full force of his polemic energies against them.

The fact is that anarchism has all of the destructive energy of communism with none of its constructive genius. Communists may be utopians in the sense that they expect the state to " wither away " after the proletarian dictatorship has destroyed all the foes of a new society. But the anarchists are pure utopians who have no realization of the necessary role of power and forces in politics. Anarchism is a dangerous doctrine. Its conceptions of human nature are purely romantic. It imagines that if it can only destroy the present instruments of power and greed, humanity will naturally and inevitably express the innate goodness of human nature, thus securing the blessings of both liberty and voluntary co-operation. Pure anarchist doctrine is dangerous because it confuses the political realities and prompts men to chase phantoms and illusions. The more realistic anarchism which dates from Bakunin is even more dangerous than the earlier and purer variety of Proudhon. It is the anarchism of terror, assassination, and insurrection. It justifies any deed of violence against men of power because it falsely imagines that to get rid of powerful men in society is to solve the problem of power. It does not know that the same power that is the source of injustice in a society is also a *sine qua non* of its public order and peace.

Radical Religion, Spring, 1937.

So destructive are the illusions and the policies of anarchism that the failure of the Spanish Government to throttle its fascist foes must be partly attributed to them. The anarchists of Spain are fighting with splendid heroism for their Government. But their help came late and their co-operation is still tentative and precarious. Only a very acute crisis can persuade anarchists to modify their creed in the interest of political co-operation. Their fanatic and utopian idealism will undoubtedly continue to be a peril to Spanish unity, even if the Government should succeed, by their aid, to stamp out fascism.

Anarchism is, in short, a disease. It is the psychosis of infantile idealists who do not know what kind of a world it is in which we are living, what human nature is really like, and what the necessities of government are. Perhaps we ought, then, to justify the Catholics and the fascists who feel so certain that they are fighting for a Christian civilization in Spain.

Before we do so we might ask the reason for the significant survival of this curious libertarian and terroristic creed in Spain. Spain and Russia were the two nations of Europe who entered the twentieth century with an unreconstructed feudalism. Anarchism flourishes in Spain for the same reason that nihilism flourished in Russia before the genius of a small group of communists transmuted its anarchism into a more realistic collectivism. This fanatic, not to say psychopathic, libertarianism is a natural reaction to an outmoded feudalism. It is a reaction to the injustices of a feudal social order, injustices that were onerous enough in the period of its flower and which grow more and more oppressive in the period of its decay. Whenever power produces only a minimal social peace and a maximum of social injustice one must expect the doctrine to arise that all power is evil.

But feudalism is not only a particular form of agrarian social order. It is also a peculiar type of culture in which religion is more intimately related to society than in the more rationalistic bourgeois and capitalistic civilization. Feudalism is in fact a religious civilization. The Catholic Church built the feudal order. The universalism of that order at its best was its glory. Its too-intimate relations to the seats of power in that order are its vice and shame. Anarchism is therefore not only a libertarian protest against unjust power. It is also a spiritual protest against corrupt religion. That must be understood if one is to appreciate the spirituality of anarchism. The genuine anarchistic Spaniard has something of the spirit of Francis of Assisi and of the Christian saints. Perhaps one might add that he has something of the spirit of many a mild liberal parson, the implications of whose moral and political theories are also anarchistic, since he believes that government could be dispensed with if only people heeded his sermons and loved one another. Of course the anarchist distinguishes himself from the Christian saints by implementing and corrupting his spiritual vision. It is nevertheless important to recognize the spiritual source of his politics and to know that it is a reaction of sincerity to hypocrisy. A utopian religion that seeks to eliminate all power from society is the curious stepchild of a religion that has given power a too uncritical justification.

A realistic religion must probably follow the Pauline doctrine to some degree and accept government as an ordinance of God (Rom., ch. 13). It is forced to regard the power that governments wield as a necessary evil, lest society fall into chaos. The difficulty with all established religion is that it stops short in its realism and fails to recognize that power is the source of social injustice as well as of social peace. Whenever religion comes into a too-intimate relation with the processes of government, it succumbs to the temptation of regarding government as only an instrument of God and of forgetting its prophetic function of declaring that the state is a rebel against God. This prophetic function is therefore usually performed by amateur rather than professional and established religious leaders. Thus Amos preaches judgment at the king's court in Bethel and is told by Amaziah the priest to get back where he came from for " this is the king's chapel and this is the king's court." This protestation of the king's chaplain contains a perfect description of all captured religion. In it the king's court and the king's chapel are so close together that it is not possible to distinguish one from the other. It is the business of prophetic religion to remind the men of power that " God resisteth the proud and giveth grace to the humble," that he will " cast the mighty from their seats and exalt them of low degree," that " he bringeth the princes to naught and maketh the judges of the earth as vanity." Prophetic religion sees how all human power is tempted to pride and to injustice. In its pride it regards itself the sole source of social peace rather than a purely ancillary factor. Thus it imagines that the inordinate privileges that it demands merely because it has the strength to demand them are really just wages that society ought to pay for its services. Thus the same power, whether priestly, military, or economic, that builds a society in its youth, destroys it by its injustices in the period of its age.

The pride of power is most significantly displayed in the religious pretensions of ancient priest-kings and god-kings, of Roman emperors and of medieval dynasties, ruling by divine right. Modern democratic governments are more rationalistic and less religious, but they may succumb to the same pride, as for instance when the Supreme Court makes pretensions of sacrosanctity. Every form of social power, whether in an avowedly religious or in an irreligious age tends to make itself god. From this sin of rebellion against God flows the sin of oppression and injustice. Whenever a purely human force seeks to transcend the limits of creatureliness, it destroys other life in the process of its aggrandizement.

Since prophetic religion discovers in God a center of life that transcends all nations and all partial values, and believes in a God who judges all peoples, it can never be completely at ease with any government. At least it cannot as long as it is true to its essential nature. But unfortunately, if its genius is perverted, its sanctification of power and injustice will be even more grievous than that of non-prophetic religions.

Catholicism is not the only form of Christianity subject to the temptation of a too intimate relation with secular power. But it is the only form of Christianity that ever built a civilization. It is therefore particularly subject to the temptation of becoming the defender, rather than the critic, of the civilization that it built. In both medieval Europe and modern Spain, its relation to its civilization has been even more intimate than that of a defender. It was the actual wielder of power. The bishop became a secular lord, the pope a secular ruler, and the church an arm of the state. Since the relation of power to society is always ambiguous, as the source of both peace and injustice, any religion that becomes either the intimate ally or the very basis of that power is bound to arouse a cynical reaction to its pretensions. The reverence that it adds to military force may actually stabilize a government for generations. But the ultimate reaction will be the more violent. Whether it is in a French, Russian, or Spanish revolution, a religiously sanctified civilization must perish in both violence and hatred. No hatred is quite so terrible as the hatred aroused by a religious institution that has taken the name of the Lord in vain. The sin of hypocrisy breeds the sin of vengeance. The most interesting aspect of the spirit of vengeance that is bred by the spirit of hypocrisy is that, though it is ostensibly antireligious, it always has its own religious genius. That was true of the middle-class revolution of eighteenth-century France and of the communist revolution in Russia; and that is true of Spanish anarchism. The most characteristic quality of this secular religion is its utopianism.

Protestantism frequently has the same relation to capitalism as Catholicism to feudalism. Even communism, which begins by setting fanatic prophets against the pretensions of established religion, ends by transmuting these prophets into priest-kings. What is Stalin but a new priest-king whose power achieves an unqualified sanctification from the official religion of his government?

The process that makes for this alliance between religion and power is not confined to any one type of Christian religion or even to the Christian religion as such. It is, in fact, such a perennial factor in human history that it must be ascribed to a basic difficulty of human spirituality. Only a religion that worships a God before whom the princes of the world are as nothing, and which is able to convict the mighty as well as the lowly of sin, is capable of dealing with this difficulty of human spirituality. But this is also the very type of religion that can be most grievously corrupted.

A church can consequently never prove itself Christian by defending a " Christian civilization." By that very effort it becomes, as church, unchristian. Every civilization stands under the judgment of God for having allowed its centers of power to become means of oppression. If the church does not see that, it does not understand its own gospel. There is a peculiar pathos in the fact that the part of the gospel that it does not understand should become the basis of a new political error, i.e., the utopianism of its foes.

12. THE HITLER–STALIN PACT

From the standpoint of power politics nothing was more logical than the pact between Hitler and Stalin. Those of us who predicted and feared it as a possibility were met with a sense of outrage on the part of the " comrades " and " fellow travelers," and the expression of frank doubts about our sanity. They usually do not know the Scriptures, but what the comrades said were modern paraphrases of

Radical Religion, Fall, 1939.

Saint Paul's words: " What communion hath light with darkness and what concord hath Christ with Belial, or what part hath he that believeth with an infidel? "

The trouble with all the comrades and semicomrades is of course symptomatic of the trouble in all modern culture. They have found a Christ in history, whereas the only true Christ is he who was crucified in history. They have found the devil in history; they saw in nazism the very incarnation of the principle of evil. Communism was Christ. Russia was the Kingdom of God. Hitler was the devil. The pluto-democracies were the Laodicean believers who were suspected of lukewarm faith and were challenged continually to choose between Christ and Belial, between Stalin and Hitler. It was regarded as unthinkable that Russia might make political choices that would be prompted primarily by instincts of survival as a nation rather than by loyalty to an international and universal cause. Russia was not a nation. Russia was the fatherland of socialism.

The true believers insisted upon this creed in spite of the fact that evidence had been multiplying for years that nationalistic motives were gaining the ascendency in Russia. The Bolshevists had begun to extol Peter the Great as a founder of modern Russia; and the Russian word for " fatherland " was popularized. Yet the comrades believed that Russia represented a force of pure disinterestedness in politics. Its only thought was supposedly the defense of the workers throughout the world. The " united front " politics of the Kremlin seemed to give some support to these ideas for a while. Russia was supporting democracy against fascism. Democracy was, of course, not as good as communism. But it was better than fascism, and Stalin was wise enough and merciful enough to support the children of light even if they were only the children of twilight.

All this was, of course, not politics at all. It was a naïve religion. People must believe something. Analyze the life attitudes of even the most sophisticated and emancipated modern, and you will discover that somewhere in his credo there is a Christ and a Kingdom of God, something that he trusts, though all else fail. If one deals with politics realistically, unhindered by the confusions of primitive religions, one must soon discover that in every national organism there is both a primal instinct of survival without reference to the " ideological," the cultural, and ideal values that the nation bears, and some loyalty to a " civilization," a " culture," a religion which transcends the nation. In each case there is also an oligarchy in each nation, whose instincts of survival cut diagonally across both the other impulses. No nation ever supports values that transcend its life if they are diametrically opposed to the preservation of its life. Nations can and do support higher values than their own if there is a coincidence between the higher values and the impulse of survival.

The international situation up to a recent date was as follows: In the so-called democratic nations there was a coincidence between the values of democracy (which are still very real, however corrupted by economic injustice) and the defensive necessities of the French nation and the British Empire. In the same way there was a coincidence between the preservation of Russia and the preservation of socialism against fascism. The defensive necessities of the capitalistic oligarchs in the democratic nations did, however, run counter to this community of interest. The Polish landlords were reluctant to allow a Russian army into Poland, even for the defense of the nation. The British Tories were equally reluctant to make a pact with Russia. Driven by desperate necessity and the urging of the common people, they did make halfhearted efforts in that direction. But the Russians were not slow to perceive how halfhearted these efforts were. They therefore counted discretion the better part of valor and made a pact with the enemy.

The Germans come into this picture as an illustration of another possible relation between national interests and those which transcend the nation. The Nazis have long proclaimed themselves the defenders of civilization against Bolshevism. But the " ideological," that is, dishonest element, in this universal value was greater than in the other cases. Nazism is, as Rauschning has pointed out, the worship of power for its own sake. Even its devotion to the racial principle is bogus. Its devotion to " civilization " certainly is. Nothing was more natural for the Nazis than to seek this pact with Russia.

The fact that Russia accepted it and set the Nazis free to attack the democratic powers places Stalin's Russia in the same relation to the cause of socialism as Napoleon's France had to the bourgeois revolution of the eighteenth century. This is not a new phenomenon of history. Nor is it anything about which good people can be particularly horror-struck. It conforms to the law of nations in so far as that is the law of the jungle.

What does strike one with horror is the communist defense of this procedure; the desperate effort that is being made to keep Russia clad in the shining armor of righteousness. The communist papers

tell us that Stalin circumvented the Chamberlain policy of appeasement, that the fear of the great Red Army brought Hitler to heel,
that Stalin broke the Axis by disassociating Japan from Germany,
etc., etc. This is to make black white and white black in a fashion
reminiscent of Nazi propaganda. The arguments outrage the simplest logic. A pact that sets Germany free to fight does not circum-
vent appeasement. It is appeasement on a larger scale than ever attempted by Chamberlain. We hope for nothing quite so fervently
than to be relieved from the necessity for arguing this matter with
ardent fellow travelers in the next months. We will have, if we do
argue the matter, the same sense of futility that we have always felt
in arguing with Nazis. When truth is made the slave of power, one
can only hold up one's hands. Truth is always partly corrupted by
power and interest. But it is in the margin of purity where truth
transcends interest partially that civilization is built and men maintain a sane world, where there is some hope of adjusting interest to
interest, life to life, and value to value.

What appalls us particularly is the spiritual poverty that forces so
many people in our era to talk this nonsense in order to save themselves from despair. One must continue to defend and to extend if
possible whatever decency, justice, and freedom still exist in this
day when the lights are going out one by one. One can do that with
clearest vision and courage if one has not placed one's faith in some
frail reed of human virtue which does not exist. It is well for all
Christians who have not fled into quietism, but who have a sense of
responsibility toward the problems of civilization, to recognize
clearly that the tragedy of our era is not merely the decay of a capi-
talistic-bourgeois social order, but the corruption of its alternative
socialist order almost as soon as it had established itself. This does
not mean that the task of advancing democracy to include economic
justice as well as political justice is a hopeless one. After all, bourgeois democracy did succeed in destroying feudalism despite Napoleon's treason, and, one might add, despite the degeneration of
Cromwell's City of God into the first tyranny of modern history.

The Kingdom of God is not of this world; yet its light illumines
our tasks in this world and its hope saves us from despair. The Christian faith stands between the illusions and the despair of the world;
it is particularly an antidote to the illusions which are stubbornly
held in defiance of the facts in order to save men from despair.

13. CHRISTIANITY AND POLITICS IN BRITAIN

The difference between the political scene in Britain and America is so great in many respects that comparisons are almost impossible. The Roosevelt Administration is ostensibly a liberal one, while Churchill's national Government is conservative. Yet labor has a significant position in Churchill's Government, while it is fighting a desperate rear-guard action in Washington. No labor leader or progressive has a position in Washington comparable to Bevin's eminence as " man power " dictator, Herbert Morrison's influence as Home Secretary, or Sir Stafford Cripps's as Minister of Aircraft Production. Lord Woolton's food administration is furthermore a more genuine instrument of democratic justice than anything we have in Washington.

The relation of socially radical Christian thought to politics in Britain corresponds to this totally different British situation. American Christian radicalism may be more consistently radical than any similar British thought; but it is much more irresponsible and much less relevant to the actual political situation. The British Council of Churches, for instance, came out in unequivocal support of the Beveridge social security plan. No corresponding religious group in America could support the report of the National Resources Planning Board. The political distance between various groups both inside and outside the church is much wider in America than in Britain.

This fact is symbolized most perfectly by the position of Dr. Temple, the Archbishop of Canterbury, in British life. It is doubtful whether the Church of England has ever had a more advanced proponent of social justice as its primate. There is no religious position in America comparable to his influence. Yet the occupants of much less influential posts of leadership could not take his advanced position on social and political matters without creating serious divisions in their organization.

This is not to suggest that Dr. Temple can count on unanimous support in his advocacy of a social order in which property interests are completely subordinated to the requirements of the community. There are members of the Church of England who regard his political pronouncements with apprehension. It may also be noted that

Christianity and Society, Summer, 1943.

certain Free Church groups, among whom bourgeois perspectives are
more powerful than in the Established Church, are quite openly
critical of Dr. Temple's politics. Nevertheless, he commands a very
wide support. Some of that support is derived from the prestige that
his great office confers upon its occupant, whoever he may be. Some
of it is derived from his personal prestige as the leading theologian
of the Church of England. These two forms of prestige combine in
such a way that one may never be quite certain whether it is because the Archbishop of Canterbury is speaking or because Dr. Temple is speaking that his words are given a special degree of respect
and sympathy.

Yet neither the prestige of the office nor the influence of the man
could account altogether for Archbishop Temple's ability to speak
for the conscience of England with a degree of support not accorded
anyone else in so advanced a position. That is due to the fact that
Britain has a wider measure of agreement upon basic social and political issues than any other modern nation. American equalitarians
are prone to think of England as a land of class distinctions; and it
must be admitted that social distinctions are still greater than in our
own country. But Americans do not always understand that the
same feudal tradition that is responsible for class distinctions is also
responsible for a political philosophy that finds nothing abhorrent
in the political control of economic processes. Thus the Right and
the Left meet across the chasm of bourgeois liberalism. The left-
wing Tories under the leadership of Quentin Hogg are actually pro-
jecting a degree of socialization of property that would strike terror
into the heart of a typical American conservative-liberal.

This does not mean that Britain is a radical nation. It was able,
as no other modern nation, to weld the virtues of bourgeois democracy upon the older feudal-monarchial world; and it may succeed
again in relating the best values of the workers' rebellion against the
injustices of a capitalistic society to the present society, without destroying the fabric of historical continuity. Britain has the most secure and least catastrophic future of any modern nation.

The defect of this virtue is that she may well maintain many
forms of capitalistic injustice because of her ability to mitigate them
more successfully than other nations. There is little prospect of a
triumph of the Labor Party. The Labor Party lacks a strong will-
to-power, and the trade-union mass of the party is jealous of any of
the more political and radical middle-class leaders who emerge in it

from time to time. This jealousy of Sir Stafford Cripps was apparent in the past. It is apparent now in the attitude toward its most promising leader, Herbert Morrison. The latter is of working-class origin, but he belongs to the political, rather than trade-union, section of the party. If anyone is to lead the party to triumph it will be Morrison. But there is little prospect of such a triumph in the next decade.

In the field of religious radicalism, the genuine achievements of national unity have the same tendency to dull the edge of a religiously inspired protest against injustice. The quasi-Catholicism of Anglicanism naturally brings the problems of human society into the orbit of religious piety in ways difficult for more individualistic Protestants to understand. A part of the Anglican Church is of course as conservative as Catholic social thought. The village church may still be intimately wedded to the squirearchy. But Anglican parishes in the cities are frequently intimately related to the life of the workers.

There is, however, no fully developed and unified socially radical movement. The Industrial Christian Fellowship, which was responsible for Malvern, has the defect of being purely Anglican and not drawing the very considerable Free Church social radicalism into partnership with it. It is, moreover, not too rigorous in analyzing the actual realities of the social struggle and frequently speaks in moralistic accents reminiscent of our own older " social gospel."

It may be observed incidentally that there is a curious hiatus between Christian social theory and social experience in Britain. If one meets with any group of " radical " clergymen, one finds them capable of making the most rigorous and shrewdest possible analysis of the social and political forces in a given situation. But most English social pronouncements seem to be taken from the pages of our old " social gospel." They seem to suggest that a " Christian " society need merely substitute the " service " motive for the " profit " one. Meanwhile every intelligent British proponent of the social meaning of the Christian faith understands quite well that politics, on any possible level, must check and channel egoistic impulses as well as harness and extend the altruistic ones. It is understood also that no conceivable " Christian " society can abolish the tensions of conflicting interests and perspectives. But the pronouncements are remarkably Pelagian and seem to envisage a frictionless society of perfect human brotherhood. This curious inconsistency in British religious thought is not unrelated to a similar aspect of British political life in general; for British political art has always been shrewder in weighing the realities of a given political situation than political science has been in stating the principles by which the realities must be interpreted.

The socially advanced portion of the British churches is in need of a unified movement through which the common testimonies of that part of the church will be clearly stated and which will exploit in more explicit terms the general atmosphere of social advance created by the Archbishop of Canterbury's leadership.

It ought to be mentioned that Sir Richard Acland's new Commonwealth Party is interesting from the Christian standpoint because Acland's own position is derived from Christian presuppositions. Others in the movement have arrived at a common position with him from other backgrounds. Tom Wintringham is a former communist. Acland, who has given up his ancestral estates and now makes a precarious living, is a most appealing figure. He stands in a long line of British radicals who represent the left wing of the Christian tradition. From Gerrard Winstanley, the leader of the Diggers in the seventeenth century, through Keir Hardie, Robert Smillie, Arthur Henderson, George Lansbury, Stafford Cripps, and Acland in the past decades, British Christianity, whether sectarian or state church, has generated prophets of religio-social criticism. In other words, the moral protest against the injustices of our society is derived from, and need not express itself against, the Christian religion. This one fact makes Britain unique in modern social history. For all the radical movements of the Continent have been anti-Christian. In America they are not anti-Christian, but they are predominantly secular. It may be that the unbroken character of the Christian ethos in Britain is also the cause of the unbroken character of the sociopolitical history since 1688.

14. SOCIALIZED MEDICINE IN BRITAIN

The necessity of surveying every problem of justice with as few dogmatic presuppositions as possible is nicely illustrated by the experience of Britain with socialized medicine. The basic provisions of the National Health Act represent a great achievement in social

Christianity and Society, Autumn, 1949.

justice. Free medical care, including hospitalization, necessary appliances, and medicine, is now available to every member of the national community. This represents an ideal for which America will have to strive for years to come. The opposition of the medical profession to our own health program is only one of the strong recalcitrant forces that must be overcome before we can offer basic health security to our citizens. Adequate medical care in this nation is still the monopoly of the well-to-do and the very poor.

But there is never a simple " ideal " in social justice. The British health service is ideal from the standpoint of the breadth of its securities. But the medical profession is taxed with tasks beyond the limits of its endurance. There is good evidence that doctors lack time for adequate diagnostic work. Furthermore, the cost of the service is greater than anticipated. This contributes to the size of a budget that the income-tax payer feels increasingly as a great burden. Sir Stafford Cripps's very honest budget message made it clear that no reduction of the tax could be expected so long as the Government financed social services on the present scale. The new budget, with no promise of relief to the taxpayer, has created an atmosphere of pessimism which has led to the loss of many Labor seats in the municipal elections.

This loss may or may not be an augury of a defeat of labor in the coming parliamentary elections. It is clear, however, that a socialized community reaches a point where it becomes obvious that its services are paid for, not by the wealthy, but by everyone. This is not, however, a serious defect in a socialized economy. More serious is the obvious waste in the time and energy of medical men if no checks are placed upon the services that the citizen may claim from the doctor. Marxism has always lacked understanding of the limitless character of all human needs, desires, and ambitions. " To everyone according to his needs " is an impossible goal, because it is not possible to set a limit to human needs. In medicine the limit of need would seem to be furnished by the health of the citizen. But no one is perfectly healthy, and there is no end of inconsequential ailments for which a patient may seek a doctor's ministrations. Human beings are, on the whole, too thoughtless to justify a community in allowing them to set their own limit on the demands which they may make of a public servant. In short, the British health service will have to find some way of placing a check upon the claims that individuals make upon it. The service must be essentially free; but some system of graduated payments above specified annual limits will have to be found.

While America is regarded by Britons as a nation lacking in a proper sense of responsibility for the welfare of the whole, we do have a more generous system of free education than even socialist Britain. But our free education above the grade school level is not absolutely free. If the proposed system of Federal scholarships should eliminate the extra charges that are now paid by the student in higher education, it will become increasingly necessary to make such scholarships subject to tests of ability and diligence. A completely free system of education up to the final limit of university education is no more possible than a completely free system of medical care.

The extension of socialized services in a modern welfare state is a greater moral achievement. It implements a Christian understanding of the limitless character of a man's responsibility for his neighbor. In so far as socialism has understood this responsibility better than conventional Christianity, it is more thoroughly Christian than conventional Christianity. But a welfare state informed by too pure Marxist thought may fail to guard against the limitless claims that may be made upon it, while it is seeking to do justice to its limitless responsibilities. Such failure means that it does not understand the problem of human egoism as it should be understood from the standpoint of a Christian interpretation of human nature.

British socialism has been much more successful than any Continental Marxism precisely because its Marxist presuppositions have been more thoroughly diluted with Christian insights than the socialism of the Continent. But its health program is a little too utopian to survive in its present form. Its weaknesses may be obscured for the time being by the theory that the undue demands upon the doctors represent a "backlog" of unsatisfied medical needs. Since there is an element of truth in this argument, it may well preserve the present program for some time to come. But ultimately it will be discovered that something more than a backlog of untended ailments prompts some people to make inordinate claims upon the doctor. Then a way will be found to protect both the doctor and the more modest patients against the claims of the thoughtless.

15. FREEDOM AS A LUXURY

Candy, or as the British say, "sweets," has been put on rationing again in Britain after being free for six months. Thereby hangs a tale which teaches us a lesson about the relation of freedom to control. When the candy manufacturers were able to produce an amount of candy equal to the total national consumption before the war, the Government felt it safe to remove candy sales from rationing control. It was glad to do this in order to satisfy a wide public clamor for more free goods. But as soon as candy was freely available the demand for it far exceeded the average consumption before the war. Either Britain had cultivated a sweeter tooth, or, what is more likely, the scarcity of other edibles led to an increased demand for sweet things. The excess of demand over supply led to long queues of customers, to favoritism in distribution, and to embarrassment for distributors, many of whom were forced to institute their own *ad hoc* rationing system. In consequence of these difficulties, the Government finally reinstituted rationing in candies in the middle of August, to the great relief of the same customers and distributors who had clamored for decontrol.

The lesson in this little bit of history reaches far beyond the problem of candy rations or of rationing in general. It proves to what degree the vaunted virtues of the "free market," upon which we pride ourselves so much in this nation, are merely the by-product of an economic situation that most of the world must regard as a luxury. In almost all modern industrial nations, with the exception of our own, the production power does not equal the demand of consumers for goods. Even in our own nation we have been involved in inflation because it proved impossible under conditions of full employment to produce enough goods to satisfy all demands. We had our own experience after the war with a too precipitate decontrol of meats, for instance, which resulted in high prices for meats. If prices rise high enough, they do of course restrict consumption, but merely upon the basis of capacity to pay. The poor are priced out of the market.

This is why the most disciplined poor nations achieve a high degree of justice through planning and control. The less disciplined nations provide every luxury for the rich while the poor are in want.

Christianity and Society, Autumn, 1949.

Nations as wealthy as our own indulge in free markets with less catastrophic results than in poor nations, but not without marked consequences in injustice. In short, the " freedom " that we celebrate as the last word in political idealism is, from the perspective of the rest of the world, merely the luxury of a very fortunate nation. That is why we have, and will continue to have, little success in commending the " American way of life " to the rest of the world. We imagine ourselves the keeper of the ark of democratic virtues; but the world regards us as a profligate rich man who can afford to be wasteful.

The controls required by poor nations for the sake of justice are not, however, the final answer to the problem of freedom and justice in a technical society. It may well be that a healthy technical society can preserve its freedom only if it has enough economic margin to permit itself the luxury of a free market in some areas of its economy. For obviously complete planning does lead to an omnicompetent state.

C. Economic Issues

16. IS STEWARDSHIP ETHICAL?

Most ethical theory in the Christian church is based upon the assumption that it is possible to make society ethical by socializing the individual, by placing an inner check upon the expansive desires and lusts of each single person and thus making him a person fit to participate in social enterprise without taking undue advantage of others.

It is not surprising that the church should hold to this assumption; for it is essentially the attitude of Jesus. He believed in a Kingdom of God, in an ideal society; but he expected to create such a society by regenerating individuals until they would have a completely social attitude toward their fellow men, until they would be thoroughly dominated by the passion of moral good will. He did not participate in any political or economic program designed to strip the powerful of their strength or the privileged of their advantages. He sought rather to convince the strong and the privileged to divest themselves of their perquisites in the interest of his Kingdom of love.

SUASION NOT ENOUGH

It would not be difficult to prove that this ideal is still and will remain the absolute ideal of social life. It is the final ideal because the individual is never completely ethical if he must be restrained by external restraint from pursuing ends detrimental to society; and society is not fully socialized if it must use force rather than suasion to bring the individual into conformity with its own ends. The recognition of this ideal must not, however, tempt us to regard the socialization of the individual through educational and religious suasion as adequate means for eliminating the injustices and inequalities of modern society. The assumption that these means are sufficient gives the whole moral life and theory of the Christian church a note of unreality, not to say hypocrisy.

The fact is, Christianity or any other religion, or for that matter any rational or educational force, has never developed a sufficient number of individuals with so perfect a passion of love as to change

The Christian Century, April 30, 1930.

the main facts of history. Pious kings have held to their power until robust nobles divested them of it. Good aristocrats took their hereditary advantages for granted until the emerging middle classes matched the strength of the aristocracy with their own newly won commercial power. Even in the family relationship, where love has been a more potent force than in less intimate social organization, the autocracy of the male was not challenged until the women gained a measure of economic independence. The industrial worker must develop power through organization before he can hope to dislodge the commercial classes from their favored position in the economic order.

There are always a few individuals in the privileged classes who, because of religious insight or rational analysis, have divested themselves of their privileges in the interest of an equitable society. Their achievements are not futile; for moral splendor in individuals always has exemplary power and persuades others to do likewise, perhaps with a lesser degree of consistency. But the total effect of the lives of such individuals mitigates without abolishing the eternal conflict in society, which the pressure of those who have not against those who have makes inevitable.

The Christian church has been singularly oblivious to this plain lesson of history. It has tried to escape the logic of the facts by its doctrine of stewardship. The idea of stewardship is plausible enough. According to it, men hold their advantages and their power as trusts from God. This trust is not used for selfish advantages. It is used only as God would have us use it. If we accept the Christian interpretation of God's will as a loving will, which seeks the welfare of all men with equal zeal, this would mean that men would use privilege only as they could justify it in terms of the greater service they could render their fellow men through it, and would use power only as it is transmuted into the kind of influence that the leader achieves in his group by the service that he renders to it. In other words, a strict interpretation of the idea of stewardship would automatically eliminate the kind of power and privilege that the church tries to moralize.

Sanctifying Privilege

What the church actually does is not to insist on such a strict interpretation of stewardship, but to sanctify power and privilege as it exists in the modern world by certain concessions to the ethical principle. The critics of the church have a right to be very scornful of this whole procedure. It could probably be proved psychologically that an unethical attitude that can get itself obscured behind a façade of moral sentiment is more dangerous than a frankly immoral one, because it confuses not only the observer but the doer.

Here, for instance, is a pious businessman who is honest in all his dealings but whose imagination does not carry him beyond the contemporary standards of honesty. Besides being honest he is fairly generous. Those two virtues give him the satisfaction of being a Christian. He regards his power in his factory much as kings of old regarded their prerogatives. Any attempt on the part of the workers to gain a share in the determining of policy, particularly the policy that affects their own livelihood, hours, and wages, is regarded by him as an impious attempt to destroy the divine order of things. He knows what is good for his workers. There is no unemployment insurance in his concern. The owner lacks the imagination to realize just what insecurity of employment means in the lives of workers or what the social consequences of unemployment are. If he has a slight comprehension of these consequences, he will make some contribution to the charities of the city and feel virtuous.

There is, of course, a wide variance between individual employers in this regard, from the owner of Procter and Gamble, who guarantees his workers forty-eight weeks of work during the year, to the employer who, while 20,000 of his workers were idle during this winter, contributed $15,000 for the relief fund and spent $300,000 to purchase rare tapestries.

NO UNIQUE BUSINESS ETHICS

There is not one church in a thousand where the moral problems of our industrial civilization are discussed with sufficient realism from the pulpit to prompt the owner to think of his stewardship in terms of these legitimate rights of the workers. The best proof of this is that there are hardly any Christian employers who have any unique business ethics. There are some, it is true, but they could be counted on the fingers of two hands. In most of our cities the pious employers of labor are just as uncompromising in fighting the labor movement and in resisting efforts to make industry responsible for old-age pensions and unemployment insurance as any other type of employer.

Meanwhile your man of power and privilege is generous. The degree of generosity varies in different cases. Sometimes his philanthropies represent a mere bagatelle in proportion to his income. It is only in rare instances that philanthropic giving changes standards of living by a hair's breadth. The church with varying degrees of sophistication and naïveté accepts these philanthropies as fulfilling all righteousness. If they actually reach the proportions of the traditional tithe, they are acclaimed with paeans of praise even though they may represent less than what the Government exacts in income tax, and they may be given partly to escape the tax. If contemporary standards of honesty are followed, part of the income thus tithed may have been made in stock speculation, in which socially created wealth is privately appropriated without a qualm of conscience; or, as is not infrequently the case, the income for the year has been derived from stock dividends, in which the productivity of the industry is used to compound the original holdings and becomes forever after a charge upon the industry.

PHILANTHROPY IS NOT STEWARDSHIP

Any theory of stewardship that operates purely upon the level of philanthropy is not only inadequate to deal with the moral problem involved in the increasing concentration of wealth and power in an industrial civilization, but it is actually inimical to a sane understanding of the problem. How inadequate it is may be recognized from the fact that in the year 1929 the total philanthropies of America amounted to two and a half billion dollars, a sum that does not equal the accretion of values in stocks on the New York exchange in a single day on more than one day in the past year. It is, of course, not impossible to interpret the doctrine of stewardship realistically. But to do so would require an honest discussion of every moral and social problem involved in modern industry, the displacement of workers by the machine, the inequality of income, the ethics of varying standards of living, the democratic rights of workers, and all the rest. If this is not done, it is idle to think of the church as a moral guide in our civilization.

But even if it is done, it will remain a fact that not a large enough number of employers will be won over to an ethical way of life to obviate the necessity of restricting power and privilege through increasing social control. Without using economic force in the form of the strike, or the strike threat, and political force through the creation of a political party that protects the interests of the less privileged members of an industrial community, there is no possibility of equalizing privilege and destroying arbitrary power.

REDUCING CONFLICT TO TENSION

This fact is no reason why we should trust social coercion alone and regard moral suasion as futile. It is not futile. The more far-sighted, imaginative, and ethical the holding classes are, the more is social conflict reduced to social tension and the more can violence be replaced by the use of more ethical types of power. However, any institution of the ethical ideal will make just as large a contribution to the attainment of an ethical goal for society by educating men in the indubitable facts of history and persuading them of the necessity of social control as by challenging them to ethical self-control. The one type of education need not exclude the other.

The realistic teacher of morals will be able to prove by examples drawn from much more ideal fellowships than that of the industrial community that even a fairly ethical individual is inclined to live his life at the expense of other men, if others do not offer resistance to his exactions. The human imagination, except in rare cases, is simply not equal to the task of completely envisaging the interests of those whose lives depend on us. There are few Americans who know that a 300 per cent tariff on French laces has, in late months, thrown 25,000 French lacemakers out of work. There are still fewer who can see that fact in terms of its human and social consequences. Such a tariff will be continued, unfortunately, until France teaches us a lesson in mutuality by raising a tariff on our automobiles.

That is not an ideal way of settling social problems. By increasing social imagination we can prevent such conflicts of interest from issuing in violence and we may perhaps be able to reduce the conflict until it is no more than tension between various interest groups in the international community. But there is no prospect of changing the facts, except in very small communities of the ideal; and an institution of the ethical ideal, such as the church, will, on the whole, make its largest contribution to the development of an ethical society by teaching its members the necessity of an increased measure of social control.

The student of history is forced to draw his conclusions in terms that come perilously near to the assumptions of economic determinism. He will, if he is wise, escape the moral enervation of complete determinism as being inconsistent with the facts. But, meanwhile, most ethical teaching is still functioning upon the basis of assumptions that are much farther from the truth than this dreaded determinism. If one had to choose between two errors, it would be truer to believe that all social action is economically determined than to believe, as the church seems to do, that ethical action develops in some kind of social vacuum. The only chance the modern man has of achieving a measure of ethical freedom and dignity is to realize with what difficulty he extricates his actions from the pressure of economic self-interest and how necessary and ultimately ethical are the restraints of an ethical society upon his will-to-power and his lust for gain.

17. THE IDOLATRY OF AMERICA

The prophets warned Israel, lest it assume that its favored position among the nations was due to its virtue rather than the grace of God. They warned the powerful nations round about Israel, lest they assume that their power gave them immunity from the perils of God's judgment. American destiny has combined the temptations to which Israel was subject with those to which Babylon was subject.

We are the most powerful nation on earth. We are also sufficiently virtuous to be tempted to the assumption that our power is the fruit of our virtue. We do not quite say as Babylon is accused of saying, " I sit as a queen and I shall never know sorrow." The fact is that we are not sure of ourselves and look into the future with apprehension, tempted to perfect the hydrogen bomb out of fear that nothing else will make us sufficiently secure. But we are very sure of ourselves morally.

The idolatrous devotion to the " American way of life" grows at a tremendous pace. We hasten to add that the whole of America is not quite as completely given to it as some of our foreign critics imagine. But the business community has never been so sure of its virtue — nor so afraid that the slightest assertion of the power of the state in the interest of human welfare is the first step down the slippery slope which leads to totalitarianism. And the ethos of the business community does influence sources of culture which ought to be more immune to the growing national idolatry.

Thus the annual report of the Carnegie Corporation of New York, in surveying the grants it has made for various educational enterprises, speaks of the " basic rules of the American system," which it declares remain unchanged but which must be reinterpreted in a day in which technology shrinks the world's distances and brings about " conflicts between our value system and those of other nations." The report also speaks of the necessity of a more adequate program of American studies in our colleges in order to " give our young people more understanding of and dedication to American values." There is nothing said here of a great and long tradition of democratic society in which America was nurtured, nor is there any mention of the necessity of correcting our unique conceptions of democracy by the experience of other free nations. This omission is the more striking since the few words which the Carnegie report has on the meaning of democracy make it quite clear that it shares the general notion that democracy and liberty are to be equated. There is no suggestion, as there is little in any of these paeans of praise for the American way of life, that democracy can never mean merely freedom. It must always relate freedom to justice, to community, and to equality as the regulative principle of justice.

The Advertising Council of America has been carrying on a campaign intended to clarify the meaning of the American way of life, in which it is suggested that the " miracle of America," namely, our vast productive power, is due merely to the spirit of initiative in our " free enterprise system." There is no suspicion that some of our wealth is derived from the fabulous natural resources of our continent, which China, for instance, could not draw on even if that nation were technically as efficient as we are. Furthermore, the Advertising Council gives no credit to the various pressures and counterpressures in our economy (unions and strikes, for instance) for achieving a tolerably just distribution of our wealth. It would have us believe that if we only produce more, everyone is bound to share equally in the abundance. Thus one of the most serious problems in a capitalistic economy, the problem of underconsumption, is obscured.

The fact is that all of the perennial problems of a free economy are momentarily obscured by the fact that an impoverished world needs American goods. We are actually wealthy enough to provide some markets for these goods by Marshall plan grants. We imagine ourselves very generous in this policy, but when the Marshall grants run out and the impoverished world will be unable to buy what it needs from us, and we will even be unwilling to buy from the world a sufficient amount of imports to finance the exports, we will not only recognize that we have not been as generous as we imagined, but we will also discover that a free economy has not solved its problems as permanently as it supposed.

Inevitably the religious world is corrupted by this idolatrous creed of America. Many businessmen will no longer support the World Council of Churches or the Federal Council of Churches because the pronouncements of these bodies on economic affairs have preserved a proper critical reserve toward the American pretensions of a perfect economic system.

Recently a pastor of a large city church sent us a brochure from one of his pious laymen on the subject of Christianity and economic life. This Christian layman is afraid that we will create " confusion " by adding mere " human opinion " to the " laws of God." For him the laws of God consist of two propositions: (1) the love commandment, and (2) the proposition that men are endowed by their Creator with the right to " life, liberty, and the pursuit of happiness." The treatise is a work of art in explicating the meaning of " love " and of " freedom " without a word about justice. The author insists that the state has only a negative function according to " God's plan," namely, to " protect the right of every man." Any more positive action in the interest of justice is deprecated. The pious layman wants good Christians to be socially minded, but he doesn't want them to be coerced to do justly, for " man's individual behavior as a social being cannot be forced on people. . . . Social qualities come from within," he declares, " and can therefore only be cultivated." One is reminded of the day when Herbert Hoover opposed unemployment insurance on the ground that it destroyed the good old American way of voluntary aid to the unfortunate.

Thus Christian sentimentality is made a cloak for a corrupt form of laissez-faire politics. What is left out of account is that a healthy society forces practically all people to be just beyond their natural inclinations. It does not do this by pure coercion. It does it by establishing standards of justice which gain the moral assent of the majority of the population but yet operate against the immediate inclinations even of some of the good people who helped to establish the standards. Any Christian political thought that exploits the law of love without considering the power of the law of self-love is betrayed into sentimentality. As David Hume observed, politics must assume the selfishness of men, however we may speculate on the degree of their unselfishness and however much we may seek to increase that degree above the level of our political arrangements.

Our present prosperity is actually creating a mood among our lay Christians that approximates the uncritical Christian adoration of the " free enterprise system " before the rise of the social gospel challenged it. The social gospel was frequently itself too moralistic, but one might be grateful now for some of its emphases, however inadequate.

If the ministers of our great urban churches become again the simple priests and chaplains of this American idolatry, subtly compounded with a few stray Christian emphases, they will merely add one more dismal proof in the pages of history that a religiously sanctified self-idolatry is more grievous than its secular variety. This is how the gospel becomes a salt that has lost its savor.

The gospel cannot be preached with truth and power if it does not challenge the pretensions and pride, not only of individuals, but of nations, cultures, civilizations, economic and political systems. The good fortune of America and its power place it under the most grievous temptations to self-adulation. If there is no power and grace in the Christian church " to bring down every high thing which exalteth itself against the knowledge of God," the church becomes not merely useless but dangerous.

We Protestants speak critical words about the idolatrous pretensions of the Roman Church. But some of these pretensions are actually more plausible than this miserable identification of the " laws of God " with a particular form of democracy, exhibiting nuances and emphases that are possible only in America and which may not be possible here for any length of time.

18. HOW PHILANTHROPIC IS HENRY FORD?

Henry Ford is America. If we may judge men not so much by their achievements as by their hopes, not so much by what they are as by what they want to be, Henry Ford reveals the true nature of the average American. Henry Ford is not a typical businessman. If he were, he could not be a typical American. There is a sentimental quality in American life which the narrow-eyed and obviously shrewd businessman type does not satisfy as a symbol. The standardized businessman is too obviously, too robustly masculine. And America is half feminine. We worship success, but we do not like to pay too high a price for it. That is why only half of America admired Carnegie and Rockefeller. The other half spoke of the Homestead strikes and Standard Oil ruthlessness. In spite of libraries and colleges, the two wealthiest men of the last generation were reviled almost as much as they were praised. Henry Ford is wealthier than either and is nevertheless the hero of the average American. The reason is that he is supposed to have accumulated his fabulous fortune without ruthlessness, and to have preserved a generous heart in the money-getting process. To pay high wages, sell a cheap product, and yet accumulate vast riches — that is a miracle which fires the imagination of every mother's son who, if the truth were known, indulges both spiritual and worldly ambitions in the secret of his heart. To be feared and loved at the same time, to satisfy natural greed without sacrificing the instincts of love — that were to solve the problem of life to the complete satisfaction of the man in the street. That is why Henry Ford is the hero not only of America, but of many a European.

A Hero with Imagination

It must be admitted that there is a quality in the character of Ford that seems to justify this universal acclaim. Ford has imagination. He has never been lost in the mechanical processes of his business. Objectively tested, his humanitarian characteristics may be inadequate enough, but there is no question but that he talks as if he were a humanitarian and that he regards himself as one. He has gone to much pains to insist that his latest venture, the five-day week, is purely a business proposition. But obviously he is doing this because he has previously seen to it that humanitarian motives should be ascribed to the new policy. His disavowal of philanthropic intentions in the institution of the five-day week are like the assurances of an old spinster that her reputation as a flirt has been grossly exaggerated.

Mr. Ford's reputation for philanthropy is a wonderful triumph of astute publicity on the one hand and an almost inevitable fruit of the peculiar psychology of the man on the other. To begin with, he has always declared himself against organized philanthropy. While his wife and son have given annually to the Detroit community fund, which embraces all the charities of the city, their contributions have never equaled the total sum given by the workers in his plant and have frequently been but a fraction of the sums given by others, much less wealthy — Senator Couzens, for instance. College endowments, libraries, and similar benefactions have never had the support of the Ford millions. A million and a half given by the family for a Y.M.C.A. building campaign recently is the first large contribution to a local charity.

Against these facts and in seeming contradiction of his own principles, it must be said that Mr. Ford has built and is maintaining one of the largest hospitals in the city. No one knows what this venture is costing him. Years ago he established the principle that an adequate wage was to be the basis of his philanthropy. One could hardly find fault with that principle, generously interpreted, if he were true to it. There is a logic in it which one might wish had been learned by a Victor Lawson and a Frank Munsey, who sluiced their wealth into enterprises — theological seminaries, art museums, and the like — which, however worthy in themselves, were totally unrelated to the institutions that created the wealth.

WAGES IN FORD PLANTS

The trouble is that the facts do not bear out Mr. Ford's contention that his wage obviates the necessity for philanthropy. Outside of a few thousand of the highly skilled workers, such as toolmakers, diemakers, and patternmakers, it is hardly possible to find a Ford worker who earned more than $1,500 during the past year. The five-day week was in fact in effect long before it was publicly proclaimed, and there were layoffs without pay besides. As a result, few Ford workers have actually averaged the $30 per week which are needed to provide an annual total of $1,500. Years ago, when the $5 a day minimum was established, which meant $30 per week, the Ford boast that an adequate wage obviated the necessity for charity was not an idle one. Today it is an idle boast, for living prices have well-nigh doubled and the weekly wage still hovers around $30. Mr. Ford declares that a third of his men have received increases. Most of these increases are either $2 or $4 per week, which means that even the best of his men are still short from $2 to $4 in their weekly pay envelope. That is, they receive either $32 or $34 instead of $36. At the present moment the five-day week has been reduced to four and one half days throughout the plant, and many workers have even less work than that. At the present rate the only workers who actually equal the money wages of 1913 are those few thousand who receive $6.80 a day or more. Whatever the pay in dollars may be, it is an established fact that the actual wage is immeasurably lower than in 1913. Every social worker in Detroit knows that the Ford wage places Ford workers in the ranks of social liabilities. The Ford worker in times of distress and sickness is thrown upon the charitable resources of the city. The statistics of practically every charity reveal not only a proportionate but frequently a disproportionate number of Ford workers who are the recipients of charity.

Not only is the Ford wage no longer a minimum subsistence wage, not to speak of a minimum comfort wage, but there is no conscience in the industry in the matter of unemployment or old-age insurance. An industry that shows regular profits from a hundred to a hundred and fifty million dollars per year does not lay aside a cent for unemployment insurance. The old argument used to be that an adequate wage would protect the worker not only against sickness disability but against periods of unemployment. It is quite obvious that the present wage is not high enough for that, if, indeed, it ever was. During the business depression five years ago, Ford managed to keep more men employed than many other automobile concerns, partly because bad times affect a cheap car less than a high-priced product and partly because he weeded out thousands of workers, speeded up production with the remaining force, and cut the price of his car. This was an effective business strategy, but it cannot be classed as humanitarian business. It shows no consideration for the average man, thrown upon the streets because he is unable to keep up.

THE DEMAND FOR YOUTH

As I write, the Ford publicity agents are flooding the country with Ford's new solution for the crime problem. He is going to employ five thousand boys from sixteen to twenty years of age to keep them out of mischief. He is doing this at a time when hardly any of his workers are working full time and many are being discharged. The net result is that Ford is substituting young men for old men. With the modern automatic machine it is a well-known fact that youth is at a premium. The automobile plant has no place for old men. Many factories refuse to employ anyone over forty-five. An industrial process that requires endurance rather than skill inevitably exploits youth and junks the aging man.

Perhaps it is unnecessary to say that there is no system of pensions to offset this ruthlessness. There is not even a contract guaranteeing tenure of employment. A man may put fifteen years into a plant, acquire no more skill than can be duplicated in a youth of eighteen by two months' training, and find himself losing in competition with the superior stamina of the stripling. Perhaps the automobile industry is too young to have acquired a conscience upon this problem. There can be no question that the conscience is lacking, and that there is rather less than more conscience upon the problem of old age in the Ford industry than in others.

If America were not so utterly naïve in matters of industrial ethics, it would long since have looked with a critical eye into the unemployment and pension policy of a wealthy industry that prides itself on restricting its philanthropy to the conduct of its business. As it is, Mr. Ford is celebrated throughout the nation as the most benevolent of employers, while human material is used with a ruthlessness and a disregard of ultimate effects which may be matched, but is not surpassed, by any industry. Mr. Ford has always maintained that one reason why he is able to perform his alleged miracle of high wages and cheap products is because he had no absentee owners to sluice dividends out of the industry. The obvious implication of this constantly reiterated observation is that he is able to maintain a smaller margin between the cost of production and the cost of the finished article than other concerns which must satisfy stockholders with big dividends. It is remarkable with what gullibility the public has accepted this explanation; for the big profits of the Ford industry are hardly exceeded by any other concern, unless it be the United States Steel Company, and, in the past year, the General Motors Corporation. What difference does it make whether absentee owners get the profits or whether they stay with one man to create the largest centralization of wealth the world has ever known, if the profits are there? The fact is that the General Motors Corporation this year underbid Ford in the cost of the finished product, comparative values considered, equaled him in wages, and yet declared dividends totaling nearly two hundred million dollars! If proof were needed, this would show that the Ford miracle is not as distinctive as has been supposed. It is simply the miracle of the modern industrial process with its tremendous productivity which permits exorbitant profits even if the product is reasonably cheap and the wage a decent, if not an adequate, one.

It is difficult to determine whether Mr. Ford is simply a shrewd exploiter of a gullible public in his humanitarian pretensions, or whether he suffers from self-deception. My own guess is that he is at least as naive as he is shrewd, that he does not think profoundly on the social implications of his industrial policies, and that in some of his avowed humanitarian motives he is actually self-deceived. The tragedy of the situation lies in the fact that the American public is, on the whole, too credulous and uncritical to make any critical analysis of the moral pretensions of this great industry. Wherefore we have the picture of a hero who is at once the most successful and the most benevolent of men. If Ford is the symbol of an America with its combination of sentimentality and shrewdness, he is also the symbol of an America that has risen almost in a generation from an agrarian to an industrial economic order and now applies the social intelligence of a country village to the most complex industrial life the world has ever known.

HENRY FORD — SYMBOL

Perhaps it is unjust to attribute Ford's vogue altogether to the simplicity of the American mind. After all, it is a universal and inveterate habit of humanity to invest its heroes with moral qualities that they do not possess and to insist that the big man is also a good man. If that should be doubted, it is only necessary to read the effusive preface to the King James Version of the Bible, in which a prince of dubious character is made to appear a very paragon of virtue. Moral philosophers and teachers of religion have ever been critical of obvious success, believing it inimical to moral perfection. But the man in the street has a fine disregard for these scruples. Nothing intrigues his fancy so much as the vision of a hero who is as good as he is great. In a recent school vote on the most famous men of history, Jesus received the highest number of votes and Napoleon the second highest. It is because most men would like to follow Jesus and Napoleon at the same time that they so credulously accept and even help to fashion the Ford myth. It is a thankless but an important task to set history against mythology.

19. FORD'S FIVE–DAY WEEK SHRINKS

Some time ago the writer took occasion in the pages of this journal to call attention to the financial losses that the workers of the Ford industry suffered through the inauguration of the widely heralded five-day week. Incidentally the soundness and sincerity of the generally accepted moral pretensions of the Ford industry were briefly analyzed. The article brought responses from all parts of the world, most of them from people who were loath to revise their previously formed and highly complimentary opinions of Mr. Ford as a great humanitarian. One critic even wanted to know how the hapless author could be so obtuse as to fail to recognize in Mr. Ford the greatest foe of capitalism in modern civilization.

It may therefore be of interest to *Christian Century* readers to receive a further report on the status of the Ford workers at the present time. The most important and significant fact is that the five-day week has given way to a four-day week. Since last Thanksgiving there are few workers in the industry who can boast of a better average than four days a week. Many of them are on three days. Thousands have worked only two days a week since the beginning of the year. The skilled workers, toolmakers and diemakers, and the maintenance men are of course in better circumstance. But the men on production, who total about 85 per cent of the total force, are in the uniform predicament of having only four days work per week if they are fortunate.

The Christian Century, June 9, 1927.

WHY THE FIVE-DAY WEEK CAME

It is now quite apparent that the five-day week was largely a device for concealing or for effecting the lower production that the decreased demand for Ford cars necessitated. The Ford industry is obviously in a slump. For the first time in its history it is not only meeting real competition but actually succumbing to it. While other automobile plants, particularly those in the great General Motors combine, are steadily increasing production, Ford sales are descending to lower and lower levels. The same autocracy that is credited with the efficiency that makes the big profits and the low prices of the Ford possible seems to lack the resourcefulness that a highly competitive market demands of the industry. No industry is immune to market fluctuations, and there are therefore those who insist that the present plight of the Ford workers is a fate that workers in the most humane industries have suffered at some time or other. Yet whatever may be the tradition of American industry in the matter of unemployment, the situation in the Ford factories clearly emphasizes the necessity for some kind of unemployment insurance in every industry that makes any pretensions to humane treatment of its employees.

Mr. Ford has had a pet dogma which salved his conscience in regard to unemployment. He has always maintained that an adequate wage would give the worker the security both against unemployment and against old age that workers so greatly covet. He has insisted that an adequate wage obviated the necessity for any kind of philanthropy, and for that reason has consistently refused to support charitable agencies. Today unemployed Ford workers are the heaviest charge upon Detroit charities of any single class of citizens. Some of the charities of the city find more than 50 per cent of their beneficiaries to be Ford workers. The adequate wage is obviously not endowed with the magic qualities to solve all industrial and social ills of which Mr. Ford dreamed.

HIGH WAGES DO NOT PROTECT

The reason is quite apparent. No wage, even the highest, can be adequate to guarantee a worker against distress through long periods of unemployment. As a matter of fact, the Ford wage before the institution of the five-day week was no more than adequate for a fair comfort standard of living without much provision for either sickness, unemployment, or old age. Following the institution of the five-day week, the wage was reduced to bare subsistence wage. After living through 1926 with an annual wage of no more than $1,500, and in most cases not more than $1,400, the average Ford worker faces the prospect of an annual wage of about $1,100 to $1,200 in 1927. Of this amount he must pay about $600 in rent. The difficulty he experiences in making both ends meet with what is left after the landlord is paid may well be imagined.

A few concrete examples may at this point aid the imagination: A is a Ford worker with wife and five children. For four months he has averaged three days of work per week. In a desperate effort to save the little home which requires $60 per month in payments, the wife has gone to work at $15 per week. The husband is on a night shift and returns at 1:30 in the morning. He rises at seven to get the children off to school, the wife having left an hour previously.

B has worked for Ford for ten years. He had not had more than three days' work per week since last November. Some of the younger men in his department get one more day a week because they are more efficient. B has a girl in high school and two other children. Two thirds of the slender savings of ten years of industry have been used up on these months, chiefly because the family did not want to take the oldest girl out of school.

PLIGHT OF FORD WORKERS

C bought a home two years ago. Unable to keep up his payments on the home, a charitable organization advanced him a loan to meet delinquent payments. He is unable to pay interest upon the loan and must secure a further loan if the home is to be saved.

D, father of a family of four, has applied for charity because he is four months in arrears for his rent and is threatened with dispossession.

E suffered from severe illness, incapacitating him from work for five weeks. His family, consisting of wife and two children, became the object of public charity and he himself became a public charge. The wife is now seeking employment. The family was without any reserves for the illness.

F is seeking charity to prevent dispossession. Sickness of two children has made it impossible to pay rent for five months.

Many of the Ford workers are holding on to their homes, which they are buying on contract merely by grace of the real estate companies who are carrying them without payments. How many of the workers have actually lost their equities it would be difficult to determine. With the rumored complete shutdown of the Ford works in prospect, many of the workers are fearful of losing their homes. It would be possible to multiply examples of distress among Ford workers by the thousands. No one is in possession of all the facts. But those who are in touch with the situation realize its gravity.

MANAGERIAL AUTOCRACY

There is no question that discontent among the workers is rising to a pitch that augurs an evil day for the industry. The grievances of the workers due to unemployment are augmented by the complete autocracy of the management, which makes protest impossible. The worker finds it impossible to reach anyone with real authority.

If a man works only two or three days a week, he finds the exacting demands of a foreman, always intent upon speeding up production, particularly revolting. Frequently workers are dismissed for the day after but one hour of work, and return home angry for the futile hours on the streetcars.

Many of the grievances of the workers are obviously due to the breakdown of management because of the very size of the industry. Other grievances have their source in the capriciousness of authority. Orders are given and countermanded without rhyme or reason, and no one can discover the source of the authority. Of late men have been discharged in cases of sickness even when they were meticulously careful to report their disability. Men who have worked at the plant for years were under the necessity, upon their return to health, to apply for a position, and were subjected to the indignities of a crude medical examination through which all recruits must pass. Worse than that, they discovered that pay increases that come through years of service were withheld because tenure of service was reckoned from the date of reinstatement rather than the actual date of first employment.

COMMUNISTIC PROPAGANDA

Dismissals of old men are multiplying. The industry is without the vestige of a pension system and old men, who spent ten to fifteen years in the plant, find themselves suddenly on the streets, the victims of the strategy of weeding out "inefficients." If the industry should continue its present ruthless devotion to the ideal of "efficiency" and throw men of fifty-five and sixty upon the industrial junk heap, the social agencies of the city will face a pretty problem caring for the discards of an industry that is blind to its obligations to these men either as a matter of justice or as a matter of philanthropy.

It is rather significant that the rising tide of resentment among Ford workers has no avenue of expression except through the communistic weekly sheet, *The Ford Worker*. This paper, which is sold surreptitiously in the vicinity of all Ford plants, boasts of a weekly circulation of ten thousand copies, though the actual number of communists is hardly one tenth of that figure in the whole city. The paper is crude enough in its temper, but fills its pages with specific instances of injustice rather than with the usual communistic propaganda. The propaganda is, of course, not wanting in the editorial pages.

For years the regular agencies of organized labor despaired of organizing Ford workers. Composed of foreigners and country boys who had little appreciation of the basic problems of industrial life, all efforts to organize them failed dismally. The time would now seem to be ripe for a real organizing effort. Yet the American Federation seems to lack both the energy and the resourcefulness to tackle the problem of organizing the automatic machine tender. A new labor strategy will be necessary for this task. What is wanting is a statesman of the type of Sidney Hillman. If such a leader does not emerge, it is quite probable that the revolutionary radicals who are now the only spokesmen of the discontent of Ford workers will gain an influence out of all proportion to their qualities of leadership.

OUR INCOMPETENT SOCIAL CONSCIENCE

The fact that an industry that develops such distressing social consequences should nevertheless still be heralded as a model of humane industrial strategy speaks volumes for the incompetence of the social conscience of our age. Here is a rather striking personality, with more than ordinary industrial success, with humane impulses, now slightly corrupted, and with a social philosophy not advanced beyond the doctrinaire individualism of the nineteenth century; and yet the world imagines that he represents something new in industrial ethics! Even in England, which has a longer industrial experience than we and which saw many of the pet theories of the Manchester school exploded in the cruel realities of an ethically emancipated industrial system, Mr. Ford is still regarded by many as a kind of demigod. Mr. Garvin of the *Sunday Observer* seems never to tire of singing his praises. In our day of enlightenment it is possible for a man to amass billions and be praised at the same time for the astuteness of his business mind and the generosity of his impulses, even though the groans of his workers may be heard above the din of his machines. Will we ever acquire enough social intelligence to match our mechanical achievements?

20. RELIGION AND THE CLASS WAR IN KENTUCKY

Pineville is in the heart of the Kentucky coal region. Of late it has received unfavorable publicity in the nation's press because of an alleged reign of terror in the region. An attorney associated with the General Defense Committee, which defends striking miners, was beaten up. Waldo Frank, the distinguished writer, and a group of investigators more or less associated with communists received similar treatment. The visiting students from New York were turned back without ceremony. Students from Commonwealth Labor College were escorted out of the county and beaten up in another county, some citizens of Pineville participating in the outrage.

Our committee of clergymen was invited to Pineville by the county attorney and the citizens' committee after twenty-one New York clergymen had memorialized the Senate to pass the Costigan-Cutting bill, which provides for a Senatorial investigation of the coal counties of Kentucky. While we were received with many courtesies, there were some evidences that the citizens resented our " investigation " almost as much as those of other more widely heralded visits to them by radical investigators. The citizens of Pineville resent the publicity that has come to them, partly because many of them regard it as giving an unfair picture of conditions there and partly because it has spoiled their tourist trade.

The Christian Century, May 18, 1932.

INVESTIGATING THE INVESTIGATORS

After visiting the county attorney who issued the invitation to us, we were turned over to a committee of ministers (not all ministers of the county were invited to this meeting) and were investigated before we were permitted to investigate. Our hosts gave an elaborate history of their religious and secular life and then demanded that we do likewise.

The effort to maintain an attitude of complete guilelessness on the part of the chairman did not succeed for long. He was out to prove us tainted with modernism. We read *The Christian Century*, were interested in pacifist activities, held connection with the hated Civil Liberties Union, believed in disarmament, did not believe in " the inerrancy of Scripture as the absolute Word of God," could not define the divinity of Jesus in terms exact enough to prove that we believed that " he was begotten by God." In short, we are not only modernists, but proved by our connections and interests that the perennial contention of fundamentalists that modernism is the mother from which springs the evil brood of atheism, communism, pacifism, and generally subversive doctrines is justified. We were told that Pineville is " fundamentalist in politics and religion " and that men under " alien influence " could not understand her ideals.

This little inquisition was very valuable to us, for it revealed one source of the temper that has driven the Pineville citizens to violence. They regard communism with an abhorrence that knows no bounds. Its frank advocacy of violence creates a fear psychosis in the hearts of timid middle-class people, and its irreligion outrages their religious sensibilities. A communist is hardly human and has no civil rights. Though citizens and county officials resent the charges of violence that have been brought against them, they make no apologies for the violence that they have used against communists. We were taken to court to hear the trial of a loose woman who had stolen an automobile and who filled the courtroom with vile oaths, but was obviously innocent and ignorant of any communist activities and opinions, in order that we might see the vileness of the breed of communist against which the county is trying to preserve its purity.

" CRIMINAL SYNDICALISM "

There is good evidence that the operators are not as worried about the atheism of the communist as are the good people of the community. They have carried on an unremitting warfare against all labor organizations for decades. They do not want the mines organized. They profess a respect for the United Mine Workers only since the communists have come in. The United Mine Workers are inert and thoroughly suppressed. Sometimes they allow themselves to be used to break up communist unions, but promises of rewards for their services are not kept. In spite of protestations to the contrary on the part of operators there is evidence that membership in any union results in the immediate dismissal of the miner. The head of the district of United Mine Workers is under indictment for murder in Harlan County because he wrote a letter to one of the defendants in the recent murder trials of Harlan union officials, encouraging him to " keep up the fighting spirit." Thirty men in Pineville are still under indictment for criminal syndicalism in Pineville, though a portion of the law has been declared unconstitutional by the state court of appeals. Indictments are freely used in all the coal counties to keep undesirable characters out of the county. One old miner ruefully declared, " If you are hungry you are a red, and if you tell your neighbor that you are hungry that is criminal syndicalism."

While the citizens' committee and the county officials assured us that everything is peaceful in the county and that tales of terrorism have been manufactured by the " reds," it is quite obvious that miners everywhere who haven't a taint of radicalism upon them are filled with resentment and fear of the brutalities of " law and order." There is, in short, every manifestation of a " class war " in Pineville, with the poor mining community arrayed against the middle-class community and, as always in wartime, charges of brutalities and atrocities on both sides.

In this warfare the church is pretty unqualifiedly on the side of the operators. The miners are mountain people who have never " belonged " to the " respectable people." They are regarded as ignorant and lazy and if, in desperation of hunger, they turn to violence and stealing, their crimes are attributed either to outside agitators or to pure " cussedness." The good people are not altogether unmindful of their plight. They have provided more relief than have the labor organizations. Sixteen thousand five hundred dollars has been raised in the county for their aid. Of course, only the completely destitute may receive aid. The funds are not large enough to help any miner who has any work. The average work week of the miners who do have work is one and a half days, and the average wage about $2.25 per day. An official in one of the best mines in the county, where the men work three days per week, confessed that the men found great difficulty in meeting minimum needs.

The picture of the church as a thoroughly middle-class institution in Pineville differs only in vividness and clear demarcation from that which may be found everywhere. The clearness of the demarcation arises from the fact that the mountaineer miner is much more clearly a class and a race apart than the worker in the cities. There is an interest in his plight but a fatalistic attitude toward it. The depression and the sickness of the coal industry are held responsible for it, and the most radical remedy that any churchman proposed for the difficulties was an association of mine operators to prevent price cutting and consequent wage reductions. Some of the ministers have denounced the violence of the officials and citizens' committee unqualifiedly, but it is only at this one point that they dissociate themselves from general community sentiment, and it might be added that a very considerable part of the community is equally critical of the reign of terror.

RELIGIOUS AND SOCIAL CONSERVATISM

From the standpoint of gauging the influence of religion upon ethical and social attitudes the most interesting aspects of the Pineville situation are two. The first is the manner in which religious conservatism and fundamentalism plays into the hands of social conservatism and prevents a thorough analysis of the human problems involved in the situation. One operator is quoted as saying, " I am a good Christian and a member of a Christian church, but I would just as soon tie a communist in a sack and throw him in the river as do anything else I know."

Lest liberal Christians raise themselves in pharisaic judgment over their fundamentalist brethren, it would be well to hasten the mention of the second aspect of the religious-social ethic of Pineville, which fundamentalist and modernist Christianity usually share. It is the tendency to make philanthropy the proof of the Christian spirit of love and of the honest interest of the church in the plight of the underdog, while every effort of the disinherited mass of miners to achieve social justice through concerted pressure is regarded with abhorrence, partly because it is believed to be " unchristian " and partly because it is felt that a union scale in the mines would wipe out the whole coal industry in the state. The middle-class community is in other words fighting for its existence, or thinks it is, and is willing that the freight differential of 35 cents a ton which operates against the Kentucky fields be taken out of the meager earnings of the miner. His wages have dropped from $1.25 a ton in the boom period to 25 and 30 cents a ton. The human problem created by this situation is glossed over by the little charity that is offered the miner.

CHARITY AND JUSTICE

Since the conscience of the Christian church has been confused by the tendency to substitute charity for justice through all the ages, one ought not be too severe on the ministers and Christian people of Pineville. One of the best ministers in Pineville refuted my analysis of this problem in the traditional Christian manner. I insisted that whenever the love ideal of Christianity degenerates into pure philanthropy without regard for the difficult task of achieving social justice, it becomes a cloak behind which social injustice hides itself. He answered by accusing me of " putting the cart before the horse." Only the Christian spirit of love, he declared, could achieve justice. Since we were told that in a revival meeting in all the churches which preceded our visit by several weeks practically everyone in town had been brought to " salvation," I naturally wondered just what one should think of the " fruits of the spirit " which the history of the town had recently revealed!

It might be added that the miners are more religious than any similar body of proletarians. It would be a wonderful thing if their religious institutions could be thoroughly related to their fight for justice. If one notes the fact that economic circumstances invariably color religious convictions and moral and social ideals, one may well come to the conclusion that no middle-class church will ever espouse the cause of the dispossessed with full vigor. The best it can do is to create an attitude of sympathy for their problems. The religious character of these proletarians would offer a splendid opportunity for the emergence of a real proletarian religion. But alas, the miners' preachers (who usually dig coal for a living) must preach in company-owned churches, and they are generally too ignorant to offer real leadership. Only occasionally one arises whose native intelligence overcomes educational handicaps, to speak with the voice of an Amos. Last year one such mining preacher was indicted in a neighboring county on a charge of criminal syndicalism. He had advised his flock to join the union. The best that can be said for the most of the preachers in the mining communities is that they are not as subservient to the companies as the company doctors. But if one knows the history of the company doctors that is meager praise indeed.

21. SPIRITUAL MOBILIZATION

The movement entitled " Spiritual Mobilization," conducted by Dr. James Fifield of Los Angeles, is one of the worst forms of religious rationalization of a class viewpoint that we have had in American history. Dr. Fifield declares that the preservation of the " free enterprise system " is a matter of religious concern because free enterprise is so intimately related to "freedom of worship" in the whole democratic system that it becomes a religious duty to defend the one for the sake of preserving the other.

He claims that his movement is purely religious and not political because he never explicitly identifies the " pagan statism " which he regards as the enemy of religious freedom. But it is quite apparent that what he is after is the general tendency toward political control of economic process which is associated in America with the " New Deal." His millionaire supporters are under no illusion about this identification. They give him all the money he needs to make this supposedly religious, but actually political, attack upon their foes.

Almost every aspect of Dr. Fifield's propaganda is dishonest. It is dishonest to identify a state that seeks for a larger measure of control of economic life with a state that makes itself God. Britain and Sweden have gone farther in political control of economics than has the New Deal. But there is no suggestion of the perils of " pagan statism " in these nations. The suggestion that only an archaic laissez-faire economics can save us from nazi totalitarianism introduces a stupid and dishonest fear into the nice calculations that modern democracy must make upon this vexing subject.

While Dr. Fifield falsely accuses the proponents of a managed economy of identifying the state with God, he actually engages in an unscrupulous identification of a particular class prejudice with the divine. The exaggerated devotion to "free enterprise" is an aberration of the wealthy classes of this country and hides and expresses their fears of social change. Even without the benefit of clergy, this fear is more exaggerated in our nation than in any other. Dr. Fifield strengthens this fear by religious sanction.

The final test of any true prophet is whether he has a word of God spoken against his group and not merely for it. By that test Dr. Fifield is a false prophet. He has not pointed out to his wealthy admirers that while they speak glibly of the value of freedom in preference to the value of security, they do nothing to establish the security of the masses and little to give social justification to the freedom of their power. There is no woe in Dr. Fifield's gospel upon "the rulers of Israel" and no judgment upon the financial oligarchy of this nation. He does not help the wealthy to realize that the demand for stronger state control upon business springs from the increased power of industry and finance in the community and from the peril to justice that resides in this power.

Even when no religious sanctities are appealed to, it is dishonest to scare people with the perils of state power if these are not considered in comparison with the perils of irresponsible economic power. The growth of state power is neither a caprice of history nor the fruit of "paganism." It is the consequence of the community's effort to protect itself against irresponsible economic power.

The whole campaign of the "free enterprise" proponents dishonestly obscures the real issues involved in the relation between political and economic power. But the religious campaign in support of free enterprise is particularly dishonest, precisely because it seeks to give an ultimate religious sanction to a particular social movement without offering a word of criticism from the religious perspective upon the perils of that movement.

Dr. Fifield claims to represent 52 per cent of American Protestant ministers. It is to be hoped that this is a falsehood. If over half of our Protestant clergy are either the knowing or the unwitting accomplices of a campaign to further the particular interests and to support the particular prejudices of the plutocratic class of the nation, the state of Protestantism in our society is even worse than we had assumed it to be.

22. IDEOLOGY IN THE SOCIAL STRUGGLE

The history of the postwar strikes in our country is instructive in that it substantiates at every point a Christian, rather than a sentimental or purely rational, analysis of human behavior.

Consider, for instance, the attitude of the National Manufacturers Association in the present difficulties. It has used expensive page ads to prove (1) that higher wages would lead to inflation and that increase in wages could be granted only if each individual worked more hours; (2) that price restrictions should be removed and that such a policy would not lead to inflation because it would encourage fuller production and would ultimately result in such a volume of goods that prices would come down through the operation of the law of supply and demand.

This propaganda is so palpably dishonest and so obviously leaves important data out of account that it cannot be attributed merely to ignorance. This is not merely the narrow view of a business class looking at the common good from its limited perspective. This is ideology; but something more is involved in this ideology than is generally assumed in Marxist analyses.

The National Manufacturers Association could not possibly believe that the way to prosperity and justice is as simple as it declares. There are too many well-known facts, which it has ignored, to permit the assumption that faulty perspective could account for the error. There must be an element of conscious dishonesty in this approach. We are confronted with the age-old sin of man, seeking to make the worse appear better reason by hiding his own interest behind a façade of assumed concern for the common good.

The National Manufacturers Association has left both the immediate perils of inflation and the ultimate perils of deflation out of account. Chester Bowles, the head of the O.P.A., has presented irrefutable proof of the fact that if price restrictions are removed before there is a full supply of consumer goods, the pressure of demand will force prices skyward, and that such a movement can get out of hand to such a degree that it will not be stopped until a catastrophic deflationary movement stops it. The deflationary movement will ultimately set in because high prices will restrict the capacity of the consumers to absorb the goods that industry can ultimately produce.

The NMA professes not to fear the ultimate peril of deflation because it is sure that more and more production will make everyone in America wealthy. Henry J. Taylor, radio spokesman of the General Motors Corporation, has given an imaginative turn to the National Manufacturers propaganda. He pictures America hungry for consumer goods after four years of dearth, and " better tools and better ways of doing things " constantly increasing production for a constantly increasing market. Finally, "American methods" will " deliver more leisure, more goods and services, and improved living standards" beyond any previous dreams of avarice. All this we can have if only we stop striking or placing price restrictions upon our goods.

The trouble with this picture is that more and more production, without a proper distribution of the ever-increasing wealth which the machine produces, eventually results in overproduction and crisis. The National Manufacturers Association seems never to have heard of the periods of unemployment we have had as a result of producing more and more goods. Take the period of 1925–1929. In that period industrial production rose 27 per cent and the productivity of labor rose 24 per cent, but wages rose only 5.8 per cent. In the steel industry alone during that period, production rose 47 per cent and profits increased by 150 per cent. Wages remained practically stationary, rising from 64 to 66 cents per hour. The National Manufacturers Association is certain not only that wages will rise but that prices will drop under the miracle of American production. But in the period preceding our last depression prices dropped only 1 per cent.

The simple fact is that the owners of industry appropriated the abundance created by the modern miracle of production; and that they were so greedy about it that they ran us headlong into a depression from which we did not emerge until war production saved us. They did not allow the great consuming public enough return on their labor to buy what this public was producing. This basic problem has not been solved, though labor is now much stronger than it was twenty years ago and is determined to use its strength, while it is undiminished, to force wages up in proportion to the new level of productivity.

The propaganda of our industrial overlords is in other words not only stupid but in such flagrant contradiction to our experience that it must be regarded as dishonest as well. One might well speculate about the character of man which makes it possible for respectable citizens to defy the known lessons of our common experience in this way in order to reap some momentary profits. Most of them would not have cheated the Government in the time of war. But they are quite willing to risk the horrors of another depression for the sake of an immediate advantage.

We still find rationalists speaking wisely about the necessity of overcoming a " cultural lag " and bringing our social intelligence to the level of our scientific intelligence. But obviously something more than ignorance is involved in this stupidity that defies all the lessons of our experience. It reveals the pathetic capacity of powerful men and groups to prefer their own and their immediate interests to the wider interests of the group and their own long-term interests.

Fortunately labor is powerful enough to prevent the wide hiatus between productivity and wages that resulted during the last boom period. But there is little likelihood that it will be powerful enough or that the nation will be wise enough to avoid all the evil consequences of the policy that our economic oligarchy is determined to follow.

23. INFLATION AND GROUP SELFISHNESS

The problem is to avoid inflation. The fact is that it is not being avoided. The reason why it is not avoided throws an interesting light upon the problems of justice in a nation. In a period of vast military expenditures money earned is greater than the goods produced for the consumer's market. Thus everybody's dollar competes with everyone else's dollar in the scant market until each dollar is worth less than before. The simplest way of avoiding inflation is to place so heavy a tax upon everyone that the dollars available for consumption are equal to the value of goods in the market. But no one dares to apply so rigorous a solution, and even the wisest citizens

Christianity and Society, Spring, 1951.

shrink in moments of self-interest from pressing what reason dictates.

The next best method of stopping inflation is a combination of price control and rationing; for without rationing, price control can become very unjust. We have price control without rationing because this policy is less subject to the charge of " socialism." We were tardy in instituting price control because even a Fair Deal Administration was reluctant to cease from burning incense before our idol of " free enterprise." This tardiness means that prices are frozen at a very high level. Furthermore, they will continue to rise, partly because the pressure on the market is too great and partly because of the guaranteed high price of food products. The " parity " principle in food prices was meant to protect farmers against unfairness in the total distribution of the national wealth. But there is no disposition among farmers to recognize that in the present situation the food consumers of the cities may need more protection than they.

Furthermore, there is the problem of wages. If wages are frozen at the same time prices are frozen, the rise in costs that immediately preceded the price freeze must be borne by the workers throughout the period of stabilization. This injustice is recognized, and the price stabilizers are willing to grant, say, 10 per cent increases. But labor can prove that this is not sufficient to cover rising costs. Furthermore, stabilization requires renunciation of the " escalator " clauses in labor contracts which guarantee labor rising wages according to the price index. Labor rightly argues that it would be willing to give up the boon of the escalator clause if prices were really stabilized. But it rightly surmises that they won't be fully stabilized. Labor argues, furthermore, that since the " escalator " contracts promise increases only three months after the price index has risen, these increases are the consequence, and not the cause, of inflation. But they cannot deny that they may well be the cause of future inflation.

The fact is that every particular group in society is more intent upon its own position in this radical readjustment of social forces than it is in the total result. Some of the reasons used in the debate wonderfully reveal the limits of reason in political debate. Thus a Senator who owns a vast industrial establishment lectures labor leaders on the injustice of their wages compared with the sacrifices that the soldiers make in Korea. But he fails to see that the contrast between his profits and the sacrifices of the soldiers is even greater. Actually the operations of a free economy become anachronistic as soon as a nation is involved in a total effort like war or quasi war. For in that moment all private advantages, compared with the great sacrifices of our actual defenders, become monstrous, even as the self-regulating tendencies of a free economy become inoperative. Yet it would not do simply to turn the nation into a vast bureaucracy. For experience has taught us that there are limits to planning as well as to freedom.

We will probably reach a tolerable solution of this problem, as we did in the last war, not because each segment of the population has learned wisdom, but because the pressures and counterpressures produce a semblance of stability. The wisdom and the virtue of a citizen is not great enough to affirm justice irrespective of interest. Democracies can remain healthy if there is enough wisdom and justice to affirm the compromises that result when no interest can fully prevail. Some interests are of course worsted in this struggle. The unorganized groups, for instance, have suffered consistently in the recent inflations of war and postwar years.

If preachers want to explain to congregations why it is sentimental to expect men to achieve pure justice, not to speak of pure love; if they want to make clear what is meant by Christian " realism " as against Christian " idealism," let them make an analysis of how we are all involved in the inflationary spiral and how we all tend to twist the spiral upward by trying to escape from the consequences of the previous twist. If pacifists, on the other hand, who think it easy to apply " pure love " to international relations, would study the anatomy of the inflationary spiral, they might be instructed in the force of collective self-interest in human affairs.

24. THE CONFESSION OF A TIRED RADICAL

This is the confession of a tired radical. I hope I will not remain tired. Time may give me new enthusiasms and save me from premature senility. But just now I am fed up. I am fed up with liberals, with their creeds, their idiosyncrasies, and their attitudes. My revolt is directed particularly against their habit of confessing the sins of their group from which they imagine themselves emancipated. There is no temptation so seductive as the temptation to be humble and proud at the same time.

Suppose I am a Nordic, a Nordic Protestant. I meet with a group of liberal people including Jews, Negroes, Catholics, and what not. I make a public confession of the bigotries and prejudices of my crowd. I ask the minority groups who suffer from the sins of my group to be generous and forgive our sins. That seems to stamp me as a humble and contrite person. But of course my very confession is supposed to impress my hearers with the fact that I do not really belong to my group, that I am superior to it. I would be greatly chagrined if anyone took my confession at its face value. For pride dictates my humble confession. Its insincerity, however, is not its only limitation. It prevents the conference from dealing objectively with the social facts and problems that concern it.

SINCERITY LACKING

Cross burning—

I have attended few conferences in which minority groups were as honest and frank in confessing limitations of their people as were the members of the majority. That may be due to the fact that minorities have developed a pride of their own to compensate for their unconscious inferiority complex. It may also be the fruit of the insincerity of the majority. Humility usually prompts humility and the contrition of one party to a conflict easily creates a sense of repentance in the other. But such a process presupposes sincerity, and the perfect sincerity is lacking in most of our present discussions on racial and religious prejudices.

A conference on race relations is in session. Someone invariably

arises to make an abject apology for the sins of the Protestant Nor-
dics, and the conference thereupon resolves itself into a discussion of
ways and means by which the sinners may be brought to see the error
of their ways. The turn of the discussion thus makes it quite impossible to deal realistically with the whole problem of group loyalties
and the resulting friction between groups. It may be true that Nordic
people have an undue amount of race pride. But racial arrogance is
certainly not a unique Nordic sin. Nor is religious bigotry and intolerance prevalent only among Protestant obscurantists.

BIGOTRY AND SELF-ESTEEM

The fact seems to be that all groups, religious and racial, tend to
preserve their self-respect by adopting contemptuous attitudes toward other groups and to express their appreciation of their own
characteristic culture by depreciating that of others. Whatever group
happens to be in the majority seems to be the most bigoted simply
because it is in a position where it can indulge its arrogance more
freely. The minority groups may commit fewer social sins, but they
probably suffer from as many spiritual limitations. They develop an
animus against the majority which makes it quite impossible to deal
scientifically with the whole problem of group animosities.

Would it not be well if the Jews realized that their racial integrity
has been maintained partly because they have lived in a hostile
world? They could probably preserve racial unity in a completely
tolerant world, but only at the price of becoming themselves in-
tolerant. Were the walls of hatred, fear, and contempt which now
divide the Jewish and the Gentile world removed, would it be possible to prevent wholesale intermarriage and the consequent assimilation of a minority group into the majority? Would the highly academic idea that variety is the spice of life, that it will make
civilization more interesting to preserve many types of culture, have
sufficient potency to restrain young men and maidens of different
groups from pooling their lives and fortunes and from thereby ef-
facing the dividing line?

The sins that the white man has committed against the colored
man cry to heaven. But might it not be well for the ultimate peace
of society if intelligent white men and colored men studied and
analyzed these sins not so much as the peculiarities of a race, but as
the universal characteristics of Homo sapiens, so-called? Colored peo-

ple who have long lived in the North and gained social and cultural advantages that recently migrated Southern Negroes do not possess, have almost as difficult a task to deal justly with their underprivileged brothers as have the white people. There are fortunately always some imaginative souls who recognize the underlying unities and the ethical obligations; but that is also true of the white group.

Adopting Majority Vices

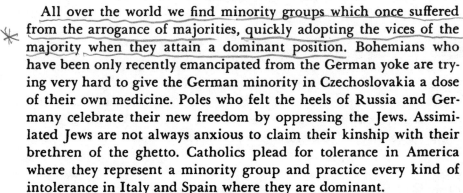

All over the world we find minority groups which once suffered from the arrogance of majorities, quickly adopting the vices of the majority when they attain a dominant position. Bohemians who have been only recently emancipated from the German yoke are trying very hard to give the German minority in Czechoslovakia a dose of their own medicine. Poles who felt the heels of Russia and Germany celebrate their new freedom by oppressing the Jews. Assimilated Jews are not always anxious to claim their kinship with their brethren of the ghetto. Catholics plead for tolerance in America where they represent a minority group and practice every kind of intolerance in Italy and Spain where they are dominant.

Is the evidence not all for the thesis that we are dealing not with the peculiar vices of particular groups and races but with characteristics of man? All human groups are essentially predatory and tend to hold desperately to their privileges against the pressure of the underprivileged, who demand a fairer share of the blessings. All human groups are essentially proud and find that pride very convenient because it seems to justify their special privileges and to explain the sad state of the underprivileged. It is this combination of selfishness and pride that makes the problems of group relationships so difficult. Thus the white man keeps the Negro in poverty and attributes the poverty to the Negro's sloth. The industrial master prevents the industrial worker from sharing the problems of industry and attributes his irresponsibility to innate defects.

The Economic Factor

In cases of conflict between groups of equal economic privilege, racial and religious prejudices frequently become a struggle for political power or social prestige. Where the conflict rages between groups of unequal privilege, race merely complicates and aggravates the

ubiquitous class struggle. In the South white men justify their attitude toward the Negro because he is supposed to be lazy and irresponsible. In California the Japanese are hated and feared because
they are too industrious. This does not prove that the economic factor is basic in race prejudice. It merely proves that the economic factor complicates every group antagonism and race prejudice aggravates every economic class struggle. If a dominant group is able to
hold a minority group in subjection, it is doubly repaid. It reaps
economic rewards and also creates the social and cultural facts that
seem to justify its pride.

Whenever these universal tendencies are attributed to the peculiar
defects of certain races and groups, the day of their elimination is
merely postponed. An animus is created which makes a scientific
approach to the problem impossible. The supposedly peculiar characteristics of races, classes, and other social groups are usually but
variations of a general pattern produced by special circumstances.
Liberal whites, Gentiles and Protestants, would do well to sit down
with members of other groups and talk as men about common human frailties and the methods by which they may be eliminated and
how the harm that springs from them may be negated. Elaborate
confessions of group sins are merely devices for establishing the
emancipation of the individual from the sins of his group. This
emancipation ought to be taken for granted, or discussion is futile.

IS GROUP LOYALTY A VIRTUE?

Perhaps the real problem to be considered in these discussions is
whether in the kind of a world in which we live all group loyalty
has not become a doubtful virtue. Group loyalty is the by-product
of group conflict, but also the perpetuator of it. Among races and
classes that are still fighting for their place in the sun, group loyalty seems a necessary virtue. Even among dominant groups some
real ethical values are involved in it. Yet on the whole it would
seem that in a world in which groups have been thrown into such
intimate contact with each other our educational and religious emphases ought to be on loyalty to standards, values, truths, and ideals
rather than to any group that is supposed to incorporate them.

What has been said about the conflict between races in the Western world applies with even greater force to the problem of the relationship of West and East. Liberals have acquired the habit of be-

wailing the sins of Western civilization and of yearning after the virtues of the Orient. The sins of the West are the defects of its virtues, and that is true of the Orient as well. The technological achievements of the West rather than any innate defects in the character of the white man have created the moral limitations of Western civilization. White men are probably no more greedy than Orientals, but they have discovered more effective methods of exploiting nature, more dangerous methods for holding up their fellow men, and a technique of group action that multiplies the peril of their ruthlessness and greed. All this spells imperialism.

The Eastern man is not so obsessed with the concrete world and, being less tempted to avarice, he is therefore more willing to live and let live. But the difference is partly a difference in physical energy created by a difference in climate. A philosophic and religious Orient permits millions to perish in poverty. An energetic and busy West spills rivers of blood in the mad scramble for the world's riches. The Western man must bring his energy under moral control. The Eastern man must learn the moral value of energy. West and East may learn of each other, and only if they do will they be able to preserve peace in the decades to come.

UNIVERSAL FAILINGS

But to learn of each other does not mean futile comparisons between incommensurable virtues and vices. Spiritual as Gandhi is, there is considerable pride in his assumption that the East is spiritually superior to the West. World peace and social harmony wait upon the men who make common war against the defects of the human heart and the deficiencies of human imagination and intelligence, which reveal themselves varyingly in various situations, but which are always more universal than they seem to be. To realize that fact is the basis of mutual repentance and forgiveness by which social harmony must be attained.

To repent of group sins has moral meaning only if the person who makes the confession has had some responsibility for the actions of the group. If not, he would do better to keep vigilance upon the pride and the selfishness of the human heart, which expresses itself most easily in group attitudes and hides itself in some new social arrogance even while it makes an elaborate disavowal of an old loyalty.

25. CHRISTIAN FAITH AND THE
RACE PROBLEM

In a *Primer on Race* issued by the Council on Christian Social
Progress of the Northern Baptist Convention some very interesting
facts are presented on the historic elaboration of the races of mankind, leading to the conclusion that " there are now no pure races."
Also brief historic evidence is presented to show that races do not
have inherent characteristics. We are told for instance that " the
Scandinavians now known as the world's most co-operative people
were once, as Vikings, the terror of coastal towns." Differences between races are the product of history and social circumstances, and
there is no evidence to support the idea that there are inferior and
superior races. " Science concludes," the pamphlet declares, " that
there is no good evidence of inborn mental differences between
races."

All this marshaling of scientific evidence for the essential equality
of the races is perfectly good propaganda for the Christian idea of
racial brotherhood. Yet there is something faulty with this scientific
treatment of the race issue from the Christian standpoint. Most of
our modern anthropologists assume that race bigots are ignorant
of the facts of life, and that they have been confused by certain superficial differences in racial traits to assume the inferiority of the
minority group. They will, therefore, spread propaganda to acquaint
men with the latest results of scientific research. They would dispel
race prejudice by increasing scientific enlightenment.

Since all forms of prejudice do feed on stupidity and since a certain amount of emancipation from bigotry can be, and has been,
effected by social enlightenment, there is no reason why the Christian
church should discourage such scientific propaganda. But it is unfortunate for the church to content itself with this scientific assurance that " there are no races " or that " there are no inferior races."
This is not sufficient because it does not measure the tragedy of racial
bigotry deeply enough. Racial bigotry, like every other form of human pride and sin, is something more than ignorance and something
less than malice, though the malice of actual sin may grow out of
the predispositions of pride and contempt that lie at the foundation
of racial bigotry.

Christianity and Society, Spring, 1945.

It is of no avail to prove that there are no pure races when actual bigotry expresses itself in history whenever a cultural, religious, ethnic, or other group diverges from the type of the majority that presumes to set the standards by which the others are judged. While there are no absolute ethnic bases for cultural distinctions, there are provisional ethnic and cultural affinities. The Irish are usually Catholic; and if the Anglo-Saxon group of some community holds them in contempt, it may justify its contempt on both ethnic and religious grounds. The power of bigotry is always greatest if the group held in contempt diverges from type, both ethnically and culturally. This, for instance, is the primary problem in anti-Semitism. Though many Jews desire to be known merely as a religious and not as an ethnic group, it is nevertheless possible to identify many Jews ethnically. Also, many of them are really concerned to be preserved as an ethnic group. But they will also have their own unique culture, as well as their own ethnic characteristics; and they affront the majority by the combination of this ethnic and religious divergence. The contempt, hatred, and fear that confront the Jew may be slightly alleviated by scientific enlightenment. But it is more important to know why the Gentile majority is inclined to accept false statements about the Jew than to refute particular false statements. The predisposition to think ill of a divergent group is a dark and terrible abyss of evil in the soul of man. If it is robbed of implausible rationalizations, it is quite capable of inventing more plausible ones.

Nor is it true that the sense of superiority of race rests primarily upon faulty premises that can be dispelled by scientific enlightenment. Very frequently the accusation of inferiority is actually a betrayal of insecurity in the face of the competition of the minority group. The Japanese were frequently hated on the West Coast because they are incredibly efficient truck gardeners, and white competitors veiled their envy and fear by various accusations. In the same way the intelligence of Jews in the competition of many colleges is feared; and the fear prompts accusations that the Jewish students are too clannish, or too pushing, or too indifferent to athletics or what not. The accusations may be plausible or implausible. They are sometimes plausible because minority groups may have special characteristics, derived from the defensive position in which they find themselves as minority groups. But the accusations may be prompted more by the fear of competitive superiority than by any real conviction of their inferiority.

Even when we consider the relation of the white man to the Negro the depth of the predisposition from which bigotry is derived becomes apparent. The Negro people of this country were once slaves and they are still subject to many forms of disinheritance. For this reason they are still "inferior" in many capacities and skills that they have not been allowed to acquire. This inferiority supposedly justifies the attitude of contempt of the majority in the eyes of those who exhibit the contempt. But even here the racial bigots give themselves away. When they are confronted by evidences of the Negro's superior gifts, as in the field of the arts, more particularly music, they are filled with rage. Furthermore, they betray a fear of the Negro's competition even while they pretend to despise his competitive competence. Most arguments against equal education for Negroes, for instance, are curiously inconsistent. It is claimed on the one hand that the Negro could not profit by these educational advantages; and on the other hand it is claimed that if he had equal educational advantages nothing would avail to keep him "in his place." Thus the majority group betrays its fears as well as its arrogance and proves that hatred and contempt of the minority group is compounded of both insecurity and a false security. It is the false security of a particular kind of man (Gentile or white man or what not) who imagines himself the ultimate man and judges those who do not conform to his standard of beauty, culture, physiognomy, diligence, laziness, or any other characteristic that he ascribes to himself, for falling short of the ultimate of which he is the exemplar. But there is a certain insecurity here also. This ultimate man has a darkly conscious sense of the fact that he is not as ultimate as he pretends, and that the groups that he pretends to hold in contempt might actually beat him at his own game if he relaxed the restraints that he has placed upon them.

Psychological science might make some contribution to the analysis of these subrational fears and hatreds. It has in fact already done so. Yet it is also inhibited from a full analysis of these complexities because it does not know the human spirit in the full stature of its freedom. Psychology is not as simply rationalistic as anthropology in dealing with race prejudice. Yet it is always looking for the specific roots of man's insecurity and sense of inferiority. It does not know to what degree the particular forms of pride and arrogance in man are prompted by a general predisposition to pride and arrogance, and how this general predisposition is man's abortive effort to hide his general insecurity. Race bigotry is, in short, one form of original sin. Original sin is something darker and more terrible than mere stupidity and is therefore not eradicated by enlightenment alone, though frequently enlightenment can break some of its power by robbing it of some of its instruments of stupidity. While the general predisposition is not malice, it does issue in specific attitudes that have malice in them. We do not finally come to terms with race pride until the soul knows itself to be under final judgment, ceases to veil its hidden fears and prides, honestly prays: " Search me, O God, and know my faults; try me and know my thoughts — see if there be any wicked way in me and lead me to the way everlasting." Race bigotry, in other words, must be broken by repentance and not merely by enlightenment.

It cannot be said that religious repentance has done much to soften the power of prejudice. Scientific enlightenment, despite its weaknesses, has actually done more to dispel race prejudice than most religion. There are many reasons for this. The liberal church merely preaches ethnic good will. It is too simply moralistic to come to terms with the hidden power of sin in the lives of men. It preaches the law of Christ and insists that " in Christ there is neither Jew nor Greek." But it preaches this as a law that all men ought to obey. When confronted with the overt and covert defiance of that law it is overcome with a sense of futility.

The orthodox church on the other hand, particularly in the South, never allows the gospel of Christ to become a cleansing force in the whole life of man. It has a simple little legalistic system of Christian morality and tries to convict men of sin because they have violated this system. It deals with sins, mostly picayune sins, and not with sin. Actually its Christian legalism, with its strong emphasis upon Sabbath observance and upon a scrupulous sex ethic, and its complete disregard of the hopes, fears, ambitions, and desires of men that create social, racial, and economic forces in society, is probably a partly conscious evasion of the moral problem involved in the race issue. The very hysteria of Southern evangelical legalism proves that something is being covered up. This pharisee would not pray quite so obviously, thanking God that he is not like other men, if he did not have an uneasy conscience.

Let the church, in dealing with the race issue, avail itself of every measure of enlightenment that modern science, anthropological and psychological, can contribute to the issue. But let it not forget its own resources, or rather the resources of its gospel. The church knows, or ought to know, that though men may be incredibly stupid, the hatred and contempt that they exhibit in their lives springs from a deeper source than stupidity. It is the consequence of the corruption of a greater spiritual freedom in man than those understand who speak of man as " rational." Both the dignity and the misery of man are greater than modern culture understands. The misery of man is derived from his idolatry, from his partly conscious and partly unconscious effort to make himself, his race, and his culture God. This idolatry is not broken until man is confronted with the real God, and finds his pride broken by the divine judgment, and learns that from this crucifixion of the old proud self a new self may arise, and that this new self has the " fruits of the spirit," which are " love, joy, and peace."

Racial conflict has become the most vicious of all forms of social conflict in this nation. And the racial tensions will become worse long before they will become better. The church has been very busy telling the nation what to do about this. The church might better try to present the national community with a greater number of truly contrite souls, truly " emancipated " of race prejudice, who express their emancipation partly in the contrite recognition of the remnant of pride that remains in the souls of even the emancipated.

26. THE RACE PROBLEM

The evacuation of thousands of American citizens of Japanese parentage from coastal states of the West in defiance of all their rights of citizenship must be added to the difficulties that Negroes are experiencing in the defense forces as indications of the seriousness of the race problem in the democratic world.

We may resist Hitler's explicit identification of virtue and race, particularly when the racial theory rebounds to the advantage of a race other than our own. But despite all democratic pretensions, there is no democracy that has fully transcended racial prejudices. Perhaps we might add that no democracy ever will transcend them completely, though of course no one can place limits upon the possibilities of surmounting them. Which is to say that race pride is one

of the many aspects of man's collective life that have been obscured
by our contemporary culture. This culture has assumed that pride
of race is no more than a vestigial remnant of barbarism and that increasing education would overcome it.

Liberal educators are fond of calling attention to the fact that
children have no race prejudice, from which they draw the conclusion that nothing but a faulty education is responsible for the prejudice. They fail to recognize that the same children who have no race
prejudice are also completely oblivious to race distinctions as such.
It would be analogous if we argued that nothing but a faulty education caused sex aberrations and proved the contention by pointing
to the absence of either sex passion or sex consciousness among children. The mistake is to identify childish innocency with virtue and
to attribute the corruption of that virtue to some social source of
corruption.

Racial prejudice, as every other form of group prejudice, is a concomitant of the collective life of man. Group pride is the sinful corruption of group consciousness. Contempt of another group is the
pathetic form that respect for our own group frequently takes. We
must not condone these sinful corruptions, but we need not condone
them if we discover that they are more inevitable and perennial than
modern idealists have assumed. But a profounder study of the
tragedy of collective sin will make us less confident of the various
panaceas that are intended to eliminate such sin in its various manifestations.

The liberal church, which has assumed that the right kind of religious education would eliminate race prejudice, might well engage
in some contrite reflection upon the fact that liberal churches have
not become interracial by force of their educational program, and
that there are not a half dozen churches in our whole nation that
have transcended race pride in their corporate life to any considerable degree.

The more orthodox sacramental churches, which make a sharp
distinction between what is possible in an ordinary human community and what is possible in a sacramental community of grace,
have actually achieved a greater degree of transcendence over race
than the liberal churches, which have assumed that " natural " man
has the capacity to rise above race pride and prejudice if only he
becomes a little more enlightened.

There are, in other words, no solutions for the race problem on any level if it is not realized that there is no absolute solution for this problem. There is no absolute solution in the sense that it is not possible to purge man completely of the sinful concomitant of group pride in his collective life.

If we understood the depth of this problem, we would not be so ready to attribute the evacuation of the Japanese from the coastal areas to the war emergency and to lack of loyalty to our institutions among them. We would know that there are undoubtedly disloyal Japanese of the first generation, and that there may be a few in the second generation of American citizens. But we would also know that the inclination to place them all in the same category is not justified by the facts. It is prompted by the inveterate tendency among men to generalize about individuals in another group upon the basis of the least favorable evidence in regard to them. We cannot deal with our injustices to either the Negroes or the Japanese adequately because we dare not confess to ourselves how great our sins are. If we made such a confession, the whole temple of our illusions would fall.

On the side of the minority groups, a little more Christian realism would also have its advantages. Negroes, for instance, tend to resist the achievement of equal rights in the Army if this means the organization of separate units for them. This policy spells segregation for them. They demand equality in mixed units and would rather have their demands denied than to compromise with their principles. Furthermore, they persist in the illusion that the difficulties that they face are caused by the particular prejudices of, let us say, Southern Army and Naval officers. Why have they not yet learned that race prejudice is a deeper disease than that? A particular culture may aggravate it, but the purest democratic culture does not eliminate it. Even if they become more realistic and attribute the sin to all white men, they would still be wrong if they did not understand that all men, and not merely white men, have race prejudice.

One salutary form of religious realism is to brush aside all illusions which have hitherto saved us from cynicism and despair, to all the facts about human nature to become fully revealed, until all men, including ourselves, are included in the disclosure. Once we have recognized that we ourselves are not free of the sin that we see in our enemy and oppressor, no matter how grievous the oppression, it becomes possible for us to deal with the sin with vigor and with grace.

This does not mean that we ought to capitulate to aggravated forms of evil, merely because we know ourselves to be tainted with them. We may deal with them more resolutely if we fully understand the situation. We can also deal with specific problems more wisely. If we imagine that race pride is only a vestigial remnant of barbarism, which civilization is in the process of sloughing off; if we do not understand it as a perennial corruption of man's collective life on every level of social and moral achievement, we are bound to follow wrong policies in dealing with specific aspects of the problem. An engineer who dammed up an ocean inlet under the illusion that he was dealing with a mountain stream would be no more foolish than our social engineers who are constantly underestimating the force and the character of the social stuff that they are manipulating.

27. JEWS AFTER THE WAR

PART I

The position of the Jews in Europe and the Western world is by no means the least of the many problems of postwar reconstruction that must engage our minds even while our energies are being exhausted in achieving the prerequisite of any reconstruction, that is, the defeat of the Axis. It is idle to assume that this defeat will solve the problem of the Jews; indeed, the overthrow of nazism will provide no more than the negative condition for the solution of any of the vexing problems of justice that disturb our consciences.

Millions of Jews have been completely disinherited, and they will not be able to obtain the automatic restoration of their rights. An impoverished Europe will not find it easy to reabsorb a large number of returned Jews, and a spiritually corrupted Europe will not purge itself quickly of the virus of race bigotry with which the Nazis have infected its culture. It must also be remembered that the plight of the Jews was intolerable in those parts of Europe which represented a decadent feudalism — Poland and the Balkans — long before Hitler made their lot impossible in what was once the democratic world. The problem of what is to become of the Jews in the postwar world ought to engage all of us, not only because a suffering people has a claim upon our compassion but because the very quality of our civilization is involved in the solution. It is, in fact, a scandal that the Jews have had so little effective aid from the rest of us in a situation in which they are only the chief victims. The Nazis intend to decimate the Poles and to reduce other peoples to the status of helots; but they are bent upon the extermination of the Jews.

One probable reason for the liberal world's failure to be more instant in its aid to the Jews is that we cannot face the full dimensions of this problem without undermining the characteristic credos of the democratic world. Even the Jews are loath to bring the problem to our attention in all its tragic depth. We will not face it because we should be overwhelmed by a sense of guilt in contemplating those aspects of the problem which Hitler did not create but only aggravated. Some Jews have refused to face it in dread of having to recognize that the solutions provided by the liberal Jewish world have failed to reach the depths of the problem.

The liberal world has sought to dissolve the prejudice between Jews and Gentiles by preaching tolerance and good will. Friends of the Jews have joined the Jews in seeking to persuade their detractors that the charges against them are lies. But this does not meet the real issue. The real question is, Why should these lies be manufactured and why should they be believed? Every cultural or racial group has its own characteristic vices and virtues. When a minority group is hated for its virtues as well as for its vices, and when its vices are hated not so much because they are vices as because they bear the stamp of uniqueness, we are obviously dealing with a collective psychology that is not easily altered by a little more enlightenment. The fact is that the relations of cultural and ethnic groups, intranational or international, have complexities unknown in the relations between individuals, in whom intelligence may dissolve group loyalties and the concomitant evil of group friction.

American theories of tolerance in regard to race are based upon a false universalism that in practice develops into a new form of nationalism. The fact that America has actually been a melting pot in which a new amalgam of races is being achieved has given rise to the illusion that racial and ethnic distinction can be transcended in history to an indeterminate degree. Russian nationalism has the same relation to Marxist universalism as American nationalism has to liberal universalism. There is a curious, partly unconscious, cultural imperialism in theories of tolerance that look forward to a complete destruction of all racial distinctions. The majority group expects to devour the minority group by way of assimilation. This is a painless death, but it is death nevertheless.

The collective will to survive of those ethnic groups in America which have a base in another homeland is engaged and expressed in their homeland, and need not express itself here, where an amalgam of races is taking place. The Finns need not seek to perpetuate themselves in America, for their collective will to live is expressed in Finland. But the Jews are in a different position. Though as an ethnic group they have maintained some degree of integrity for thousands of years, they are a nationality scattered among the nations. Does the liberal-democratic world fully understand that it is implicitly making collective extinction the price of its provisional tolerance?

This question implies several affirmations that are challenged by both Jewish and Gentile liberals; it is therefore important to make these affirmations explicit and to elaborate them. One is that the Jews are really a nationality and not merely a cultural group. Certainly the Jews have maintained a core of racial integrity through the ages. This fact is not disproved by the assertion that their blood is considerably mixed. There are no pure races. History develops new configurations on the bases of nature, but not in such a way as to transcend completely the natural distinctions. Who would deny that the Germans have a collective will to live, or think that this simple statement can be refuted by calling attention to the admixture of Slav blood in people of German nationality?

The integrity of the Jews as a group is, of course, not purely biological; it has also a religious and cultural basis. But in this Jews are not unique, for there are no purely biological facts in history. The cultural and religious content of Jewish life transcends racial particularity, as does the culture of every people, though never so absolutely as to annihilate its own ethnic core. The one aspect of Jewish life that is unique is that the Jews are a nationality scattered among the nations. I use the word " nationality " to indicate something more than " race " and something less than " nation." It is more than race by reason of the admixture of culture and less than nation by reason of the absence of a state. The Jews certainly are a nationality by reason of the ethnic core of their culture. Those Jews who do not feel themselves engaged by a collective will have a perfect right to be so disengaged, just as Americans of French or Greek descent need feel no responsibility for the survival of their respective nationalities. But Jews render no service either to democracy or to their people by seeking to deny this ethnic foundation of their life, or by giving themselves to the illusion that they might dispel all prejudice if only they could prove that they are a purely cultural or religious community.

The fact that millions of Jews are quite prepared to be *spurlos versenkt,* to be annihilated, in a process of assimilation must affect the program of the democratic world for dealing with the Jewish question. The democratic world must accord them this privilege, including, of course, the right to express the ethos of their history in purely cultural and religious terms, in so far as this is possible, without an ethnic base. The democratic world must resist the insinuation that the Jews are not assimilable, particularly when the charge is made in terms of spurious friendship, as it is by Albert Jay Nock. They are not assimilable but they have added to the riches of a democratic world by their ethnic and cultural contributions. Civilization must guard against the tendency of all communities to demand a too simple homogeneity, for if this is allowed complete expression, it results in Nazi tribal primitivism. The preservation of tolerance and cultural pluralism is necessary not only from the standpoint of justice to the Jews but from the standpoint of the quality of a civilization.

The assimilability of the Jews and their right to be assimilated are not in question; this conviction must prompt one half of the program of the democratic world, the half that consists in maintaining and extending the standards of tolerance and cultural pluralism achieved in a liberal era. But there is another aspect of the Jewish problem that is not met by this strategy. That is the simple right of the Jews to survive as a people. There are both Jews and Gentiles who deny that the Jews have such a survival impulse as an ethnic group, but the evidence of contemporary history refutes them, as does the evidence of all history in regard to the collective impulses of survival in life generally. Modern liberalism has been blind to this aspect of human existence because its individualist and universalist presuppositions and illusions have prevented it from seeing some rather obvious facts in man's collective life.

One proof of the Jews' will to survive is, of course, that they have survived the many vicissitudes of their history. They have survived in spite of the fact that they have been a nationality scattered among the nations, without a homeland of their own, since the dawn of

Western European history. They are a people of the Diaspora. Modern assimilationists on both sides sometimes suggest that the survival of the Jews through the centuries was determined on the one hand by the hostility of the feudal world and on the other by the toughness of an orthodox religious faith; and they suggest that the liberal era has dissipated both the external and the internal basis of this survival. They assume that the liberal ideals of tolerance are infinitely extensible and that the breaking of the hard shell of a traditional religious unity will destroy the internal will to live.

The violent nationalism of our period proves the error of the first assumption. While we need not believe that nazism or even a milder form of national bigotry will set the social and political standards of the future, it is apparent that collective particularities and vitalities have a more stubborn life than liberal universalism had assumed. The error of the second has been proved by the Jews themselves. For Zionism is the expression of a national will to live that transcends the traditional orthodox religion of the Jews. It is supported by many forces in Jewish life, not the least of which is an impressive proletarian impulse. Poor Jews recognize that privileged members of their Jewish community may have achieved such a secure posi-tion in the Western world that they could hardly be expected to sacrifice it for a Zionist venture. But they also see that for the great multitude of Jews there is no escape from the hardships a national-ity scattered among the nations must suffer. They could, if they would, be absorbed in the Western world. Or they could, if they de-sired, maintain their racial integrity among the various nations. But they know that the price that must be paid for such survival is high. They know from their own experience that collective prejudice is not as easily dissolved as some of their more favored brothers assume.

The poorer Jews understand, out of their experience, what is fre-quently withheld from the more privileged — namely, that the bigotry of majority groups toward minority groups that affront the majority by diverging from the dominant type is a perennial aspect of man's collective life. The force of it may be mitigated, but it can-not be wholly eliminated. These Jews, therefore, long for a place on the earth where they are not " tolerated," where they are neither " understood " nor misunderstood, neither appreciated nor con-demned, but where they can be what they are, preserving their own unique identity without asking " by your leave " of anyone else.

It is this understanding of a basic human situation on the part of the less privileged portion of the Jewish community which has given Zionism a particular impetus. There are of course individuals in the more privileged groups who make common cause with the less privileged because they have the imagination to see what their more intellectualist brothers have not seen. But on the whole Zionism represents the wisdom of the common experience as against the wisdom of the mind, which tends to take premature flights into the absolute or the universal from the tragic conflicts and the stubborn particularities of human history.

The second part of any program for the solution of the Jewish problem must rest upon the recognition that a collective survival impulse is as legitimate a " right " as an individual one. Justice, in history, is concerned with collective, as well as with individual, rights. Recognition of the legitimacy of this right must lead, in my opinion, to a more generous acceptance of the Zionist program as correct in principle, however much it may have to be qualified in application.

The Jewish religionists, the Jewish and Gentile secularists, and the Christian missionaries to the Jews have, despite the contradictory character of their various approaches, one thing in common. They would solve the problem of the particularity of a race by a cultural or religious universalism. This is a false answer if the universal character of their culture or religion demands the destruction of the historical — in this case racial — particularism. It is just as false as if the command " thou shalt love thy neighbor as thyself " were interpreted to mean that I must destroy myself so that no friction may arise between my neighbor and myself.

The author, who happens to be a Christian theologian, may be permitted the assertion, as a postscriptum, that he has his own ideas about the relation of the Christian to the Jewish religion. But he regards all religious and cultural answers to the Jewish problem that do not take basic ethnic facts into consideration as the expressions of either a premature universalism or a conscious or unconscious ethnic imperialism.

PART II

I offer " a " solution rather than " the " solution to the problem of anti-Semitism precisely because a prerequisite for any solution of

a basic social problem is the understanding that there is no perfectly satisfactory formula. A perennial problem of human relations
can be dealt with on many levels of social and moral achievements,
but not in such a way that new perplexities will not emerge upon
each new level. The tendency of modern culture to find pat answers
and panaceas for vexing problems — one aspect of its inveterate
utopianism — has confused rather than clarified most issues with
which it has occupied itself.

I have previously suggested that the problem of the relation of the
Jews to our Western democratic world calls for at least two different
approaches. We must on the one hand preserve and if possible extend the democratic standards of tolerance and of cultural and racial
pluralism that allow the Jews *Lebensraum* as a nation among the
nations. We must on the other hand support more generously than
in the past the legitimate aspiration of Jews for a " homeland " in
which they will not be simply tolerated but which they will possess.
The type of liberalism that fights for and with the Jews on the first
battle line but leaves them to fight alone on the second is informed
by unrealistic universalism. If its presuppositions are fully analyzed,
it will be discovered that they rest upon the hope that history is
moving forward to a universal culture that will eliminate all particularities and every collective uniqueness, whether rooted in nature or
in history. History has perennially refuted this hope.

The late Justice Louis D. Brandeis illustrated in his person and
his ideas exactly what we mean by this double strategy. Brandeis was
first a great American, whose contributions to our national life prove
that justice to the Jew is also a service to democracy in that it allows
democracy to profit from the peculiar gifts of the Jew — in the case
of Brandeis and many another leader, the Hebraic-prophetic passion
for social justice. But Brandeis was also a Zionist; his belief in the
movement was regarded by some of his friends, both Gentile and
Jewish, as an aberration that one had to condone in an otherwise
sane and worthy man. Brandeis' Zionism sprang from his understanding of an aspect of human existence to which most of his fellow liberals were blind. He understood " that whole peoples have an
individuality no less marked than that of single persons, that the individuality of a people is irrepressible, and that the misnamed inter-
nationalism that seeks the elimination of nationalities or peoples is
unattainable. The new nationalism proclaims that each race or people has a right and duty to develop, and that only through such

differentiated development will highest civilization be attained."
Brandeis understood in 1916 what some of his fellow Jews did not
learn until 1933 and what many a Gentile liberal will never learn.
"We Jews," he said, "are a distinct nationality of which every Jew
is necessarily a member. Let us insist that the struggle for liberty
shall not cease until equal opportunity is accorded to nationalities
as to individuals."

It must be emphasized that any program that recognizes the rights
of Jews as a nationality and that sees in Zionism a legitimate demand
for the recognition of these rights must at the same time support the struggle for the rights of Jews as citizens in the nations in
which they are now established or may be established. This strategy
is demanded, if for no other reason, because there is no possibility
that Palestine will ever absorb all the Jews of the world. Even if it
were physically able to absorb them, we know very well that migra-
tions never develop as logically as this. I cannot judge whether
Zionist estimates of the millions that a fully developed Palestine
could absorb are correct. They seem to me to err on the side of optimism. But in any case it would be fantastic to assume that all Jews
could or would find their way to Palestine, even in the course of
many centuries.

It is more important, however, to consider what democracy owes
to its own ideals of justice and to its own quality as a civilization
than what it owes to the Jews. Neither democracy nor any other
civilization pretending to maturity can afford to capitulate to the
tendency in collective life that would bring about unity by establishing a simple homogeneity. We must not underestimate this
tendency as a perennial factor in man's social life. Nor must we fail
to understand the logic behind it. Otherwise we shall become involved in the futile task of seeking to prove that minority groups
are not really as bad as their critics accuse them of being, instead
of understanding that minority groups are thought "bad" only
because they diverge from the dominant type and affront that type
by their divergence. But to yield to this tendency would be to allow
civilization to be swallowed in primitivism, for the effort to return
to the simple unity of tribal life is a primitive urge of which nazism
is the most consistent, absurd, and dangerous contemporary expression. In the case of the Jews, with their peculiar relation to the
modern world and the peculiar contributions that they have made
to every aspect of modern culture and civilization, any relaxation of

democratic standards would also mean robbing our civilization of the special gifts that they have developed as a nation among the nations.

The necessity for a second strategy in dealing with the Jewish problem stems from certain aspects of the collective life of men that the modern situation has brought into tragic relief. The Jews require a homeland, if for no other reason, because even the most generous immigration laws of the Western democracies will not permit all the dispossessed Jews of Europe to find a haven in which they may look forward to a tolerable future. When I say the most " generous " immigration laws, I mean, of course, " generous " only within terms of political exigencies. It must be observed that the liberals of the Western world maintain a conspiracy of silence on this point. They do not dare to work for immigration laws generous enough to cope with the magnitude of the problem that the Jewish race faces. They are afraid of political repercussions, tacitly acknowledging that their theories do not square with the actual facts. Race prejudice, the intolerance of a dominant group toward a minority group, is a more powerful and more easily aroused force than they dare admit.

A much weightier justification of Zionism is that every race finally has a right to a homeland where it will not be " different," where it will neither be patronized by the " good " people nor subjected to calumny by bad people. Of course many Jews have achieved a position in democratic nations in which the disabilities from which they suffer as a minority group are comparatively insignificant in comparison with the prestige that they have won. A democratic world would not disturb them. Their situation would actually be eased to an even further degree if the racial survival impulse were primarily engaged in Palestine. Religious and cultural divergences alone do not present a serious problem, particularly under traditions of cultural pluralism. But there are millions of Jews, not only in the democratic world, but in the remnants of the feudal world, such as Poland and the Balkans, who ought to have a chance to escape from the almost intolerable handicaps to which they are subjected. One reason why Jews suffer more than any other minority is that they bear the brunt of two divergences from type, religious and racial, and it is idle for the Jews or Gentiles to speculate about which is the primary source of prejudice. Either would suffice, but the prejudice is compounded when both divergences are involved.

Zionist aspirations, it seems to me, deserve a more generous support than they have been accorded by liberal and democratic groups in Western countries. Non-Zionist Jews have erred in being apologetic or even hostile to these aspirations on the ground that their open expression might imperil rights painfully won in the democratic world. Non-Jewish liberals have erred equally in regarding Zionism as nothing but the vestigial remnant of an ancient religious dream, the unfortunate aberration of a hard-pressed people.

Whether the Jews will be allowed to develop a genuine homeland under their own sovereignty, within the framework of the British Empire, depends solely upon the amount of support that they secure in the two great democracies, for those democracies will have it in their power if Hitler is defeated to make the necessary political arrangements. The influence of the American Government will be indirect but none the less effective — which is why American public opinion on this issue cannot be a matter of indifference. It is obviously no easy matter for British statecraft to give the proper assurances and to make basic arrangements for the future while it is forced to deal with a vast and complex Arab world still in danger of falling under the sway of the Nazis. Yet it must be observed that the Arabs achieved freedom and great possessions in the last war, and that this war, in the event of victory for the United Nations, will increase the extent and cohesion of their realm. The Anglo-Saxon hegemony that is bound to exist in the event of an Axis defeat will be in a position to see to it that Palestine is set aside for the Jews, that the present restrictions on immigration are abrogated, and that the Arabs are otherwise compensated.

Zionist leaders are unrealistic in insisting that their demands entail no " injustice " to the Arab population since Jewish immigration has brought new economic strength to Palestine. It is absurd to expect any people to regard the restriction of their sovereignty over a traditional possession as " just," no matter how many other benefits accrue from that abridgment. What is demanded in this instance is a policy that offers a just solution of an intricate problem faced by a whole civilization. The solution must, and can, be made acceptable to the Arabs if it is incorporated into a total settlement of the issues of the Mediterranean and Near Eastern world; and it need not be unjust to the Arabs in the long run if the same " imperial " policy that established the Jewish homeland also consolidates and unifies the Arab world. One may hope that this will not be done by making the Jewish homeland a part of an essentially Arab federation.

It must be noted in conclusion that there are both Jews and Gentiles who do not believe that Palestine is a desirable locus for a Jewish homeland, though they do believe that a homeland must be created. They contend that there is as yet no evidence of Palestine's ability to maintain an independent economic existence without subsidies; that the co-operative agricultural ventures of the Jews, impressive in quality but not in size, offer no hope of a solid agricultural basis for the national economy; that the enmity of the Arab world would require the constant interposition of imperial arms; that the resources of Palestine could not support the millions whom the Zionists hope to settle there; and that the tendency to use Arab agricultural labor may once more create a Jewish urban caste. It is difficult to know to what degree such criticisms are justified. The fact that 25 per cent of the Jewish settlers in Palestine are engaged in agriculture tends to refute the argument that the Palestinian economy has no adequate agricultural base. The criticism that Palestine cannot, under the most favorable circumstances, absorb all the Jews who must find a new home and security after the war is more serious. However, even if fully borne out, it would not affect the thesis that the Jews require a homeland. It would simply raise the question whether a different or an additional region should be chosen. It is barely possible that a location ought to be found in Europe.

The whole matter is so important that it should be explored by an international commission, consisting of both Jews and Gentiles, both Zionists and non-Zionists. The Jews were the first, as they have been the chief, victims of Nazi fury. Their rehabilitation, like the rehabilitation of every Nazi victim, requires something more than the restoration of the *status quo ante*. We must consider this task one of the most important among the many problems of postwar reconstruction. We cannot, in justice either to ourselves or to the Jews, dismiss it from our conscience. ✓

28. THE NEGRO ISSUE IN AMERICA

The increasing tension between Negroes and whites in America is proof of the fact that basic social issues become more complicated in the very process of their solution. The Negroes have more rights in this war than in the last one. Yet they are more resentful of the injustice done them. The reason for the increasing resentment undoubtedly lies in the fact that a much larger number of Negroes have by education and other advances achieved the ability to resent and to resist injustice than in the past. If a community desires to keep a race in permanent subjection, it can only do so by consistent Nazi methods. It must destroy the capacity to resist injustice among those who suffer from it.

The tortuous process of democratic justice fortunately makes it impossible for a total community to follow the principles of discrimination which one part of the community would like to apply. Thus the best impulses of our democratic society have expressed themselves in providing ever increasing educational advantages to the Negro race, even while our worst impulses express themselves in seeking to prevent those higher forms of justice which this more equal education makes logical and necessary.

Increasing race tension is due, however, not merely to increasing resentment among Negroes but also to increasing fear among the proponents of " white supremacy " who feel their privileged position in a caste society imperiled and who become more and more desperate in seeking to ward off further concessions of justice. This is why certain reactionary white Southerners express themselves more and more hysterically in their attitude toward the race question. This is particularly apparent in the Southern opposition to the elimination of " poll tax " restrictions upon the franchise and in the recent hysteria occasioned by the decision of the Supreme Court that Negroes have a right to vote in the primaries of Southern states. We must expect this tension to heighten until it reaches its climax after the war. The frightened reactionaries regard the returning Negro soldier as a particular threat to their peace, and not without reason. For it is undoubtedly a fact that the Negro soldier in America has conceived a profound resolve to claim some of the democratic justice for which they have been fighting a foreign foe.

No easy solution can be offered for this vexatious problem. All the spiritual resources of our nation will be required to effect even a tolerable minimal solution by achieving some advances in justice between the races and yet avoiding overt conflict.

It may be worth observing that at the present moment the Christian church is making no great contribution to the solution of this issue. The churches of the North absolve their conscience by passing idealistic resolutions in which all race discrimination is condemned. Most of the churches of the South are completely enslaved and cowed by the prevailing hysteria. There are fortunately leavening minorities in the South in the universities and the churches, who are doing what they can to lessen the tension and to mitigate the pride and the fear of the white man.

There are several tasks that the church might perform in terms of its own peculiar genius that would make its idealism more relevant to the present situation. If, for instance, the church were to make a rigorous religious analysis of the motives that underlie the white man's pride and fear, if it allowed the Word of God to be sharper than a two-edged sword, if it searched the conscience of men in the light of that Word, it might help white people to see to what degree the very hysteria of their attack upon the Negro is the evidence of an uneasy conscience.

It is not possible to travel in the South or to mix in the complex race relations of a Northern municipality without noticing that the most brazen forms of injustice are partly due to the effort of men of disquiet conscience to hide the uneasiness of their inner life. Even the worst sinners against God's law of brotherhood have some testimony in their inner life to the wrong they do. Such uneasiness may prompt repentance; but it may also prompt despair; and despair may express itself in frantic professions of righteousness and unjust attacks upon the minority. Only religiously astute and profound pastors of the souls of men understand to what degree men make public accusation against their fellows in order to cover up the secret accusations that the dispossessed make against them in God's sight. Cain protests the more loudly that he is not his brother's keeper because he knows in the secret of his heart that he is.

The preaching of the ideal possibilities of brotherhood that is not accompanied by a careful and pitiless analysis of the motives, of the inner fears, self-accusations, and self-justifications of those who deny brotherhood is not religious. It moves on the plane of secular idealism and does not bring the terror of the judgments of the living God to bear upon the soul. Only if this is done can the mercy of God also heal the hurt that men have in their own heart and that prompts them to hurt each other.

There is one other point at which the church fails miserably in its attack upon the race issue today. It is always calling upon the community to abolish this or that discrimination, but it makes no contrite admission of the fact that the church in America is almost consistently Jim Crow in its pattern of segregation. There are few cities of the South in which even ministers of the same denomination have any fellowship across race lines. Even in the Northern churches there is frequently no fellowship below the level of the general conference of the entire church.

The real fact is that the Christian church in America lacks even minimally adequate symbols of the reality of a community of grace that does not recognize race as basic to its fellowship. In the South, denominational divisions are still so strong that there is little fellowship even between white pastors and congregations across denominational lines. Protestantism thus reveals its pathetic particularism and proves that the forces of history, whether they be racial or national, cultural or economic, can divide it without the church having the power and the grace to preserve even a symbol of its ultimate unity in Christ. It might be well for the church to make fewer ideal demands upon the community for a while and center upon this problem in its own life. If the church is the body of Christ, and if in Christ there is neither Jew nor Greek, there must be some dimension in the life of the church where this is recognized and actualized. If it is not, the church ceases to be a true church. If the salt has lost its savor, if the inner life of the church has ceased to be a real leaven in society, it cannot hide that fact by making brave and idealistic public pronouncements.

Let the church approach the race issue with greater humility and perhaps some fruits meet for repentance will develop in its own life.

29. FAIR EMPLOYMENT PRACTICES ACT

The F.E.P.A. has been defeated in the United States Senate, at least indirectly. It has been impossible to win a two-thirds vote to impose cloture, which means that a Southern filibuster can prevent passage of the act. Southern liberals were without exception opposed to the bill, though some of them were also opposed to the practice of filibuster.

The act, which sought to bring Government pressure upon employment practices, is part of a general program of the Fair Deal, which also includes a federal antilynching bill and an anti-poll-tax bill, designed to force the Southern states to grant the Negro minority more equal rights. This is a laudable end. It is important that all our moral, spiritual, and political resources be used to give our Negro fellow citizens every democratic privilege that we enjoy. The Negro problem in this country is on the one hand a contest between the old institution of slavery and the spirit of democracy. History has proved that an institution like slavery, even when abolished by law, lives on vestigially. On the other hand, the problem is older than our nation, being a manifestation of race pride that expresses itself in every encounter between different races, particularly when one race has a minority status.

Recent Supreme Court decisions, forcing Southern states to grant Negroes equality in interstate transportation and in college education, prove that law may be a potent weapon in enforcing rights. Within limits it is possible for a total national community to insist legally that every portion of the community observe its minimal standards of justice. Thus, too, court decisions have forced some of the Southern states to admit Negroes to party primaries. It is clear, in other words, that the power of law is considerable in raising democratic standards of a community.

But the law is not omnipotent. The very fact that the Emancipation Proclamation did not abolish slavery absolutely, and that the Federal grant of suffrage to all Negroes has been circumvented in Southern states for two generations proves that there are limits to the power of law. A study of these limits may lead to the conclusion that a Federal act, enforcing fair employment, is futile. It obviously cannot be passed. It probably could not be enforced if it were passed. In stating such a conclusion we are flying in the face of an almost unanimous "liberal" opinion, inside and outside of the churches. But liberal opinion has again and again failed to observe that the potency of law has its limits. We learned a lesson in the Prohibition movement that we seem already to have forgotten. That lesson was that a determined minority, if it is locally a majority, whether in a city or a state, is able to defy, evade, or nullify a law passed by a national majority. It will do so if the law goes too far beyond the moral or social standards of community. Laws can be enforced only upon recalcitrant minorities. The majority of the community must accept a law without enforcement if it is to be enforceable. But if individual recalcitrance has the support of a local community, if the " conscience " of the community aids and abets defiance, no amount of enforcement by coercion avails.

This is why laws enforcing fair employment in individual states differ from Federal laws. In a state, e.g., New York, such a law proves efficacious because the majority behind the law registers a moral climate that makes the law enforceable. But if the Federal Government forces such a law upon a reluctant state, it tends to produce a reaction of defiance rather than compliance. This is particularly true in our South where " Yankee interference " is regarded as almost synonymous with " foreign " interference. This is a legacy of the Civil War. It proves that the Northern victory did not, and could not, completely heal the breach in the national community.

It must not be denied that a law has considerable power in changing the moral climate of a community. If, say, 53 per cent of a population is in favor of a certain social standard, the enactment of that standard into law gives it sufficient majesty to persuade possibly 90 per cent of the population that the law ought to be obeyed. But if only 33 per cent of the population accepts the standard that the law embodies, it is always possible that the effort to enforce the law will arouse such resentment that the proportion of the population in its favor will be dissipated rather than enhanced. These proportionate figures are, of course, quite arbitrary. A good deal depends upon how fervently and stubbornly majorities and minorities hold to their position.

It would be quite wrong to draw the conclusion that only educational and religious influences upon moral and social standards are of avail, and that it must be regarded futile to change social structures and systems by legal pressure. Too often religious leaders draw this conclusion and assert that goodness by coercion is abortive. A considerable proportion of our social virtue is derived not from our own resources but from the restraints and influences of the community. But the most effective restraints are not those of pure law, particularly not if the law is in conflict with the conscience of the community.

In the case of the racial problem of the South it would have been much better to begin with antilynching and anti-poll-tax legislation. The South has an uneasy conscience about the problems against which these laws are directed and the liberal portion of the South would have supported them. The conscience of the best people of the South would have converged with the conscience of the nation upon these issues. It was because it was felt that the Fair Employment bill had less chance of passing that President Truman was persuaded to place it first upon his program. Its proponents felt that it would not pass at all if it came last. It is now quite clear that it will not pass, first or last.

One might, as most liberals, nail the flag to the mast and fight on this issue without regard to immediate success or failure if one could be certain that the law could be enforced, once passed. But a fair employment act requires, above all, a tremendous degree of community co-operation. In states in which it has been successful it has relied chiefly upon administrative procedures and persuasion and has availed itself as little as possible of sanctions. The more sanctions are used or threatened, the more voluntary co-operation vanishes. No type of legislation lends itself so easily to evasion.

In short, it is important in the field of political reality to be as wise as the serpent as well as to be as harmless as the dove. Politics is still the art of the possible. This remains true even when we deal with racial injustices that affront the conscience of the nation. Progress toward better race relations is still too slow in both North and South. But there is real progress. From the Christian viewpoint it is more important that the church of the South should give more solid proof that the Christian community is a community of grace, transcending race, than that the church of the North (which is incidentally almost as completely segregated as the Southern church) should seek a purely legal solution for a deep moral and spiritual problem.

30. THE SUPREME COURT ON SEGREGATION IN THE SCHOOLS

In an age of sorry realities and dread possibilities, one is grateful for any cheerful news. The Supreme Court decision on school segregation gave every American of good will a large measure of cheer in a cheerless age. Our children may well remember this decision long after the antics of the demagogues and the confusions of our

Christianity and Crisis, June 14, 1954.

statesmen are forgotten. The prerequisite for such a consummation is, of course, that their confusions will not result in disaster.

The statesmanship of the Supreme Court decision is displayed in its combination of boldness and concern for the political realities. It declares a principle, applies it to a situation without compromise. But it wisely postpones application of the principle for most of the affected states until they have time to adjust themselves to the conditions created by the decision. Thus any undue shock is avoided, and the danger is lessened that the decision will provoke resistance by Southern authorities. The Court seems quite conscious of the fact that no law can be enforced if it is not generally accepted by the people. When local recalcitrance becomes armed with the sense of the moral rightness of its cause, the case is lost.

What is at stake in this whole enterprise is the contest between the moral sense of the national community and the local communities in which there are vestigial remnants of the slavery ethos, at which the postwar amendments were directed, but which cannot be quickly eliminated by any law. Therefore, the decision was, on the other hand, an excellent example of the power of law and of ethical norms in directing the moral growth of a community. For the law ordained " equality." It embodied the principle of justice that was responsible for the rejection of the institution of slavery. But communities do not always conform their actions and attitudes to " tasks in hours of insight willed." The hiatus between the ideal, embodied in law, and the social facts was most glaring in the states that enjoined school segregation by law. But it was a universal characteristic of our nation. It was in fact the " American dilemma " in Gunnar Myrdal's phrase. The dilemma was that we could not conform our race attitudes, at least to the one race that had at one time had slave status among us, to the basic presupposition of American democracy, eloquently stated in the Declaration of Independence, which affirmed " that all men are created equal," and given a new significance by the war that abolished slavery and that left the residue of the Fourteenth and Fifteenth Amendment in our basic law. Since the facts of history do not, however, conform readily to the challenge of a law that states the ideal, rather than some minimal of conduct, American democracy was subjected to long years of tortuous experience in trying to conform to the ideal, incorporated in the law.

In 1896, the Supreme Court tried to ease the hiatus between the ideal and the social realities by its doctrine of " separate but equal " rights before the law. It was a very good doctrine for its day; for we must remember that the present Supreme Court decision would, at the beginning of the century, merely have prompted revolt. And revolt that is so widespread that police power cannot suppress it represents the defeat both of the law and the ideal. History had to prepare the nation for the present Supreme Court decision. By " history " we mean something more embodied than that abstract concept. We mean the thoughts· and aspirations of a people, and the dozens of hesitant or bold actions that were taken by individuals and groups to overcome racial bias, to lift the educational standards of the allegedly inferior group and to breach the bar of segregation in every walk of life and in every communal relationship.

We must, as Christians, humbly confess that the world of sports has given the most vivid proofs of the spirit of brotherhood and fairness in allowing athletes to prove their worth without bar of color, proofs that undoubtedly affected the public temper more than the segregated churches could do. We must also include in this capillary action, the splendid proofs of worth furnished by the Negroes in all walks of life, in all disciplines of culture, and in every manifestation of moral character. The Negroes have most obviously excelled in the arts and in sports; but they have shown the validity of the doctrine of equal worth in every department of life. Thus the way was prepared for the next step.

Meanwhile the doctrine of " separate but equal " facilities was used effectively by the Supreme Court in the last two decades to open up new opportunities for Negroes, particularly in transportation but also in the schools of higher learning where the force of the Court ruling frequently opened the way for nonsegregated education in cases where equal, but separate, institutions were unavailable — in other words, where law and medical schools had to be opened up to Negroes because the states could not furnish separate professional schools for them. The fact that " nothing happened " in these revolutionary steps under the prodding of the law prepared the way for the next step, which the Supreme Court has now taken.

In fact, the progress has been so rapid that it would have seemed plausible to " let well enough alone " and continue upon this course. But the court refused to adopt this policy. Challenged with the idea that separate school facilities could not be " equal " because they left a mark upon both white and colored children by the implication of inferiority for the colored group, the Court met the challenge by admitting this indictment of segregated education and proving the correctness of the indictment by an analysis of the " intangible " as well as the tangible factors of education. Thus the Court wrote a great State paper as well as rendering a wise decision. Its rejection of segregated education is so persuasive that no one will probably have the hardihood to challenge it. It has fixed a point in our advance in democratic racial relations. Of course, the fact that the decision was unanimous served to increase its moral authority.

The court might have been satisfied with this show of statesman-ship; but it gave additional proof of its wisdom by deferring the date on which most of the states, not directly involved in the litigation, would have to meet the new norms. This policy did much to deflect any incipient revolt against the decision.

The reaction in the South to the decision is almost as cheering as the decision itself. Only the Governors Talmadge of Georgia and Byrnes of South Carolina are in open opposition. Most of the Southern journals have accepted the decision as " inevitable." Some have regretted that the South was not allowed to make further progress under the old norms. There will no doubt be evasions and circumventions of the law, even as the " white primary " is an evasion of the equal suffrage law. But there will evidently not be a wide-spread revolt against the Court's interpretation of the law, so that the decision would be negated in fact.

Thus we have had another demonstration of the way in which an " open " community may grow, with the ideal furnishing the norm of conduct with progressive interpretations of the ideal, rendering it more rigorous and with social and moral history furnishing the stuff to give body to the ideal.

To illustrate the significance of the Supreme Court decision and its light upon the health of our democracy, we must report on a recent visit by a South African visitor. He was a pious Christian of peculiar Dutch African persuasion. But he had an uneasy conscience about race relations in South Africa, which he tried to assuage by a visit to this country to study race relations. But such are the quirks of the human conscience and the capacity of the self for self-deception, that our visitor spent his time proving to himself that there was a wide hiatus between our ideals and our practices; that there was in fact much evidence of bias in our race relations, and that, therefore, South Africa was justified in its policy of rigorous segregation of races, which our visitor declared were created by God to be " different but not unequal." We tried to prove to him that if he and his fellow countrymen really believed that the difference did not spell inequality and if they did not regard " creation " as fixed, but as part of the historic development to which every race and person was subject, they could not maintain the rigor of their policy. We argued further that the sin of South Africa was in closing the doors of hope. This would create increasing hardness of heart among the dominant group who had an uneasy conscience, and would leave the minority group resentful and outraged. We told him that our society undoubtedly had an unsolved race issue. But we had many citizens in the white group who had dedicated themselves to the cause of justice and many Negroes who hoped for the future, and allowed their hopes to console them about present bitter realities. We did not pretend that our community was free of race prejudice, but we asserted that the difference was in the way a society was closed or kept open for future possibilities. The Supreme Court decision has justified every argument used in that encounter. We hope our South African will hear of this decision and learn from it.

31. WHAT RESOURCES CAN THE CHRISTIAN CHURCH OFFER TO MEET CRISIS IN RACE RELATIONS?

Evidence multiplies that our nation is facing the most serious crisis in race relations since the Civil War. Ironically, the crisis has been brought about by a Supreme Court decision, which even those who think more time should have been allowed for the gradual processes of history to take their hitherto hopeful course do not criticize because it simply affirms a Constitutional guarantee of equality before the law that if realized would solve the age-old " American dilemma."

Both Hodding Carter, a Southern editor with a long record of fairness on the race issue, and the distinguished novelist William Faulkner insist that, whatever may be the ultimate issues of justice in this problem, it is now unwise to push the cause of desegregation too consistently, lest the Southern white people are pushed, in Faulkner's phrase, "off balance" and are not allowed time to get their balance.

The question is what resources the Christian church can offer for the solution of these grave issues. It would be wrong to assume that there are automatic resources of grace and wisdom even in the church. The fact is — and it is a disturbing one — that the church is not now, and has not been, very creative on this issue. Perhaps it lacks resources for discriminate judgment — and that is the kind of judgment that the problem demands.

If we turn to the gospel, we shall come first of all upon the rigor of its moral demands. It challenges all partial loyalties in the name of an absolute loyalty. "For if you love those who love you, what reward have you?" asks Christ. "Do not even the tax collectors do the same?"

But the gospel is not simply a system of rigorous idealism; it knows that all men fall short of this universal love. Perhaps the first thing we must learn from the gospel is the sense of our common involvement in the sins of racial loyalty and prejudice. It is not a Southern sin, but a general human shortcoming. Such humility will prevent Northern liberals from self-righteous judgments, which, in the present instance, will aggravate the crisis.

Nevertheless, the realization of our general involvement in the evils of racial prejudice must not prompt us to inaction when particularly flagrant forms of the sins we all commit challenge our conscience. The fact that we all violate the law of love in some way or other ought not to obscure to our conscience the force of that law. Every Christian, for instance, should have some sympathy for a group of Negroes, who have long smarted under the contempt of their fellow men and who now see a chance, under the changing environment, to challenge age-old customs of segregation on public buses. Their boycott must appeal to sensitive men everywhere as another assertion of the dignity of man.

But this does not mean that we can have no sympathy for anxious parents who are opposed to unsegregated schools. The cultural differences between the two races are still great enough to warrant a certain amount of disquiet on the part of the parents. One may hope that ultimately the Negro people will have the same advantages that all our children have. But there must be a measure of sympathy for those who are afraid of the immediate effects of present educational plans. It might help if we all realized that, in all our judgments about each other across racial lines, we do not judge with pure hearts and reason. Our judgments, however honest, are corrupted by the most perennial sin of group pride.

There seems nothing in the Christian ethic about prudence, and prudence is what is demanded in such critical situations as this one. But a genuine charity is the father of prudence. For genuine love does not propose abstract schemes of justice that leave the human factor out of account.

Perhaps there ought also to be a Christian witness of integrity and courage whenever fears prompt cruelty and oppression as they do today in some communities.

32. PROPOSAL TO BILLY GRAHAM

I have no business making any proposals to Billy Graham. We are not acquainted. But I share a general approval of his modesty and sincerity in the Christian community and also a certain uneasiness that his type of evangelism may seem to be irrelevant to the great moral issues of our day.

My proposal is prompted by the fact that in the revival that swept the nation a century ago, under the inspiration of the great Finney, the abolition of slavery was made central to the religious experience of repentance and conversion. As a result the revival led to the manumission of slaves in some instances and to various abolition movements in others. Warner, in his book *The Anti-Slavery Impulse,* gives us a good account of the reality of this type of evangelism. It sharpened the religious awareness of the central moral problem facing the nation a hundred years ago.

CHURCH LAGS IN JUSTICE

A hundred years later we still confront the same moral issue, though in a different historical context. The slaves have long since become emancipated. But the Negroes have not been freed from the contempt that the white majority visits upon the ex-slaves, partly

because of their color and partly because of their " previous condition of servitude." Men are very slow in their collective life in meeting the elementary norms of the Christian life. They violate the simple commandment, " Thou shalt love thy neighbor as thyself." So
here we are a hundred years after the emancipation of the slave in a
new crisis because our Government, based upon a conception of law
that makes " equal protection under the law " the cardinal principle
of justice, is challenging the mores of the community that incorporated a remnant of the pattern of slavery into its customs.

The Christian church did not seriously challenge these customs.
The political community proved itself more rigorous than the Christian community in guarding the dignity of man. The church, as our
Negro friends constantly remind us, was the most rigorously segregated institution in the nation. That segregation wittingly or un-
wittingly gave a religious aura to racial prejudice. Even now, while
many a heroic Southern minister has defied the congregation and
the community in upholding the standards of both the gospel and
the law, the church as an institution has lagged behind the trade-
union movement in supporting the Supreme Court decision.

It would be idle to mention all this were Billy Graham totally unconscious of the moral crisis in our nation on the age-old race issue.
Though a Southerner, he is " enlightened " on the race issue. He
does not condone racial prejudice. But neither does he incorporate
the demand of love transcending racial boundaries into his evange-
listic appeal. He does not suggest that the soul, confronted with the
judgment and the forgiveness of Christ, should regard racial prejudice as an element in the " life of sin " from which the conversion
experience redeems. And he does not suggest that among the " fruits
meet for repentance " there must be a whole-souled effort to give the
Negro neighbor his full due as a man and brother.

A Jewish friend, after witnessing one of Billy Graham's revivals
in the city of Richmond, Virginia, made some pertinent remarks
about the nature of the revival. " We Jews," he wrote, " are naturally
critical, not only because such a revival, with its emphasis upon a
commitment in religious terms to which Jews cannot subscribe, tends
to widen the chasm between Jews and Christians, which common devotion to civic decencies has tended to bridge, but also because the
commitment does not include a new attitude on the race issue, which
is so desperately needed today." In other words, the revival does not
revitalize the Christian faith on the one point where Jews and secu-

lar idealists who do not share our faith would find a Christian witness most relevant and impressive.

This Jewish comment is much more searching than the innumerable Christian comments that find Billy Graham's interpretation of the Christian life too simple and perfectionist but counsel the rest of us to be sympathetic rather than critical because, they argue, Billy will bring people into the Christian church, and then the rest of us will have the opportunity to reveal all the duties and possibilities that a Christian commitment implies. These proposals might be relevant to the problem of the relation of a perfectionist version of the Christian faith to all the ambiguities that any man, including the Christian, must face in the realm of international politics. Even in this realm it is clear that Graham's insights, gained as a world traveler, are in conflict with his perfectionist solutions of the problem of the hydrogen bomb, for instance.

Minds Dull to Racial Sin

But these counsels do not apply to the race issue. There the moral dimension of the issue is fairly simple. It is whether the Christian recognizes the validity of the Biblical observation, " If a man sayeth that he loves God and hateth his brother, he is a liar." If the issue is as simple as that, the question arises why an obviously honest man, such as Graham, cannot embody the disavowal of race prejudice into his call to repentance. Perhaps the answer to that question takes one into the very heart of the weaknesses of " evangelical " Christianity, particularly evangelical Christianity in its pietistic versions. This form of the Christian faith relies on an oversimplification of the issues in order to create the " crisis " that prompts conversion and the acceptance of the Christian faith. The best way of inducing this crisis is to call attention to some moral dereliction of the person, in which some accepted moral norm has been transgressed and the conscience is consequently uneasy.

The moral transgressions that are embedded in the customs of the community, the sins that we do, not " one by one," but with the approval of our community, are not such effective means of creating the sense of crisis upon which the revivalist depends. .If the " sinner " is to be convicted of involvement in some collective sin, it is necessary to appeal not only to the emotions but to the mind; that is, it is necessary rationally to analyze the social situation, conformity to which means the violation of the love commandment. This is true even in such an uncomplicated problem as the issue of desegregation.

CALCULATIONS IN JUSTICE

Perhaps this is the reason why revivalistic Christianity has not been particularly effective in challenging collective evil. It grew to power on the frontier, where its moral appeals were limited to the condemnation of drunkenness, adultery, and Sabbath violations. It may not be entirely unfair to observe that the section of the country in which the present crisis in race relations is most acute is precisely that section which has experienced annual " revivals," all calculated to " redeem " the sinner and guarantee the perfection of a truly " committed " soul.

I well remember a rather pathetic experience more than a quarter century ago in Harlan county, Kentucky, at the time when industrial violence engulfed the county because of a strike by its miners. Their wages were very low because that was the only way the Kentucky mine owners were able to meet the competition of the Pennsylvania coal fields. The middle-class community was solidly arrayed behind the mine owners. We, who were members of a church delegation, met with the ministers of the county in order to convince them that it was dubious for the middle-class community to be so indifferent to the plight of the miners, simply because they felt that the community itself was endangered by a higher wage scale.

These calculations in justice, which touched the collective interests and challenged the moral complacency of the middle-class churches, were quite beyond the moral comprehension of the Harlan county ministers. We were assured that they had just had a collective revival in the town and would have another one, and that these revivals were bound to generate the kind of Christian perfection that would make the collective sins we spoke of quite impossible. The ministers were naïvely good men who did not think in terms that were even remotely relevant to the moral issues their community faced.

LOST WITH THE SOCIAL GOSPEL

The only difference between the situation a quarter century ago and now is that Protestantism as a whole was then informed by the social gospel and regarded the viewpoint of the Harlan county ministers as a quaint vestige of an outmoded form of piety. But now, whether because of the many personal excellences of Billy Graham or because of a widespread naïve enthusiasm for any kind of religious revival, we have official church federations committing themselves to this kind of revivalistic Christianity, assuring us that if only Billy can bring the people into the Christian fold, the ordinary pastors can then proceed to instruct the new recruits in the full implications of the Christian life.

There is more hope that Graham himself will see the weaknesses of a traditional evangelical perfectionism in an atomic age than that his clerical and lay sponsors, with their enthusiasm for any kind of revival, will see it. For Graham is a world traveler and a very perceptive observer of the world scene with its many collective problems. His instincts are genuine and his sense of justice well developed. He could embody the cause of justice — particularly where it is so closely and obviously related to the love commandment as on the race issue — into his revival message. The only thing that could prevent such a development is that it is contrary to the well established " technique " of revivalism. That technique requires the oversimplification of moral issues and their individualization for the sake of inducing an emotional crisis. Collective sins are therefore not within the range of a revival. It may be that Graham is good enough to break with this traditional and obvious technique. In that case he would cease to be merely the last exponent of a frontier religious tradition and become a vital force in the nation's moral and spiritual life.

PART III

Love and Justice
in International Relations

A. A Variety of Issues

---

33. THE CONFLICT BETWEEN NATIONS AND NATIONS AND BETWEEN NATIONS AND GOD

THE BIBLE NEVER DENIES THAT THERE ARE SIGNIF-
icant conflicts between good and evil forces in history, between just and unjust nations, and between righteous and unrighteous men. The prophets of Israel had no doubt about the special mission and virtue of Israel as compared with the Gentiles; and they saw the meaning of history as partly derived from this conflict. They hoped for the victory of the righteous over the unrighteous.

But these distinctions did not prevent the prophets from understanding that there was a profounder conflict between all nations and God, and all men and God. They were not afraid to pronounce the judgment of God upon Israel in even severer terms than upon the pagan nations. The prophet Amos combined these two facets of prophetic interpretation in the classic lines, "You only have I chosen; therefore will I visit you with your iniquities." Jesus was later to justify the seeming perversity of the severer judgment upon the righteous with the words, " To whom much hath been given, of him much shall be required."

Nothing gives Biblical faith a greater consistency than this subordination of the struggle between good and evil men to the more

Christianity and Crisis, August 5, 1946.

significant struggle between all men and God in "whose sight no man living is justified." If there was any inconsistency in the Old Testament upon these two strains of interpretation, it is certainly overcome in the New Testament. There only the one conflict is dealt with so consistently that one sometimes wonders whether the conflict between justice and injustice in history is considered at all. This is why in times of such conflicts, as in the recent war, we turn with a certain relief to the Old Testament and thank God that it is a part of the Bible. For the faith of the New Testament, which knows little of this distinction, seems almost too sheer for us. The insights of faith upon the conflict between good and evil men and upon the conflict between just and unjust nations rightfully belongs to the Bible, and we have no reason to be ashamed for including it in our Christian life. In times when some Christians are tempted to evade their responsibility for maintaining a relative justice in an evil world, we must actually turn to this level of thought in the Bible. But in times of victory, when the so-called righteous nations have prevailed, we had better not forget the words of our Lord, " Judge not that ye be not judged," and the words of Saint Paul, written in the same spirit, " Who art thou that judgest thy brother; for we must all be made manifest before the judgment seat of Christ." These words are spoken out of the ultimate insights of New Testament faith. They are, furthermore, remarkable sources of insight into our contemporary experience.

Consider our relations to our vanquished enemies. We were certainly righteous when we fought the Nazis, that is, righteous by comparison. But how quickly our righteousness runs out, not only because we have destroyed the evil with which we compared ourselves, but also because we inherited some of the irresponsible power through our victory, which tainted them with evil. As far as Japan is concerned we seem to have less reason for an uneasy conscience; for there the administration of victory has some semblance to justice. In Germany it has hardly had a semblance to justice at all, unless we regard the meticulous impartiality of the Nuremberg court as a good symbol of justice. From every side the cry of the anguished comes to our ears, out of the chaos and confusion of Germany. People are dying of hunger. People cannot find work. With millions of houses destroyed, others are now dispossessed to make room for the families of the army of occupation. The occupying powers do not trust each other and make the confusion worse confounded by their

mistrust of each other, fighting as it were the next war over the prostrate body of the vanquished foe of this war. Every once in a while
some self-righteous journalist takes a casual glance at this prostrate
figure and pronounces that there is no health in it. The irony of
such judgments is almost too perfect.

There are people in Germany fighting desperately for freedom
against new totalitarian threats. We are not certain that we can support them because we are afraid they mean something different by
freedom than we do. If they are going to have democracy, it will have
to be a kind that fits an impoverished nation. We, in our pride, are
inclined to identify democracy with luxuries of economic freedom
that only a wealthy nation can afford.

The whole social and economic chaos of Europe, beyond Germany, is an indictment of our virtue, or at least of our wisdom. All
the nations of the world who have the power of victory in their
hands are too stupid to exploit the fruits of victory for the sake of
justice. As Christians we ought to know, however, that stupidity is
never merely stupidity. There is always a perverse taint of sin in it.
In this situation the taint of national self-interest and national pride
is very obvious.

As the proofs of the confusion in the wake of our victory multiply,
we find some of our commentators trying to save our conscience by
logic. Were we not righteous yesterday, they ask, when we fought
the Nazis? Very well; quiet your conscience, we still are. But the
logic of the Bible and the logic of history both run against this
kind of reason.

Statesmen must work out the details for giving our vanquished
foes the economic and political basis of a sane and healthy life. But
certainly it is the business of the Christian church to create the spiritual atmosphere in which this can be done. The primary engine of
injustice in victory is still the pride of victors who have no idea of
the fact that the judgment of God is upon them as well as upon
their foes. It is a question whether nations, as such, can ever have
any other but a semipagan arrogance, though they call themselves
Christian. But those individuals who are really informed by the
mind of Christ must have some conception of the more ultimate
conflict between all nations and God; and from that conception
there must flow some decent pity and mercy to leaven the arrogance
of nations.

II

Unfortunately we face this issue not only with a vanquished foe but with the uneasy partner of our victory. The rift between the Western world and Russia is growing. Again it is a conflict between justice and injustice, or at least between freedom and totalitarianism. On the level of politico-moral judgments, I do not see how it can be denied that the distinctions between the Russian morality and our own are valid. The Russian tyranny is pretty vexatious. In a recent series of articles *The New York Times* correspondent Brooks Atkinson has come to the conclusion that the Russians do not want our friendship, that they look at the world through Marxist spectacles, that they expect the Western world, which we call democracy and which they call "monopoly capitalism," to be destroyed by its own mistakes and errors. There seems no doubt but that the Russians, besides other mistakes, are grievously miscalculating the residual health of a not-too-healthy Western world. These errors and stupidities may cost the Russians dearly, and us also.

But Mr. Atkinson also reports that the Russians are afraid. That is a different point, which reveals the perpetual relevance of the Biblical viewpoint. They are, let us say, the unjust and we are the just. (One might stop to think, by the way, of the curious fact that no matter how the vicissitudes of history run, the Lord always puts us on the just side. Such qualms give this author a momentary pause, but he would still go on to insist that the distinctions between Western justice and Russian totalitarianism are significant.) But the Russians are afraid, and so are we. Those are the marks of our common humanity. Out of these fears they generate strategies of defense, and so do we. Those are the marks of our common sin. Sin is always trying to be strong at the expense of someone else. The Russians want to make themselves strong by dominating Eastern Europe, and as much more beside as they can. They would probably swallow both Turkey and Iran if they thought they could get away with it. They deny that we have a will to peace; and their propaganda falsifies the almost pathetic desire of the Western world for peace most ludicrously. It is difficult to restrain one's self-righteousness when one contemplates all these facts.

Only we cannot be certain whether we are really more righteous than they, or merely stronger. Perhaps they are hysterical because they know that they are not really as strong as we. Some of our strength is actually derived from our virtue. The smaller nations will flock to us because they trust us a little more, just a little more. But some of our strength is derived not from our virtue, but from the atomic bomb and the threat of it.

We are so righteous that we offer the Russians a pretty fair solution for the control of the atomic bomb. We actually surpass ourselves by that offer which looks forward to the suppression of atomic destruction by international action. Yet in practically the same week in which the offer is made we demonstrate at Bikini the destructive power of the bomb, which we say we are never going to use any more. There is something very unlogical in this. It is in fact the lack of logic of a man or a nation which has a law in its members that wars against the law that is in its mind.

If the Baruch proposals prove our righteousness, the Bikini experiments prove that the Bible is still right and that the contest of greatest significance is not between good and bad nations, but between all nations or men and God. We do want peace, but we would like it to be our peace, just as the Russians. We are just; but we are also afraid. We are almost as inclined as the Russians are to generate false strategies out of our fears.

Perhaps the vicious circle of mutual mistrust between us will work itself out to the final chapter of another universal conflict. Such a conflict would give a new kind of vivid historical proof of the fact that the conflict between nations and God is more significant than the conflict between good and bad nations. For in that conflict we would call ourselves the " democracies "; but our enemies would call us " monopoly capitalism." We would call our enemies totalitarians and tyrants. But they would continue to think of themselves as the fatherland of a new utopia. We would of course condemn the pretension of their self-righteousness; but we would also have a sneaking suspicion, stronger than we had when we fought the Nazis, that only God could make a just judgment between these conflicting pretensions of righteousness.

If we could, by faith, somewhat anticipate this divine judgment, we might still avoid the conflict. For a very wise statesmanship does manage to insinuate some vestige of the divine judgment into human judgments. The Christian faith, in so far as it understands the conflict between God and men, stands right across and transcends all historical conflicts. But in so far as it can insinuate something of this ultimate perspective into the competing and contradictory judgments of men and nations, it introduces some leaven of pity, mercy, and forebearance into the conflicts of men and nations.

34. ON THE ETHIOPIAN WAR

The political and moral problems raised by Mussolini's venture in Africa are almost too typical to be true. The Italian venture is a venture of a modern robber state, seeking to solve its internal problem at the expense of the freedom of another people. The economic benefits promised Italy by the conquest of Ethiopia are said by experts to be small. The real motives animating Mussolini are therefore not immediate economic advantages but the possible prestige which a victory would give his harassed dictatorship and the more solid advantage which might accrue if he could make this victory the basis of continued encroachments in Africa at the expense of British imperialism in Africa.

Mussolini is opposed by the League of Nations on the one hand and by the British Empire on the other. The intervention of the League is not typical but novel. This is the first time that the League has acted with energy in such a situation. Many of the lovers of peace are therefore filled with enthusiasm at the prospect of a new world order arising from this new energy of the League. Such enthusiasm is too unqualified. For the fact is that British energy is the real core though not the total circumference of this League vitality. If British imperial interests were not at stake, the League would not act so energetically, particularly since France is a most reluctant partner in the game of sanctions. Whether spoken or unspoken, a bargain between England and France underlies this reluctant partnership of France with England against her Latin neighbor. The bargain is that Britain will support France in the eventuality of an attack from Germany as France now supports Britain — and probably with the same degree of reluctance.

One might draw the cynical conclusion from all this that we are confronted with the old game of power politics behind the façade of the League. Such a conclusion would be nine tenths correct. Yet there is a one-tenth particle of novelty in the situation. Without Britain the League would not now be functioning. Yet more than

Britain is involved. The conscience of Europe is arrayed against Italy. " Collective security " is operating. It is operating only in minimal terms, but in politics one must be satisfied with very minimal beginnings and not ascribe too much moral worth to them.

Typical in the situation is the self-righteousness of Britain. The stability of social orders is always maintained by self-righteous robbers who have stopped robbing because they have what they want and try to prevent the hungry " have-nots " from emulating their imperialism. That means that the apostles of law and order can be supported only with moral reservations. It does not mean that they ought not to be supported. The support that Russia and the Communist Party is giving to this imperialistic anti-imperialism is an instructive and typical piece of realism. One supports law and order (collective security) if the alternative to it is worse than the injustice that it maintains and not otherwise. In this case the alternative is worse. Therefore one ought to support both the League and Britain — and be thankful that there are George Lansburys who call attention to the hypocrisy involved in the cause of law and order.

The problem that Christian pacifists face in this situation is typical, too, of the relation of morals to politics. Most pacifists believe not only in abstention from war but also in creating a system of collective security that will prevent war. Now they have the opportunity of supporting it. But how is the League going to " enforce peace " against Italy? By economic sanctions. Very well, is not the pacifist able to support such sanctions since he objects only to violence? But sanctions may lead to war. Shall they be supported only until they lead to war? or not supported at all because they may lead to war? These questions prove how impossible it is to deal with political problems from the standpoint of an absolutist credo. One must support sanctions in the hope that they will not lead to war. But if they should, one can hardly withdraw from the political consequences of such a policy. It is a great pity that a Christian saint in politics like George Lansbury should bring his official life to a close because he has pacifist scruples against these sanctions. His religious penetration into the hypocrisy of British imperialism is a part of his saintliness. His effort to translate this judgment into a political policy leads to confusion. He has no policy for restraining Mussolini. Politics must deal with immediate necessities as religion deals with ultimate insights by which the danger and hypocrisy of these immediate necessities is revealed.

All this does not suggest that American pacifists ought above all to support the League. The League happens not to be a live alternative in American politics. The best we can do is to seek the enlargement of American neutrality provisions so that they will operate to support League sanctions. Such neutrality embargoes will operate against both Italy and Ethiopia. That cannot be helped. They will hurt Italy more than Ethiopia, and we must be content with that.

We are living in a very anarchic world. We are not building the Kingdom of God in it. The best we can do for the moment is to prevent the outbreak of a world war, in the hope that its postponement may increase the possibility of its prevention. Meanwhile we will not prevent it if we cannot build a totally new economic system that will relieve the imperialism of the hungry nations. Even Sir Samuel Hoare admits that. We radicals might well underscore this admission of Hoare. In it capitalistic imperialism confesses that there is no peace within terms of its own economic presuppositions. But meanwhile the consequences of a world war are too terrible to permit irresponsibility toward any measure calculated to mitigate the international anarchy or postpone international conflict.

35. THE WILL OF GOD AND THE VAN ZEELAND REPORT

Reading, as I do, everything that Ernest Fremont Tittle writes with the respect that both the integrity of his character and the lucidity of his mind deserve, will you permit me to say that I have never read an article on the relation of Christianity to the international order that seems to me so full of the moral confusions that will probably make it impossible to save a democratic civilization from the perils of a new barbarism as his article in *The Christian Century* on " God and National Policy."

In this article he rejects two possible policies — war to end war and economic pressure against aggressors — as completely unchristian. The third policy that he proposes is virtually the adoption of the van Zeeland report. About this policy he declares, " Such an attempt and no other might confidently claim the support and approval of God." This statement literally took my breath away. How can Dr. Tittle be so sure about God's will? " Such an attempt and *no other*" will meet with God's approval, declares Dr. Tittle." Has he no appreciation of the ambiguity of all human actions and the endless relativities in which political policies, particularly, are involved?

The whole history of Christian faith is filled with the tragedy of righteous fanatics who were certain about God's will. The Catholic hierarchy is certain that it is God's will that General Franco be supported. One is reminded by Dr. Tittle's rash statement of the words that Stephen Vincent Benét puts, with historic justice, into the mouth of Abraham Lincoln:

> They talk to me about God's will
> In righteous deputations and platoons,
> Day after day, laymen and ministers.
> They write me Prayers from Twenty Million Souls
> Defining me God's will and Horace Greeley's.
> God's will is General This and Senator That;
> God's will is this poor colored fellow's will.
> It is the will of the Chicago churches;
> It is this man's and his worst enemy's.
> But all of them are sure they know God's will.
> I am the only man who does not know it.

Aligning myself on the side of Lincoln's skepticism about God's will, at least for any policy that is short of the love that transcends all political justice, I must confess that the van Zeeland report is in my mind just as certainly not God's will for us in this crisis as for Dr. Tittle it represents God's will.

At its best the van Zeeland report is an effort to cure the ills of modern international anarchy by returning to the policies of classical laissez-faire capitalism. Unfortunately for the theory that this is a magnanimous way out, the dictators treated the van Zeeland report with scorn, for a good reason. The poverty of their populations is caused not so much by trade barriers which their foes have erected as by the barriers that they have themselves erected in order to organize their economy for military purposes. German living standards have dropped about 25 to 30 per cent since Hitler came to power and a good third of the higher living costs are due to the expensive manufacture of ersatz (substitute) materials in order to prepare for economic autonomy in wartime. Furthermore, the dictators have discovered that by setting up barriers to the free exchange of money and securities across national boundaries they can use their money over and over again without limit, or in other words increase their debts indeterminately.

At its best the van Zeeland report is therefore a counsel of perfection that is completely irrelevant to the situation because the dictators would sign their abdication if they accepted it. At its worst the van Zeeland report is just one of the many efforts of the Chamberlain government to beguile Germany into partnership in the imperial business in order to overcome the threat of a rival imperialism. It would take more space than could be granted me to prove that point, but I do think it is slightly pathetic that simple-hearted moralists and pacifists are constantly talking of the virtues of the van Zeeland report. If one gives it the best rather than the worst interpretation, it is still true that modern capitalism cannot, by taking thought, reverse the dynamics of history and return to its simple laissez-faire innocency.

In regard to the first two points of Dr. Tittle's article, they are meant to present the only two alternatives to the policy that he regards as indubitably God's will. These two alternatives are either to fight the dictators or to use economic pressure upon them. The second is as bad as the first because it will force the dictators to fight you. In other words one must not use force, nor the threat of force, nor economic pressure if that means that it will elicit the use of force. Now the simple fact is that, if neither the threat of force nor nonviolent force can be used in politics because both have the risk of the use of overt force in them, the nations who profess such moral scruples are completely at the mercy of any nation that publicly disavows these scruples. That is one reason why Hitler had his way at Munich, though he had less force at his disposal than his opponents. He had been counseled for years by Himmler and Ribbentrop that the democracies would not fight. I do not mean to suggest that Chamberlain and Daladier were prompted by these moral scruples. I do think it is increasingly patent that they could not have sold democracy out as they did, for reasons of their own, if they had not been certain to be able to count on the moralistic illusions that have filled the so-called liberal world for generations. Is it really "Christian," is it God's will, never to call the bluff of a bully for fear that you might be involved in violence? Then we had better

· prepare for the complete victory of the barbarism that is spreading over Europe.

On whether the dictators were bluffing or not a letter from an anti-fascist Italian to an English friend, published in *The New Statesman and Nation,* may be instructive. He writes: "You say that Chamberlain had all the cards in his hands. But you do not know that in the days preceding the criminal encounter at Munich Italy was inundated by an exposition of joy, of the certainty of her coming liberation from slavery every day more cruel. We were all certain that the people would not have marched beside Germany. The soldiers were not responding to the call of arms. Mussolini's bluff was apparent in its tragic magnitude. In a few weeks, but for Munich, we would have been liberated from the octopus of fascism."

Of course our pacifist friends will insist that such hopes may have been illusions. They are right. They may have been. But desperate political struggles must take such factors into account. Risks have to be taken. Violence must be avoided. But there is no political struggle that does not have some risk of violence in it. That is because political arguments are never pure exercises in persuasion but the clash of resolute wills. If any Christian wishes to say that it is incompatible with Christianity to fool with such terrible and sinful relativities of the political world, I for one will accord him my genuine respect and admiration if he leave the world of politics alone entirely and seek simply to live by the love commandment in terms that demand an irresponsible attitude toward the problem of collective justice in international and economic terms. Let him, in other words, be a pure pacifist and remind the rest of us, who fool with politics, that we are playing a dangerous game. But for heaven's sake leave the van Zeeland report out of this Kingdom of God.

On reading my vehement tirade against my friend Tittle, I fear that the lust of battle betrays me into passions that seem out of accord with the opening sentence of the letter. I can only say that for many years I have constantly held up Dr. Tittle as an example of the kind of integrity and courage that saves the church from futility. I should hate to be in a church that did not include him in its ultimate communion. But the church that he has set up will exclude many of us. For we are determined upon political policies for the saving of democratic civilization — boycott of Japan, lifting the boycott on Spain, etc. — which in his opinion are counter to God's will.

Perhaps the only church to which both groups could comfortably belong would be one in which there was some knowledge of the defiance of God's will in even the best of human intentions.

36. A NEGOTIATED PEACE

Certain sections in the Protestant Church persist in their belief that there is something uniquely " Christian " in the advocacy of a negotiated peace. This idea was first advanced at the very beginning of the war and has been given periodic impetus by various groups since that time. If we are informed correctly, we may expect a new campaign along this line shortly.

This stubborn belief, held by men whose sincerity cannot be doubted, is a perfect revelation of the lack of political realism in American Protestantism. Hitler bestrides the Continent of Europe, and nothing stands between him and the complete victory, which he undoubtedly regards as within his grasp, but the stubborn resistance of the British and the increasing aid of America. Naturally Hitler has visions of the possibility of a complete triumph. His success against British shipping has been so great of late that he may not even attempt the hazardous adventure of invasion. This is not to say that Hitler will be victorious. The point is that he still has good reason to hope for victory and therefore no incentive at all to make a peace that would conform to even minimal standards of justice. The only possible peace that Hitler would accept now would be one that left an unredeemed continent under the heel of his dictatorship and that would give him the possibility of a more complete triumph later.

To insist that it is the religious duty of Christians to advocate a negotiated peace under these circumstances means that Christian " idealism " has been compounded with one of two possible errors:

1. It may mean that the Christian idealist considers any kind of peace, without regard to the quality of its justice, as morally preferable to the continuance of the war. Although there are few Christian idealists who will admit that they actually prefer a tyrannical peace to continued resistance, it is a fact, nevertheless, that many are driven to this unwilling conclusion. Since they begin all their

reasoning on the question of war with the premise that nothing can be worse than war, they can hardly escape the conclusion that the enslavement of Europe is to be preferred to the continued resistance of Britain.

2. Most isolationists and political pacifists seek to escape the necessity of arriving at such a conclusion by holding out the hope that if only someone, the President or the pope or some other leader, would be willing to call a conference, the matter in dispute between the nations could be arbitrated or mediated, and a just peace might be achieved. Sometimes this hope is supported by the belief that such a conference would be able to appeal over the head of Hitler to the German people and prompt them to force Hitler to yield. This belief obviously does not take into consideration that a modern dictatorship is able to mold the public opinion of its nation so thoroughly and to suppress dissident opinion so completely that it is fatuous to expect a rift between a dictator and the people. Furthermore, the hope does not take another very ugly fact into account: the fact that in every nation there are millions of people for whom nothing succeeds like success. Even though disaffection among German masses may be wide and deep, it is not likely that the prestige of the Nazi dictatorship can be broken without a military defeat. If there had been such a possibility, it would have been realized more easily before the war than now.

More frequently the hope of a just peace by negotiation is expressed even more naïvely. It is simply the hope that if only the cool discussion of a conference room can be substituted for the "passions" of conflict, a just settlement is bound to be worked out. Sometimes we are told, rather piously, that what is desired is a peace of "reconciliation," and that such a peace is quite different from one of "appeasement." But these pious words can hardly hide the ugly fact that any possible peace now would be worse than the peace of Munich. It would represent not appeasement but capitulation to a ruthless foe.

All these illusions are due to the simple moral sentimentality that does not understand that any justice that the world has ever achieved rests upon some balance between the various interests and vitalities that enter into a structure of justice, and that, whenever power is completely disproportionate, there injustice grows. The people who are unable to recognize this fact in the present situation are equally unable to assess the realities of a problem of justice in peacetime. They do not understand why Hitler might not be made to yield now, for the same reason that they cannot understand how difficult it is to achieve justice in domestic and economic problems and how tentative and precarious every scheme of justice is.

The failure to understand the political implications of a problem of justice is not due merely to a moralist's, perhaps excusable, ignorance of the technical aspects of political life. These technical aspects are overlooked because the whole human situation is not understood. The basic error is the modern moralist's inability to appreciate the stubbornness of self-interest, particularly collective self-interest. We fail to understand Hitler, not because we are too good to gauge an egoistic mania that has broken all internal and external checks. We do not understand Hitler because we do not understand ourselves and fail to realize to what degree men achieve justice against our interests, not merely by appealing to our consciences, but by resisting our pretensions. If we understood the stubbornness of sin in all men, including ourselves, we would realize more perfectly why the collective egotism that Hitler embodies is not to be beguiled at a conference table and why Hitler would regard any effort to bring him to a conference as merely a proof of the weakness and irresolution of the foe. The conflicts of life and history happen to be more tragic than the philosophies and theologies of many of our contemporaries envisage.

There is something rather ironic in the fact that we must be on our guard lest those who regard the peace of the Kingdom of God as a simple alternative to the difficult justice and precarious peace of the world deliver us into a peace of slavery. They would not do it willingly; but they willingly nourish illusions that obscure the difficulties of achieving justice and the sorry realities of a peace without justice.

37. ALLIED PEACE AIMS

In his Mansion House speech Anthony Eden mingled wisdom with something less than wisdom. There was justification for a dash of realism in his reference to Germany in the postwar world; for to suppose that a victorious Britain will conclude a peace that will not carefully guard against a repetition of German aggression is naïve in the extreme. Worse than that, it is to overlook a plain material and moral requirement of the peace. It is just possible that Mr. Eden was addressing himself, on the one hand, to what the British Government fears is a dangerous sentimentalism at home and, on the other hand, to the manifest tendency in France to accept German hegemony in Europe.

Be this as it may, Mr. Eden's declaration is disappointing. Not because he gave no blueprint for reconstruction — no one can do that — but because of his broad intimation that the old concept of exclusive German guilt is being officially revived to furnish a rationale for an anticipated settlement. Five times in a century, he says, Germany has violated the peace. Thus Hitler, whose emergence has been pictured as something so horrendous as to array the civilized world against him, is assimilated to German history. This is particularly regrettable because Mr. Eden's speech contains so much that is commendable and might otherwise have been reassuring. There are many people in Britain, particularly in the ranks of labor and the church who fully understand that a British victory has its own perils, however devoutly it is hoped for and however preferable it is to a German victory. To judge by the applause that Mr. Eden's thrust received — greater, we are told, than for any other part of his address — a mood is developing under the pressure of war that proves how real the anticipated peril is. One shudders to think, moreover, of the use that German propaganda will make of this and similar utterances by Allied statesmen, since it has long been apparent that only the fear of destruction keeps many strong anti-Nazi Germans loyal to Hitler.

It would be unfair to assume that Mr. Eden was consciously echoing Duff Cooper's demand that Britain be not " fooled again " by a hypocritical German nation. But what he said about Germany was ill designed to keep alive the consciousness, so gratifyingly evident in other British utterances, of common responsibility for the international anarchy that led to this war. As victory approaches, vindictiveness is likely to be harder to smother. If this word of Mr. Eden can be said in the green tree, what will be said in the dry?

The matter comes down to this: the recognition of the necessity of guaranteeing Europe against a revival of Hitlerism should have been accompanied by a much more specific elaboration of the constructive intentions of the Government toward the whole of Europe and the world. Mr. Eden said not a word about the abandonment of the principle of unlimited national sovereignty and the creation of a truly international government. He said nothing about the necessity of fundamental economic reconstruction such as the pronouncements of the Labor Party and of British churchmen have clearly implied. There is no hint — or at most, no more than a hint — of the requirement that the victors shall impose limitations upon themselves corresponding to those which are to be imposed on Germany.

This criticism has no relation to the uncritical demand so often repeated that Britain should tell the world what she is going to do about India, or precisely how she will move to correct her failure to find a constructive solution of the problems of the Empire in the Near East. All such demands overlook the requirements of a war strategy where an avaricious and conscienceless dictator is ready to take immediate advantage of every promise of a revision of national policy. What was lacking in the Eden speech was a clear statement of Britain's intention to participate in the creation of a truly new order in which justice and security will not depend on mere restraint in the use of power but on a mutual abandonment of the political and military instruments of power. It is a first principle of democracy, re-enforced by Christian insights, that power itself engenders the will-to-power, that political justice and security have only a precarious foundation so long as the exercise of power is unilateral.

All this is immensely important for America at this moment. The commendable efforts of our political realists to convince the nation of the necessity and wisdom of full British-American co-operation, and of the consistency of such a policy with our whole history, have in them an element of serious danger. It is one thing to use the combined might of our two nations to preserve " freedom of the seas," but quite another thing for these nations to claim the role of permanent keepers of the world's peace. Facile assumptions that Germany is by permanent nature a potential bad " master " lead directly to the conclusion that peace must be maintained by an arsenal of democracy in the keeping of other governments. An Anglo-American peace will not be a real peace. There is at this moment grave danger that the gradual overcoming of American isolationism may have an unwholesome sequel. It is said that the A.E.F. returned from Europe with a strong conviction that the peace should have been made in Berlin. It would take little en-couragement from Britain to give impetus to a boisterous demand in America that " this time " no halfway job shall be done.

It may indeed be argued that in failing to make any distinction between Hitler and the historic German nation Mr. Eden is more realistic than Mr. Roosevelt, who never fails to make it. There is a surprising degree of continuity in the foreign policy of a nation regardless of what group administers it. But the inference drawn from this fact is precisely the point at issue. A nation's foreign policy is formulated and carried out within a complex of interna-tional relationships, and it is not likely to undergo radical and permanent change except in response to a change in the system of which it is a part. The counterpart of this truth in personal rela-tions is one of the basic assumptions of Christianity. This is the meaning of redemption. If a Christian justifies war, it is because he recognizes no permanent limits upon this redemptive principle: he believes that while criminality on a national scale must be met with stern justice, it can and must be followed by a regime in which every nation concerned shall participate, as of right, in the creation and maintenance of a juster peace.

Perhaps the admirable, but rather cryptic, portions of Mr. Eden's address concerning political and economic co-operation in the post-war world imply that he did not mean what has been inferred from his remarks about the restraints to be imposed on Germany. If so, his statement should be clarified without delay.

38. REPEAL THE NEUTRALITY ACT!

There are weighty considerations of national interest that require the immediate modification or repeal of the Neutrality Act of 1939. Some of these considerations are strategic; others are political and economic. But for Christians the decisive factor is moral. We demand the immediate repeal of the Neutrality Act because it is one of the most immoral laws that was ever spread upon a federal statute book. Its immorality was accentuated by the misguided idealism that was evoked in its support. The essence of immorality is the evasion or denial of moral responsibility. When a man refuses to recognize his obligations as a member of a community, when he isolates himself from the affairs of his community, and acts as a completely unrelated individual, he is an immoral man. Morality consists in the recognition of the interdependence of personal life. The moral man is the man who acts responsibly in relation to his fellows, who knows the duties that communal life requires, and who is willing to accept the consequences that these duties impose.

As with men, so with nations. An irresponsible nation is an immoral nation, while a nation that is becoming dimly aware of its responsibilities and acts accordingly is moving toward morality. The Neutrality Act of 1939 was the culmination of a recent immoral trend in American life that needs to be recognized for what it is and dealt with accordingly.

Two or three hundred years ago it was possible to set out from Europe to a New World in the hope of gain or of building a better society. The oceans were then so vast that there was some reason for thinking of the Americas as a separate world from Europe. But the mechanical revolution of the last one hundred years has destroyed the distinction between the Old World and the New. Air transportation has hurdled the vast barriers of the oceans; space has shrunk. The peoples of America and Europe are now becoming members one of another. We belong to a common community and we have acquired immense communal responsibilities as a result of that fact. To deny these responsibilities is unchristian and unethical. This is exactly what the Neutrality Act did.

The normal channels of human intercourse provide the occasions when responsibility expresses itself. To withdraw from the use of these channels is to attempt to escape from responsibility. The man who shuts himself up in his house, and refuses to go out on the village street because he doesn't like conditions in his neighborhood, is not a type that Americans admire. He is either a weak, timid soul, afraid of being contaminated by what is going on around him, or he is a moral prig who considers himself too good to associate with his disreputable neighbors. In either case he is a pharisee. We have far more respect for a fellow who knows what conditions are like in his town and who, because of that knowledge, takes off his coat and goes out on the street to help change them.

The normal channels for human intercourse between this continent and other continents lie across the oceans and through the air — the highways of our world community. Moral responsibility requires us to use these highways. To put the matter bluntly, freedom of the seas is a condition of developing a responsible national policy. To say that Americans are not to sail the seas is to say that they are to do nothing about their world.

The advocacy of national do-nothingness in the interests of peace has been justified by an appeal to Christian ideals. No argument could be more fallacious. Do-nothingness for the sake of peace is not moral. It is pure escapism in a world where nations can escape no longer from the ethical consequences of their interdependence. The dream that our forefathers had when they sailed from Europe of building a better world in the Americas has been perverted by selfish minds into a desire to evade moral obligation to the rest of the world. This degenerative trend in our national life must be arrested. The Christian ethic demands that we turn and face the world.

When a great fire has broken out in a small town, responsible citizens who are in a position to do something about it do not draw their shutters, lock their doors, and crawl under their beds. To do so would be to forfeit forever moral authority in their community. The Christian ethic requires these citizens to go out on the street and do whatever may be necessary to help their fellows bring the fire under control.

The passage of the Neutrality Act of 1939 was a signal to the world that the United States had gone indoors and drawn the shades. To repeal the Neutrality Act is to crawl out from under the bed, throw open the shutters, unlock the doors, and go out on the street to help law-abiding neighbors who are in trouble and who need assistance.

This we will do. We will repeal the escapist sections of the Neutrality Act because our national policy has been declared through the passage of the Lend-Lease Act and the effect of these sections is to make that policy increasingly null and void.

We will repeal the Act because we recognize the irresponsibility of promising to supply the soldiers of freedom while withholding the transportation necessary to deliver the supplies.

We will repeal the Act because freedom of the seas is a condition of a free world and the destiny of the United States is to serve mankind by helping to establish such a world.

39. CHASTISEMENT UNTO REPENTANCE OR DEATH

It is now apparent that we are in for a long war. The Axis has been able to gain so many points of strategic advantage, while we are still in the process of arming, that only long and costly military and naval operations can overcome, can regain what we have lost. It is in fact quite likely that in another six months our nation will confront one of the most momentous decisions of its history. At that time we may be in the position of having been defeated essentially, except of course that we cannot be defeated absolutely as France was. That means that we will have the possibility of rescuing victory from defeat, provided we are willing to pay the price. Whether we understand the consequences of capitulating to, or conniving with, a Nazi world sufficiently to be ready to pay the price of victory is a question that is not yet decided. It is quite obvious that the superficial unity, achieved by the Pearl Harbor attack, is pretty well dissipated now. The isolationists are beginning to come out of their storm cellars. We can expect a fairly strong propaganda in favor of a negotiated peace should we continue to suffer further military reverses. The determination to carry on can certainly not be generated out of interpretations of the war that assume that we are at war only because we were attacked by the Japanese. Only if we understand this war in its profound revolutionary setting, is it possible to generate the will to fight it to its final conclusion. For only then can we see how important it is to overcome the revolt against our civilization, and how equally important the inner renewal of our civilization is.

Isolationist liberals have believed, and still believe, that we must not strain the resources of the democratic world too much, that we must not submit it to too strenuous exertions, lest it suffer some kind of apoplectic stroke and die as France died. This is a counsel of despair, which assumes that democratic civilization is a very sick old woman whose life would be endangered by any exertions beyond the sickroom. If our civilization is as sick as that, it would of course die in any event, whether it exerted itself or not.

The experience through which we have already gone in a few months of belligerency suggests a different thesis about the relation of our war efforts to democracy. The thesis is that only the chastisements of a fairly long war can prompt a really thoroughgoing repentance and conversion from those sins of the democratic world which helped to produce the Nazi revolt against our civilization. We were much too soft and fat, much too heedless and indifferent to the ultimate issues of life to be changed by the only casual chastisements of a brief belligerency. This is not to say that war as such is the only possible source of repentance to nations. We must think not abstractly but historically about these questions. When we are guilty of sins that make a revolt against civilization possible, we can hardly repent of those sins until bitter experience has taught us what the consequences of the sins are and by what kind of sacrifices and change of heart the evils we have done can be overcome.

How for instance can the sins of national irresponsibility, by which the democratic nations invited aggression, be overcome? They are overcome partly by learning how terrible are the consequences of an international anarchy, which we aggravated by our effort to escape from it into our own continental security. They are overcome partly by forms of international co-operation that the exigencies of war force upon us and that we would not accept except under the pressure of necessity. It is idle, for instance, for idealists to wash their hands of the war and then speculate upon what kind of a system of international co-operation they will be able to build. The Constitution of the United States grew out of the experience of the Revolutionary War, in which the inadequacies of colonial particularism were glaringly revealed and the necessity of the abridgement of the state sovereignty became apparent.

The forms of international co-operation that we adopt during the struggle may of course be disavowed after the struggle, as we did after the first World War. But it is quite certain that they will not in any event rise higher than the level to which the pressures of war forced them.

In the same manner the sacrifices of the war will greatly reduce the inequalities of our economic system. The discipline of wartime taxation has had strong equalitarian effects upon British life and will have similar consequences in our life. The gross inequalities of capitalistic democracies are disappearing under the wartime necessity. These gains are not necessarily permanent. We must expect the privileged classes to make desperate efforts after the war to regain their imperiled position in society; and we cannot deny that these desperate efforts may imperil democracy itself. But on the other hand, it is not likely that democratic society will reach higher standards of equal justice, after the pressure of war is removed, than it achieved under the pressure of war.

In so far as one of the basic weaknesses of bourgeois society is the love of ease and the identification of civilization with the comforts and gadgets that technical achievements have made possible, the chastisements of war are, again, the primary prompting to repentance. The fact that we have lost our rubber and may thereby become bereft of our automobiles is a highly symbolic form of chastisement for all of the most characteristic sins of bourgeois life. For what could be a more perfect symbol of our idolatries than our automobile? If we can stand its loss, we can bear almost anything. On the other hand, there is the possibility that we might prefer to give in to the Axis rather than be without our automobiles. If fatness was our sin, the war is quite obviously making us more lean. But of course such experiences in themselves do not bring repentance. There is always the possibility that we might decide to be fat slaves rather than lean freemen. It is in that sense that the issues which we face in coming months are so tremendous, and that the resolution to continue our battle against external foes also involves our desire to be quit of our internal weaknesses, which made the revolt against our civilization possible.

In so far as democratic society was guilty, not only of sins of omission and of weakness that made the more virulent evils of nazism possible, but was also guilty of sins similar to those of the Nazis (imperialism for instance), we face the same necessity of chastisement. India will probably gain its freedom under the pressure of necessity. It would not have secured it, at least not for years, if the British Empire had not come so close to defeat. The similarity between the white man's arrogance in the democratic world and Nazi race theories is apparent. If we do not repent of this arrogance, we cannot win the war. Our co-operation with China and the British co-operation with a free India are fruits meet for repentance, brought forth by the rigors of war.

One could only wish that our Negroes had a strategic position comparable to that of the Hindus and the Chinese. In that case they would win more concessions from our pride than they are likely to get. Nevertheless, they are going to win some concessions, provided we are hard pressed enough to find their disaffection as a serious threat to our victory.

Moralists may find this trait of human nature, its grudging concessions, its unwillingness to repent except under chastisement, abhorrent, and they may dream of another kind of history than the actual history of man. But if they examined their own conduct scrupulously, they would find evidences in it of this same reluctance and would learn to appreciate the tragic elements in history as manifestations of divine judgment, without which men would remain in the stupor of sin.

It must be observed in conclusion that while a long war may be the only discipline that will bring a democratic world completely to its senses, it is also possible that too long a war would make the burdens too grievous to be borne. It might drive us to despair and finally to death; which is to say that it might so aggravate the social issues through general poverty that the democratic way of life would break down under the tensions created by this general poverty and exhaustion.

We are thus in the position of going through an ordeal that may make or break us. We do not know what the residual health of our world is. We do not know how much punishment it can stand, or even how much it needs.

40. ANGLO–SAXON DESTINY
AND RESPONSIBILITY

It is becoming increasingly apparent that, whether any other conditions of a stable peace will be fulfilled or not, an Anglo-American alliance, which must be the cornerstone of any durable world order, is in the process of formation. Mr. Churchill's unequivocal words at Harvard, Governor Dewey's statement in favor of lasting co-operation with Britain, and the Republican postwar statement in which isolationism is renounced, all point to at least one step forward in our foreign policy.

This partnership between the English-speaking peoples can of course become a new menace to international justice and peace if it stands alone. The world cannot be organized by an Anglo-Saxon hegemony. Such a leadership could be ten times more just than the Nazis were and yet not be just enough to avoid arousing the resentment of Europe and Asia, in fact, of the entire world. Whatever Britain and America do together must be immediately related to a wider co-operation with the other two great powers, Russia and China, and must finally be made a part of a total constitutional or quasi-constitutional system of the world order in which all the nations, large and small, will have their due responsibilities and rights.

Nevertheless the further steps that must be taken to insure a stable peace all depend upon this first step of Anglo-American solidarity; for if Britain and America cannot agree together, all other necessary agreements become improbable.

The position of the Anglo-Saxon peoples at the crucial and strategic point in the building of a world community is a fact of such tremendous significance that it can only be adequately comprehended in religious terms. It is a position of destiny and carries with it tremendous responsibilities. Without a religious sense of the meaning of destiny, such a position as Britain and America now hold is inevitably corrupted by pride and the lust of power. We may in fact be certain that this corruption will not be absent from our political life. But if the churches in Britain and America are able to speak to the several nations as the prophets spoke to Israel, it may be possible to mitigate the pride sufficiently to allow these two nations to serve the world community creatively.

THE PROPHETIC IDEA OF DESTINY

The prophet Amos was certain of two things. One was that Israel had been particularly chosen of God; and the other was that this special mission gave the nation not a special security but a special peril. " You only have I chosen," he declared in God's name, " therefore will I visit you with your iniquities." It would serve no good purpose to try to compare the special destiny of the Anglo-Saxon peoples with that of Israel in olden times. Certainly no one would be so rash today as to claim the kind of destiny for our nations that the prophet's word " only " implies. Nevertheless only those who have no sense of the profundities of history would deny that various nations and classes, various social groups and races are at various times placed in such a position that a special measure of the divine mission in history falls upon them. In that sense God has chosen us in this fateful period of world history.

The world requires a wider degree of community. It must escape international anarchy or perish. If the world community is to be genuine, it cannot, of course, be superimposed by Anglo-Saxon or any other power. All peoples and nations must find their rightful place in the fellowship. Nevertheless, neither the world community nor any other form of human society ever moves as logically or abstractly as some of the " planners " and blueprinters imagine. Some nation or group always has a higher degree of power and responsibility in the formation of community than others.

It so happens that the combined power of the British Empire and the United States is at present greater than any other power. It is also true that the political forms in which these nations move and the moral and political ideals that are woven into the texture of their history are less incompatible with international justice than any other previous power of history.

THE COMPONENTS OF DESTINY

Yet as soon as one has said this, one is forced to make qualifications. All historical destiny is compounded of virtue and grace. If the position that any nation or group of nations holds is attributed to the virtue of those nations alone, one has the beginning of that pharisaism which destroys virtue, whether in individual or in national life. The fact is that no nation or individual is ever good enough to deserve the position of leadership that some nations and individuals achieve. If the history that leads to a special mission is carefully analyzed, it always becomes apparent that factors other than the virtues of the leader are partly responsible for the position the individual or collective leader holds. Those who do not believe in God's providence in history will call these factors " accidents " or " fortune." The religious man perceives them as gifts of grace. The grace that determines the lives of men and nations is manifest in all the special circumstances, favors, and fortunes of geography and climate, of history and fate that lead to eminence despite the weakness and sinfulness of the beneficiary of such eminence.

These elements in history are either purely accidental or they stand under divine providence. If they are purely accidental, then history itself has no meaning; for in that case it would be the fruit of caprice. That is why secularists usually obscure these factors of history; for it is not possible for man to live in a completely capricious world. But if they are obscured, the sense of destiny becomes purely a vehicle of pride. Those who achieve a special position in history claim a right to it either by virtue of their power or by virtue of their goodness. The Nazi sense of destiny is completely amoral because it regards power as the sole source of eminence. This amoral sense of destiny has been developed more explicitly by the Nazis than by any other modern nation; but no powerful nation is completely free of the pretension that its power is the sole source of its right to rule. Ideas of " manifest destiny " in our own history have this same source.

The Rule of the Virtuous

The idea that we have a right to rule because of our superior virtue is of a higher order than the amoral idea that we have a right to rule because of our power. It recognizes the moral element in history. It is nevertheless a dangerous idea because it obscures the immoral elements in all historical success. If Germany has been the particular bearer of the idea of destiny through power, the Anglo-Saxon world has been constantly tempted to express its sense of destiny pharisaically and to claim eminence by the right of its virtue. It is this element in Anglo-Saxon politics that has subjected it to the charge of " cant " from Continental nations. We have not heard the end of this charge from either Germany or France, from either the Continent or Russia, because there is an element of truth in the charge.

There is no cure for the pride of a virtuous nation but pure religion. The pride of a powerful nation may be humbled by the impotence that defeat brings. The pride of a virtuous nation cannot be humbled by moral and political criticisms because in comparative terms it may actually be virtuous. The democratic traditions of the Anglo-Saxon world are actually the potential basis of a just world order. But the historical achievements of this world are full of violations and contradictions of these principles. " In God's sight " they are not just; and they know it if they place themselves under the divine scrutiny, that is, if they regard their own history prayerfully rather than comparatively and measure themselves by what is demanded of them rather than by comparing their success with the failure of others.

Thus a contrite recognition of our own sins destroys the illusion of eminence through virtue and lays the foundation for the apprehension of " grace " in our national life. We know that we have the position that we hold in the world today partly by reason of factors and forces in the complex pattern of history that we did not create and from which we do not deserve to benefit. If we apprehend this religiously, the sense of destiny ceases to be a vehicle of pride and becomes the occasion for a new sense of responsibility.

THE PERILS OF EMINENCE

If we know that we have been chosen beyond our deserts, we must also begin to realize that we have not been chosen for our particular task in order that our own life may be aggrandized. We ought not derive either special security or special advantages from our high historical mission. The real fact is that we are placed in a precarious moral and historical position by our special mission. It can be justified only if it results in good for the whole community of mankind. Woe unto us if we fail. For our failure will bring judgment upon both us and the world. That is the meaning of the prophetic word, " Therefore will I visit you with your iniquities." This word must be translated by the church today into meanings relevant to our own history. If this is not done, we are bound to fail. For the natural pride of great nations is such that any special historical success quickly aggravates it until it becomes the source of moral and political confusion.

Without a religious sense of humility and responsibility the Anglo-Saxon world will fail to come to terms with the two great non-Christian nations, Russia and China. It will fail to understand to what degree what is good in the new Russian order represents values of equal justice that we should have, but did not, achieve, and to what extent the evils of tyranny in Russia are simply a false answer to our own unsolved problem of social justice. It will fail to understand to what degree the white man's pride is the chief obstacle in building a world community that brings Asia fully into the world community. It is worth remembering in this connection that long before the Nazi elaborated the idea of Nordic superiority the Anglo-Saxon world betrayed an arrogance toward the darker peoples of which the Latin world, for instance, was comparatively free. Our racial pride is incompatible with our responsibilities in the world community. If we do not succeed in chastening it, we shall fail in our task.

If we should imagine that our victory in this great World War were a justification of our virtue and if our moral pride thus becomes accentuated, we shall fail in our task of finally bringing the fallen foes into the world community on terms that will bring health both to them and the total community. If we should give ourselves to the illusion that this war was a simple contest between right and wrong, and that the victory was a simple triumph of right over wrong; if we fail to understand to what degree Nazi tyranny grew on the soil of our general international anarchy; if we lack the spiritual humility to see these facts of history, we shall be bound to corrupt the peace by vindictiveness.

SELF-RIGHTEOUSNESS LEADS TO VINDICTIVENESS

There are already many ominous signs of this vindictiveness, and a careful analysis of various manifestations of the spirit of vengeance reveals very clearly how self-righteousness is the presupposition of vengeance. It is also quite easy to foresee the consequences of any peace that is built upon the assumption that the elimination of Nazi evil will eliminate evil from the world. All these perils are the insecurities to which we are exposed in our historical eminence. They represent the always overhanging divine judgment. They are the modern counterparts of what Amos foresaw in his words, "Therefore will I visit you with your iniquities."

We may be fairly sure that the Anglo-Saxon world will not be good enough or sufficiently contrite to fulfill its historical mission with complete success. It nevertheless has a great opportunity to fulfill it with relative success. But if this is to be accomplished, the Christian church must understand its prophetic mission. It must cease to vacillate between ascetic withdrawal from the world "power politics" and a too simple identification of the nation's purposes with the divine Will. It must contend against both irresponsibility and complacency in our national life.

The world community cannot be realized if the Anglo-Saxon world fails in its historic mission. If it is afraid of the perils of that mission and is affrighted by the moral ambiguities of " power politics," it will fail just as seriously as if it accepts its mission without a religious sense of contrition. It may be that the former temptation is still the primary temptation for America, and the second one that to which Britain is particularly prone. But the differences between the two great parts of the Anglo-Saxon world are less than the similarities. In both cases the Christian faith is still in sufficiently close relation to the national life to encourage the hope that it will help to purify the nations for their mission; in both cases, however, the Christian forces are to some degree the salt that has lost its savor. If the nations should fail therefore, the failure would be the consequence of the prior failure of the Christian church.

41. AIRPLANES ARE NOT ENOUGH

Before we entered the war, we were forced to challenge many idealists, religious and secular, who refused to believe that if an evil idea became embodied in tanks and used airplanes as its instruments, it could be defeated if we did not set corresponding force against it. It has since become quite apparent that tyranny would have conquered the world if the material resources of civilization had not been organized and harnessed so that force could be met by superior force.

Simple moralists may draw melancholy reflections from the fact that history places us under such a necessity. But profounder souls will recognize the relation of power to ideas as part of the unity of life that man has, in body and soul. The spiritual and the physical aspects of life are not identical; but neither can they be easily separated.

We have now come to a phase of the world struggle when it is important to remind the statesman of the democratic cause that while political struggles are never purely spiritual, neither are they ever purely physical. Our journals are filled today with promises and prophecies of victory, based upon the facts that our material resources are immeasurably greater than those of the Axis, that we now build nine thousand airplanes a month, and that we will be able to reduce the principal cities of Germany to rubble before the invasion begins.

Christianity and Crisis, February 7, 1944.

It would be foolish to deny that part of our certainty of victory is derived exactly from such calculations, and it would be hazardous to draw absolute distinctions between what is, and what is not, permissible in a total war. The melancholy necessities of total war were invented neither by the Nazi nor by us. They are the consequences of a technical society that makes the harnessing of the total resources of a society for the destruction of the foe possible and therefore necessary. The necessity follows from the possibility, because once the instruments of a total war are unloosed they will guarantee defeat for the side that fails to use them, whether from want of resolution, or failure of organization, or moral scruple.

Nevertheless it is becoming obvious that our reliance upon our physical superiority has become so preponderant because we are failing in giving the war its true spiritual meaning. The problem of the world is the problem of anarchy. Europe, with its multicolored national and ethnic life has been the particular source of world anarchy. We have proved in the past year that our statesmanship has no clear answer to the problems of Europe. We have no program that would rally the creative forces of Europe to our cause, though the oppressed nations of the Continent naturally look forward to the negative solution of their problem that our victory will bring.

We make much of the fact that the three great hegemonous powers have reached an agreement. It must be admitted that this agreement represents a real achievement. But Europe does not know what an agreement implies. It could mean the partitioning of the Continent into spheres of influence; in which case Europe would remain a cockpit for power rivalries. It could mean the subjugation of the Continent by the three great powers; in which case the unity of the Continent would be a coerced order. The cultural vitality of Europe is too great, whatever its present political and economic weakness, to give lasting value to such a solution.

We may well require more guns and airplanes to produce the collapse of our enemies precisely because we are not using the most effective spiritual weapons against them. By confronting them with a future seemingly without hope, we give the dictators the opportunity of exploiting the despair of the people and using it as the final resource of a fatigued nation. If we were wise, we would induce them to despair of the possibility of their victory but not of the meaning and virtue of ours.

If the whole of Europe is reduced to rubble before we destroy our enemies, that will partly prove how great a loyalty an evil cause can claim before it is finally defeated. But it may also prove that a good cause can be emptied of its essential meaning in the heat of conflict. We are not pleading for dishonest promises as weapons of " psychological warfare." What is needed is a more meaningful definition of our positive aims. The defeat of tyranny will give this war a negative justification in any event. But it cannot be positively justified if it does not give Europe and the world a working alternative to the twin evils of international anarchy and international tyranny.

It is significant that the same statesmanship that would make the war meaningful in the long, as well as in the short run would also hasten the victory; all of which proves that ideas and ideals are important in conflict, even though they are never disembodied as the idealists imagine.

One tragic aspect of such a world conflict as that in which we are engaged is that preoccupation with the immediate issues and urgencies among both statesmen and people, occasioned by the war, seems to render us incapable of lifting our eyes to the wider and more ultimate issues. But we must not succumb to this peril. Physical weariness could cost us the victory, but spiritual weariness or complacency could rob our victory of its virtue.

42. THE LIMITS OF MILITARY POWER

As we receive day-by-day news of the agonies of disunity and potential chaos that South Vietnam is undergoing in trying to achieve order and unity, it is well to remember that only a few short months ago our whole nation was excited by the crisis in the war between Vietnam and the Communists involving the obscure fort of Dienbienphu. The fortress was besieged, and we were given to understand that its fall would seriously alter the whole strategic picture in Asia. Vice-President Nixon, speaking to an editors' dinner, hinted that it would probably be necessary to support the French military effort if catastrophe was to be avoided. The Administration seemed on the verge of committing at least our Air Force to this struggle. President Eisenhower, standing on the brink of war, finally re-

The New Leader, May 30, 1955.

treated — partly because he had the sixth sense to know that such a commitment would not be popular, and partly because the Senatorial leaders were reluctant to give him the authority. In any event, we seemed about committed to "save" the last bastion of freedom by military action.

No doubt military action must frequently be the ultima ratio in a struggle with a foe. We saved the whole situation by prompt military action in Korea. But the contemporary situation in Vietnam should certainly instruct us on the limits of military power in the long cold war. For what we are witnessing is the revelation of the poverty of our cause in moral and political terms in a nation that we sought to save from communist aggression by military defense. That poverty is revealed by the still-lingering resentment against French imperialism, by the opposition to the puppet "Chief of State" Bao Dai on the part of the people of the budding nation, and by their own inability to achieve unity against divisive forces within their nation. The Government's desperate victory over military formations, which are alternately described as "river pirates" and "religious sects," reveals the lack of solidity and unity in the community; and the trouble with Bao Dai, regarded as a puppet of the French, is a reminder of the old trouble that made the Vietnamese struggle against communism so ineffective. Military power is, in short, ineffective when it lacks a moral and political base. It is the fist of a hand; but the hand must be attached to an arm, and the arm to a body; and the body must be before the fist can be effective.

Military power is, therefore, necessary, particularly in moments of crisis when the community faces recalcitrance and anarchy at home, and dispute with another community abroad. It is more effective in international disputes than in domestic ones because the order and peace of a community is primarily dependent upon forces of cohesion and accommodation for which pure force is an irrelevance. But, even in international disputes, military force has its limits. It is primarily limited by the morale of the community that exercises the force. That is why pure military power was so ineffective in Vietnam and why, incidentally, no amount of military aid could save the Chinese Nationalist cause. It lacked the cohesion and morale to avail itself of the proffered aid.

Despite these obvious limits of military power, the American nation has become strangely enamored with military might. We treat the Asian continent, with its nationalistic and social upheavals, as if it were possible to establish order out of chaos by the assertion of military might. We are preoccupied with our "defense perimeter" in Asia and have little interest in the vast political complexities of the great continent except to express consistent contempt for the great uncommitted nation, India, though that nation's neutralism is not informed by the slightest degree of sympathy for communism. It is not so certain that it may not possess illusions about this tyranny; but we ought at any rate to have more patience with neutralism, particularly since we emerged only so recently from a like mood vis-à-vis Europe.

Our attitude toward India is typical of our indifference toward the political complexities of a continent in ferment, our blindness to the hazards that our cause inevitably faces on that continent. The resentments of the Asian people against the white man's arrogance and against the imperialist impact of a technical civilization are bound to prove handicaps to our cause even when it is contending against a vicious tyranny. These moral and political hazards cannot be overcome by the show of military power. In fact, military might may tend to aggravate our moral and political embarrassments.

Thus, our preoccupation with military power and strategy places us in a false light in Asia, particularly since it creates a picture that seems to conform to the communist slogans that identify "militarism" and "imperialism" with "capitalism." The question is why we permitted ourselves to appear in this unfavorable light in the whole of Asia. Our nation is singularly innocent of the military tradition and bereft of the military caste traditionally associated with Prussia. Yet we are made to appear in Asian eyes as the new Prussians. There are probably two reasons for this strange turn of events.

The first is the fact that a serious predicament may persuade even a pacific man to rely upon his fists. We are in a serious predicament in Asia and are therefore tempted to rely too much on our fists to extricate ourselves from our seeming hazards.

The second reason is that our leadership in the world is drawn primarily from our economic and the consequent military strength. Economic power can be quickly transmuted into military power, particularly in a technical age, and more particularly in an atomic age. We are therefore tempted to an undue reliance on the obvious might that we possess, particularly since our apprenticeship in the leadership of world affairs has been brief, and we have not had time to accustom ourselves to the acquisition, and to know the importance, of prestige as a source of power, or to learn patience with the endless complexities of loyalties and resentments of traditions and established forms of cohesion that govern the actions of nations.

This impatience is the more grievous because the very technical achievements that have endowed us with superior military power have also given us living standards that are beyond the dreams of avarice of the nontechnical cultures and that militate against our moral prestige. The combination of fear and envy, which our power and good fortune excites, militates against our moral and political prestige, which is the real source of authority in the political realm. This fact is probably the cause of the paradoxical fact that Britain, which only recently divested itself of its Asian empire, is more popular in Asia than we, and that we, who have always been " anti-imperialist " at least in theory if not in consistent practice, are now regarded as the primary exponents of " imperialism " to the nascent nations of Asia.

Having resisted the temptation to resolve the Indo-Chinese situation purely by force and by the support of a French imperialism that came to terms with the rising tide of nationalism too tardily, we are doing rather better than the French in coping with the complex problems of a nation that desires freedom but cannot find the unity that would give substance to its independence. There are, in fact, suspicions that the French have aggravated the problem of Vietnam both by their support of Bao Dai and by possibly covert support of the rebellious forces. We are certainly more disinterested than the French in desiring only the health of the new nation, and its sufficient strength to ward off the communist peril from the north. Perhaps we have done well enough to give us a better reputation in Asia as a political, rather than a military, power.

It must be taken for granted that no amount of political skill or wisdom in the tumultuous affairs of the Asian revolution can obviate the necessity of strong military power, nor obscure the importance of our supremacy in atomic weapons. We cannot dispense with military power as the ultima ratio of international relations. But we do have to keep it in that position of the ultimate instance and not use a meat ax in situations in which a deft manipulation of loyalties or channeling of aspirations is called for.

It is well to remember that in collective, as well as individual, life the force which coerces the body but does not persuade the will can have only negative significance. It can prevent something that we abhor more than conflict, and it can enforce our will and purpose momentarily on a recalcitrant foe. But the loyalties and cohesions of the community are managed and transfigured not by force but by a wise statecraft. Therefore, our military power cannot be as potent as we think in making our world hegemony sufferable either to our friends and allies or to ourselves. Britain learned the limits of force in Ireland and then in India. We have not had comparable lessons, which may be the reason we do not have a comparable wisdom.

43. THE POSSIBILITY OF A DURABLE PEACE

One of the most tragic aspects of this war is that it offers little prospect of anything more than a negative justification in the sight of God and history. Nazi tyranny had to be defeated. There are certain crises of evil in history in which we are forced to move against a threatening evil without too much regard for the ultimate consequences of our action. If the whole world had not been finally aroused against Nazi tyranny, it would have lived for decades in slaveiy. On the other hand, the very fact that it was not aroused to this peril until each nation in turn became the victim of tyranny proves that we did not understand the deeper meaning of this war. We did not understand that the peril of tyranny grew out of the soil of anarchy: the anarchy of our irresponsibility toward each other. The children of darkness are wiser in their generation than the children of light. The Nazis understood the global character of this war long before the so-called democratic nations understood it. They knew that they would have to conquer the world if they were to preserve their conquest of the Continent. We did not know that until the Nazis proved it to us.

It now appears that, though we have learned many things about the character of life and history from this war, the nations are not likely to learn enough to build a secure peace. We are not fully conscious of the depth and breadth of the world revolution in which we stand.

The problem of the peace after the war may be divided into two aspects. The one is the creation of a durable world order. The other is the development of justice within the new system of order. Order will have to be maintained for some time to come by the organization of preponderant power. There is no other way of overcoming the anarchy of rival national sovereignties. Justice can be achieved within this system of order only if and as the nations that control the preponderant power have the conscience and imagination to set up constitutional instruments that will guarantee the weaker nations their just rights.

It is not altogether surprising that there is some prospect of

Christianity and Society, Summer, 1943.

achieving the first goal, but little prospect of achieving the second in any adequate measure. For the first merely requires that each of the powerful nations understand that it has become impossible for any one nation, no matter how powerful, to control the world's economic and political life. The second requires a degree of imagination and self-abnegation of which the powerful nations do not yet seem capable.

There is some possibility that Britain, America, China, and Russia may preserve and extend the mutual relations that the urgencies of the war have forced upon them. It is not at all certain that they will achieve this end; but there is a possibility of it. It is not certain because each of these nations has impulses toward solitary dominion; and some of them (particularly America and Russia) have tendencies toward isolationist irresponsibility, which must be overcome before a stable alliance between them can be formed. Of the four nations Great Britain is prompted by geographic circumstances and political experience to espouse the cause of mutual security with fewer reservations than any of the other nations. It is not tempted to the isolationist alternative at all, because that would quite obviously mean suicide. It has some temptation in the direction of solitary dominion. That expresses itself in ideas such as the possibility of extending the " British Commonwealth " idea until all nations would be included in it. Obviously there is no possibility of arriving at a real partnership between Russia, Britain, and America, merely by extending the scope of the British Commonwealth. While there are such ideas in British political thought today, they are generally not held in authoritative circles. On the whole, Britain holds the promise of playing a creative role in forming a genuine alliance of the larger powers.

It must be observed that such an alliance would degenerate into nothing more than a new global balance of power if Britain merely became the broker between the other powers. We must have a direct and intimate relation with Russia and must not depend upon Britain to act as broker between us. But at best Britain will have a special function in the alliance because she will be closer to each of the other partners than either is to the other.

The organization of preponderant power represents tremendous difficulties; and we may therefore fail in achieving it. It is, however, significant that both Britain and America (and probably Russia also) know that the basis of world order must be laid, not in some abstract world constitution that will not really engage the sense of responsibility of the large powers, but in a partnership of power. Power and responsibility must be made commensurate in the new world order, in a way the League of Nations was unable to accomplish.

When we move from this aspect of our problem to the second one — the use of order for the achievement of justice — we have less reason to be hopeful. There is little indication that any of the larger powers are thinking significantly on how their combined power is to be used for the achievement of justice. There is little prospect of their arriving in time at a basic agreement on how either the Continent of Europe or the Pacific region should be reorganized. Russia is intransigent on the acquisition of a vast strategic area, stretching from the Black Sea to Finland. Whether she could be beguiled from this venture in unilateral security, if the other powers had a really creative plan for the reorganization of the Continent, is an open question. She will, at best, be unable to overcome her mistrust of the Anglo-Saxon, capitalistic world completely.

There are ominous rumors that she would like to persuade Poland to compensate herself for the loss of the Polish Ukraine to Russia by the acquisition of Eastern Prussia. If this happens, there will be small prospect of bringing Germany into a wholesome relationship with a Continental community of nations.

The general preoccupation in the Western world with the problem of what kind of punishment should be meted out to Germany, reveals how little the depth of our crisis is understood. The German problem is in all conscience a perplexing one. The corruption of German life by nazism has been deep and wide, and the dynamic and demonic evil of German nazism will not yield to some simple prophylaxis. Nevertheless, this evil must be understood against the background of the Continent's static corruption. If Germany suffers from cancer, France suffers from consumption. Germany must ultimately be related to a healthy continent; and the Continent itself cannot be healthy without a wholesome German political life. This can certainly not be achieved by punishment alone.

It may be observed that the nice calculations of how much or how little Germany ought to be punished are in obvious violation of the Scriptural injunction: " Vengeance is mine. I will repay, saith the Lord." Obviously the moral, political, and economic bankruptcy that Germany faces in the hour of her defeat represents a more terrible punishment than anything in our power to add or subtract.

Nor are there any indications that the Western powers will allow the socialization of property to which it would naturally be prompted by its poverty and by the socialization that has already taken place under a war economy. It is much more likely that abortive efforts will be made to undo what the war has done, and thereby to lose the chance of creating a property system upon the Continent that would give a new unity and health to its economic life.

It is probable, moreover, that irrelevant political sovereignties will be maintained just as much as irrelevant economic authorities. The small nations have been promised the return of their independence. If they get no more than that, they will not have it long. They ought rather to be persuaded and forced into a council of Europe in which there would be perfect cultural autonomy for each nation but something less than absolute independence, either politically, or economically.

We may count it as a gain since the last war that the nations understand the historical process of the coalescence of power and authority. But there is little significant thought in high places in either Britain or America about the way this power is to be used. There is wide apprehension in Britain lest American power be expressed in purely reactionary and imperialistic terms. But Britain's best insurance against such an eventuality would be a generous plan of Continental and Pacific rehabilitation, for which she would ask our support. So far there is little evidence of such a plan.

If Britain and America are not careful, we will waste our time and spiritual substance in repenting of each other's sins. British liberalism will express abhorrence of the tendency toward economic imperialism in American politics, and our liberalism will profess itself morally affronted by British political dominion in all parts of the world.

Britain will have the preponderant political power in the world after the war, and we will have the preponderant economic power. The possibilities are that Russia may surpass both of us in both forms of power within the next century. The important problem for each of the great nations is to use this power responsibly, neither withdrawing from the world nor yet seeking to dominate the world alone. The important problem for all the great nations in partnership is to relate the smaller nations to this preponderant power by such constitutional means that the injustice of power will be checked and a system of justice be developed inside of the system of order created by their power.

There is at present little prospect of such developments. Unless we do better than now seems probable, the world is still far from finding a stable and secure peace.

44. AMERICAN POWER AND WORLD RESPONSIBILITY

There is a fateful significance in the fact that America's coming of age coincides with that period of world history when the paramount problem is the creation of some kind of world community. The world must find a way of avoiding complete anarchy in its international life; and America must find a way of using its great power responsibly. These two needs are organically related; for the world problem cannot be solved if America does not accept its full share of responsibility in solving it.

Analogies between individual and collective life have only limited application. It may therefore seem dubious to speak of America's " coming of age." Nations do not have well-defined periods of infancy, adolescence, and maturity. Nevertheless, the analogy is more than usually applicable to American life. The period of our infancy can be clearly defined. We were once a small and weak nation, and we seemed justified in that period to abjure all " entangling alliances " while the nation established itself upon a vast and virgin continent. There followed a period of adolescence (roughly between the Civil War and the first World War) in which we exhibited a typically adolescent disparity between growing physical strength and lack of social experience. Our relations to the world were tentative and diffident. We were furthermore relatively " innocent " rather than virtuous. Our domestic life was free from great social tensions because an expanding economy and a retreating frontier solved or mitigated all our social problems. Our two vast ocean moats gave us external security. These simple solutions for vexing problems prompted us to underestimate the difficulties of all problems of human togetherness and gave both its political and moral thought an overtone of adolescent sentimentality. Nor was it free of adolescent self-righteousness; for it was unmindful (as young

Christianity and Crisis, April 5, 1943.

people prove to be) of the favored circumstances that had contributed to its virtues; and it did not understand the difference between untempted innocency and the virtue that has surmounted temptation. From this strain of self-righteousness was drawn that dubious note in our foreign policy, according to which the other nations of the world appeared in the guise of " city slickers " who would, if we came too close to them, corrupt our morals and take advantage of our guilelessness.

If we have now " come of age," we have done so only in the sense that it is gradually dawning upon us that we are really a very powerful nation, perhaps the most powerful upon earth. We have not had sufficient experience in the complexities of international relations to have lost all remnants of our adolescent vices. They will still rise to plague us. And we may add a few vices of youthful maturity to them. Thus we may add a heedlessness toward the problems of the community of nations, which is derived from our sense of power, to a feeling of irresponsibility, which was derived from our favored geographic position. The real peril to the soul of America lies in the fact that both our power and our favored position make the establishment of a system of mutual security less urgent for us than for other nations. Though we speak of this war as a war of survival, our survival is not at stake in the same sense that it has been for Russia, Britain, China, and the smaller nations. We would have had to come to terms with a tyrannical world overlord in the event of an Axis victory, and would have lost our soul in the process; but our actual survival as a free nation would not have been at stake in the same way as that of the other nations. It is this fact that makes it quite impossible to overcome the impulse toward irresponsibility in our national life as absolutely as we might desire. The fires of history have not, and will not, purge us as completely as they have some other nations. Nor will the lash of fear support the gentler persuasion of conscience to the same degree as in the experience of others.

ISOLATIONISM IMPOSSIBLE

Meanwhile, the world has grown smaller while we have grown more powerful. The advances of a technical civilization have made our continental security almost as untenable as Britain's island security. Britain has finally learned that she cannot withdraw from the Continent, and we may have learned that we cannot withdraw from the world. Yet there is a difference between the width of the Channel and the ocean, and that geographic difference is almost perfectly matched by the difference between the British and the American temper toward world problems. We have become successively involved in two wars from which we (or many of us) believed we could remain aloof if only this or that policy had been different. The first World War should have proved to us that our fancied continental security was in reality partly parasitic upon the power of the British Navy.

More exactly, it was a security presaged upon the ability of British policy to maintain a semblance of order in the world by a European balance of power. When this balance was challenged we knew ourselves to be insecure. We chose (in terms of adolescent sentimentality) to justify our participation in the first World War as an effort to make the world " safe for democracy." We would have done better to admit that it was merely an effort to make the world safe. Order, mutually secured, is the first purpose of the international, as of every other, community. Democracy is an ideal form of such order, and is not easily established. Our disillusionment in failing to establish world democracy contributed to our cynical irresponsibility after the war. Cynicism is, in fact, the usual reaction of disappointed sentimentalists. It is always wrong to interpret political tasks purely in terms either of ideal ends or of purely egoistic ones. No political program ever completely lacks the inspiration of the one and the corruption of the other. But the substance of it deals with minimal standards of mutual justice and security.

Our reaction from our first large-scale effort on the world scene was so deep as to have amounted to a psychosis. And the effects of the psychosis were so great that we refused to recognize the realities of the international scene when the second crisis came. We might still be in a mood of withdrawal and irresponsibility had it not suited the strategy of the dictators to awaken us from our slumbers, though it must be admitted that our sleep had been for some time uneasy and full of nightmares.

The two wars coming after each other have proved that our continental isolation does not guarantee our safety. In profounder terms they have proved: (1) that balance of power politics is not sufficient to guarantee the world's peace; (2) that in any event a European balance of power is certainly unable to maintain order in a total world (Europe having lost its position as the world's strategic center) ; and (3) that even if the first two points were not true, Britain does not have sufficient power to manipulate a balance of power alone.

Thus the world faces the task of finding more adequate instruments for preventing anarchy while we must recognize that both conscience and interest compel our participation in this task. We may not have learned as much as some other nations during this tragic era; but there are indications that we have learned enough to know that we cannot completely evade this issue. The immediate symbol of the difference between our mood now and twenty-five years ago is that the Republican Party is no longer solidly isolationist.

Our greatest peril today is not the temptation to a complete withdrawal from world responsibility. There will indeed be some impulses in that direction; and they will be supported not merely by a conscienceless indifference toward the plight of the world community, but also by the secularized and sentimentalized conscience of those Christians who are so affronted by the moral ambiguities of world politics, as of all politics. They therefore prefer immoral irresponsibility and inaction to the moral taint that is involved in all political action. But we have gone through too much experience to make the isolationism of 1920–1940 a live option. It is more likely that we will combine the impulse to dominate the world, to which we will be prompted by our undoubted power, with the impulse toward withdrawal, to which we are prompted by our comparative geographic security. To be sure our power is not great enough to give us security, even as our isolation is not complete enough to guarantee it. But our temptation lies in the fact that we have just enough power to make the policy of seeking security by an unmutual expression of power seem plausible; just as we have enough continental isolation to obscure the urgency of the problem of mutual security, which other nations feel so strongly.

ISOLATIONIST IMPERIALISM

The danger that we will combine two contradictory impulses in our life in a compound of isolationist imperialism is heightened by the fact that such a policy nicely combined the diffidence of our recent adolescence with the pride of our mature strength. Already the

signs are multiplying that the isolationists of yesterday are the imperialists of today. They will not yield any of the strategic points
that we have secured in the world conflict. They even want more air
and naval bases. They know that we have the economic power to
maintain a larger air force and navy than anyone else; and they intend to do it. But they do not intend to make any international
commitments that would bring our strength into mutual relations
with other nations, either great or small.

We need not assume that the present Administration will give itself to such ideas and ideals. Its orientation runs, on the whole, in
the opposite direction. But there are powerful opposition forces in
Congress and in the country working partly consciously, and partly
unconsciously, toward isolationist imperialism. Furthermore, some
military ideas, developed under the aegis of the administration, fit
into the general imperialist pattern. The fact that we disavow " imperialism " consciously is no guarantee against the expression of
this impulse to dominate with our power, without regard to the
rights and interests of the rest of the world. It is one of the perils of
adolescence and early maturity to display power without full regard
for the consequences.

Sometimes our more idealistic newspapermen and some of our
religious leaders piously inform Britain that we are through with
imperialism forever, meaning thereby that we have a critical attitude toward traditional imperialism, with all of its stereotyped
marks of identification. But the same newspapermen may give voice
to sentiments of isolationist imperialism in the next moment; and
some religious leaders of sentimental persuasion will regard any tolerable solution of the world's problems with as much disfavor as
British imperialism, because it would fail to conform to the ideal
requirements of world brotherhood. If I were British, I would find
nothing quite so difficult to bear as these American criticisms, leveled against British policy, from sources that have little or no understanding of the greater perils of American imperialism.

One reason why isolationist imperialism is, in fact, so great a danger is because the more " idealistic " forces of America, whether secular or religious, are inclined to plan for a world community in such
abstract terms as not to engage the actual historical realities at all.
Their plans are so completely irrelevant to the real problems that
the world faces, and so far from the actual possibilities of a tolerable system of mutual security, that the realists can afford to disre-

gard them. Thus our policy moves toward a cynical expression of American power, while our avowed war aims are as pure as gold.

It would be fatal to assume that the wiser and more sensitive forces of America have already lost the battle against an irresponsible expression of American power in the postwar world. But if the battle is to be won, we will have to draw upon profounder insights of our Christian faith than is our wont. Nothing is quite so important for the Anglo-Saxon world in general, and for America in particular, as the knowledge that it is not possible to build a community without the manipulation of power and that it is not possible to use power and remain completely " pure." We must not have an easy conscience about the impurities of politics or they will reach intolerable proportions. But we must also find religious means of easing the conscience, or our uneasy conscience will tempt us into irresponsibility.

Most Urgent Problem

The world's most urgent problem is the establishment of a tolerable system of mutual security for the avoidance of international anarchy. Such a system will not meet all the requirements of perfect justice for decades to come. There is a sense in which it will probably never meet them. Yet it is possible to avoid both a tyrannical unification of the world, and the alternative anarchy, if each nation is ready to make commitments commensurate with its power. If America fails to do this, the world is lost for decades to come. In that case we would gain little satisfaction from the knowledge that some of our idealists had perfectly splendid schemes for the federation of the world, which would have been adopted if only the nations had been wise or good enough to recognize their worth.

But America must not fail. This will be the great battle of the next decades. It will not be easy to win, but it is certainly not yet lost. We may be grateful that the religious leadership of America has with its secular leadership been chastened by history. The pronouncements on world problems by the Federal Council Commission on a Just and Durable Peace have become increasingly realistic and continue to stress America's responsibility to the world community. Other unofficial groups, such as the Committee on War and Peace under the chairmanship of Bishop McConnell are making the same emphasis. We must find a way of placing the power of

America behind the task of world order. We must overcome the impulse toward domination toward which we are tempted by our power and the impulse toward irresponsibility to which we are tempted by our youth and comparative security.

45. PLANS FOR WORLD REORGANIZATION

In the various plans and programs for postwar reconstruction and world organization, it is possible to discern two general types of approach to the problems of international politics. One might be defined as the historical and realistic school of politics. The other is rationalistic in method and idealistic in temper. In the first all plans for the future are dominated by the question, Where do we go from here? The broken process of history is emphasized, and it is believed that new ventures in political organization, however broad their field and bold their purpose, remain under certain conditions and limitations which human history never transcends. In the second school, the primary concern is not with perennial conditions but with new possibilities, and not with the starting point but with the goal.

The historical school realizes that certain perennial problems of political organization emerge in new forms, but are of the same essence on each new level of the political integration of human society. The idealists are more conscious of novel and radical elements in a new situation and are inclined to believe and hope that old problems and vexations will disappear in the new level of political achievement.

In the present situation the idealists rightly insist that the economic interdependence of the world demands new international political organization. They believe in the necessity of some kind of world government, which will make our economic interdependence sufferable and which will organize the potential world community and make it actual.

The realistic and historical school does not deny these new necessities and possibilities. But it views the task of realizing them in the light of its knowledge of the stubborn inertia of human history. It wants to know how nations are to be beguiled into a limitation

of their sovereign rights, considering that national pride and parochial self-sufficiency are something more than the mere fruit of ignorance but recurring forces in all efforts at social cohesion.

All these differences of temper and viewpoint are finally focussed
upon one crucial issue: the problem of power. The historical realists
know that history is not a simple rational process but a vital one.
All human societies are organizations of diverse vitalities and interests by power. Some dominant power lies at the center of every social
organization. Some balance of power is the basis of whatever justice
is achieved in human relations. Where the disproportion of power is
too great and where an equilibrium of social forces is lacking, no
mere rational or moral demands can achieve justice.

The rationalists and idealists are inclined to view history from
the standpoint of the moral and social imperatives that a rational
analysis of a situation generates. They look at the world and decide
that its social and economic problems demand and require a " federation of the world." They think of such a federation not primarily in terms of the complex economic and social interests and
vitalities, which must be brought into and held in a tolerable equilibrium. Least of all do they think of the necessity of some dominant
force or power as the organizing center of the equilibrium. They
are on the whole content to state the ideal requirements of the situation in as rigorous terms as possible.

Sometimes they wring their hands in holy horror when the tortuous processes of history do not conform to their ideal demands.
They declare in self-righteous pride that since the statesmen of the
world refused to heed their advice, and since the people of the
world were too obtuse to see the light, they themselves can do nothing more than consign the world to its deserved doom. During the
past decades they have been too preoccupied with the task of condemning the nations for their obvious defiance of the new requirements of a world civilization to be much concerned with the immediate perils that the crisis of our civilization has brought upon us.

This word of stricture upon the idealists will betray the bias from
which this analysis of the two schools is attempted. This analysis
assumes that, on the whole, the task of world organization must be
attempted from the standpoint of the historical realism. This conclusion could be justified by the simple fact that no historical process has ever, even remotely, conformed to the pattern that the idealists have mapped out for it. It must be added immediately, how-

ever, that the truth does not lie simply on the side of the realists. Without an admixture of the temper and the insights of the other school, there could be no genuine advance in social organization at all.

The realists understand the perennial problems of politics, but they are usually deficient in their sense of the urgency of a new situation. They know that politics is a problem of the manipulation of power. But they easily interpret the problem of power in too cynical terms. Sometimes they forget that political power is a compound of which physical force, whether economic or military, is only one ingredient. They do not fully appreciate that a proper regard for moral aspirations is a source of political prestige, and that this prestige is itself an indispensable source of power.

II

In the present situation the idealists, in making plans for world organization, either disregard the problem of power entirely, or they project some central pool of power without asking what tributaries are to fill the pool. In the former case they are sometimes under the illusion that " national sovereignty " is merely the fruit of faulty conceptions of international law. They would write new international laws in which the absolute sovereignty of nations is denied; and they believe that such a legal refutation of national claims would be sufficient to tame the stubborn self-will of nations and to maintain " law without force." (This phrase is the title of a recent book upon that subject, written in the temper just defined.)

In the latter case they conceive of some federation of the world with an international police force, and with a newly and abstractly created moral and political prestige, sufficient to maintain itself against the divisive forces that will inevitably challenge its authority. Usually they refer to the creation of American nationhood as analogy and proof of the possibility of creating such a new authority. It happens that the history of the American Constitution and of American Federalism conforms more nearly to this pattern than any other national history; but it does not conform as completely as the idealists imagine. They forget to what degree the sovereignty of the several states was actually abridged in the heat of a desperate conflict; that even this conflict did not persuade the states to go as far as it was necessary to go; and that when they did take the final step, many of them did so with mental reservations in the direction of separatism, which finally resulted in a civil war. That war was necessary to prove that the nation was really one and that the Constitutional commitments, by which it was formed, were irrevocable.

Generally the idealists think it possible to create such a new international authority and then make a moral demand upon the nations to submit themselves to it. They do not realize that no collective group in human history has ever made decisions in vacuum. Sometimes nations are able to say B if history has previously established the A upon which the B follows. But that is about as far as collective volition goes.

As against these illusions of the rationalists and idealists, the historical realists are more correct. They are right in looking to mutual commitments made by the United Nations in the war as the real source of possibly wider commitments for the future. They are right in looking to the immediate necessities of a war situation for the compulsion that will abridge the self-will of nations, and in hoping that the necessities of the peace will be obvious enough to persuade the nations to extend, rather than to disavow the commitments thus made. It is always possible, of course, that the necessities of peace will, though equally urgent, not be equally obvious; that nations will refuse to conform to them and that another and even more tragic chapter in world history will have to be enacted before the nations bow to the irrefutable logic of history. This logic is irrefutable because an economically interdependent world must in some sense become a politically integrated world community or allow potential instruments of community to become instruments of mutual annihilation.

The weakness of the realists is that they usually do not go far enough in meeting new problems and situations. They are so conscious of the resistance in history to new ventures, and are so impressed by the force of the perennial problems of politics, which manifest themselves on each new level of history, that they are inclined to discount both the necessity and the possibility of new political achievements.

III

In the present situation, both the idealists and the realists may be divided into two subordinate schools of thought. One group of idealists does not deal with the problem of power at all. They would simply organize the world by law without asking where the power and authority to enforce the law is to come from. The other group is conscious of the problem of power, but they deal with it abstractly. Among the realists, one school of thought would merely reconstruct some new balance of power among the nations, having no confidence in international political organization. The other group believes in some kind of imperial organization of the world, with some small group of dominant nations furnishing the imperial power.

The most brilliant exposition of the school of thought that thinks in terms of reconstructing the balance of power as a principle of world peace is Professor Spykman's very able book *America's Strategy in World Politics*. The book has the merit of recognizing all the geographic, economic, and other elements that must enter into any kind of international equilibrium and which cannot be disregarded on any level of political achievement. But it does not fully realize that an unorganized balance of power is potential anarchy and cannot preserve peace. The introduction of a single new factor into the precarious equilibrium, or the elaboration of a single new force of recalcitrance (as for instance the air power of Germany) may destroy the balance. The world community requires instruments for the manipulation of its social forces. Without them it is bound to fall into periodic anarchy.

For this reason the imperialistic realists actually have a more hopeful program than the " balance of power " realists. They know that a balance of power must be organized and that a dominant power must be the organizing center. They expect either America, or the Anglo-Saxon hegemony, or the four great powers, Russia, China, Britain, and America, to form the organizing center of the world community. I think they are right in this thesis and that there is no possibility of organizing the world at all that will not be exposed to the charge of " imperialism " by the idealists who do not take the problem of power seriously.

But the imperialistic realists usually do not take the problem of justice seriously enough. An Anglo-Saxon imperialism might be a great deal better than a Nazi one; but the Nazi order is so purely destructive that a new imperialism could be a great deal better than nazism and yet not good enough to bring peace to the world. The new understandings with Russia, which cannot be overestimated, probably preclude the possibility of a pure Anglo-Saxon imperialism; and that is a great gain, however difficult the adjustments between Russia and the Western nations may prove to be.

But the real question is to what degree smaller nations can be drawn into the postwar reconstruction constitutionally so that their voice and power will be fitted into the whole scheme so that it will prevent the power of the dominant elements in the organization from becoming vexatious. Fortunately, many small nations are already related to the inchoate world scheme in the United Nations. But unfortunately the policies of the United Nations are not being democratically conducted. The Roosevelt Administration, despite its great superiority in political astuteness over the Wilsonian one, is failing at this point. Washington negotiates with many partners separately, and with Russia and Britain jointly to a considerable degree. But there is little indication of the gradual development of a democratic process on an international scale in the deliberations of the United Nations.

IV

It would be unjust to claim that the realists are consistently unaware of the problem of democratic justice in the realm of a gradually coalescing unity. There are many shades of thought among them. A few even manage to be imperialists in one breath and to speak of the " imposition of order " upon the world by dominant power, while in the next breath they elaborate plans for an ideal democratic federation of the world. But it is fair to say that, on the whole, the realists do not take this problem seriously enough.

It is of course a desperate problem. It includes not only the relation of smaller powers to the dominant ones, but the relation of undeveloped nations, who have no power at all, to the nations that do have power — in other words, the problem of imperialism in the stricter sense of the word. It includes the necessity of apportioning responsibility to the proportions of power as they actually exist. For constitutional arrangements that allowed smaller nations to determine policies, which they lacked the power to implement, could become as fruitful a source of new anarchy as unchecked dominant power could become a new source of tyranny.

Nor will any amount of forethought be able to solve all these problems. The solution of some of them depends upon the internal structure of the nations participating in world community. While it is not true that a just world order depends altogether upon political and economic democracy prevalent in the constituent nations, it is true that the stronger the internal political and moral checks upon the imperialistic impulse are, the easier will it be to solve the problem of external checks. If a stable peace depended altogether upon the achievement of an ideal democracy in the constituent nations, we would have to resign ourselves to decades of further purgatory. For obviously history does not move consistently in these matters; and we will have to include many nations of varying internal structures in any new world arrangements. The proposal for the federation of democratic nations only is a fantastic one, no less fantastic than, let us say, a plan for the exclusion of " poll tax " states from the Federal Union.

When all the difficulties are surveyed and all the necessities are kept in mind, it becomes almost axiomatic that anything like a perfect world organization is bound to elude us. There must be a tolerable equilibrium in it, and that equilibrium must be politically implemented; there must be an organizing center for it, and that center must be surrounded by checks to prevent its power from becoming vexatious; the organization must include many regional arrangements, and yet these regional arrangements must not run counter to the basic fact that the economic and political life of the nations is integrated in world, rather than regional, terms. The hazards to success are so great that we must be prepared to accept anything that keeps the future open; but we must also be prepared to contend for everything that represents a basic requirement of justice.

From the standpoint of Christian faith it is important to recognize that Christianity cannot be equated with "idealism" and that the Christian answer to a problem is not simply the most ideal possible solution that the imagination can conceive. A profound Christian faith knows something of the recalcitrance of sin on every level of moral and social achievement, and is, therefore, not involved in the alternate moods of illusion and disillusionment that harass the world of idealists and secularists. It knows something of the similarity between our own sin and the guilt of others, and will therefore not be pitiless if ideal possibilities are frustrated by the selfishness of others. But it also hears the divine command in every new historical situation. The Christian ought to know that the creation of some form of world community, compatible with the necessities of a technical age, is the most compelling command of our day.

46. THE SAN FRANCISCO CONFERENCE

On paper the San Francisco Conference has greatly improved the character of the United Nations organization, first outlined at Dumbarton Oaks. In reality the conference was unable to solve the main problem that confronted it, which was the establishment of a genuinely mutual accord between Russia and the West.

On paper the character of the charter was improved because the small nations made themselves heard and because general public discussion served to bring a greater degree of moral idealism into the charter. The power of the general assembly has been considerably enlarged and the veto power of the great nations has been slightly abridged. A preamble has been added which gives the charter a moral meaning that it did not have in the original document. An international bill of rights has also been added, the significance of which has been lauded by all international idealists, despite the fact that there is no international sovereignty that could enforce its provisions upon any constituent states. All in all the instrument that has come out of San Francisco deserves all the praise that the hopeful have bestowed upon it, provided you do not look too much beneath the surface.

Under the surface of this document the political realities are such as to give little assurance for the future. The simple fact is that no significant forms of mutual accord between Russia and the West have been reached though fairly plausible formulas have been found to cover up that fact. Hundreds of observers among the " consultants " at San Francisco, who have kept their various constituent bodies informed on the developments of the conference, have made their reports of the conference without once penetrating to the realities under the conference verbiage.

Thus for instance the conference was for a time in conflict on the problem of trusteeship. The Russians demanded that the trustees of backward regions should be committed to the proposition that the purpose of trusteeship was the ultimate independence of these

Christianity and Society, Summer, 1945.

regions. This was very smart of the Russians because they used almost the identical phrases, and certainly the very ideas, which American liberalism, Christian and secular, had advanced. Our religious delegation did in fact address a communication to Mr. Stettinius expressing embarrassment over the fact that the Russians, rather than we, were assuming leadership in championing the rights of the backward regions. But the communication did not mention, and its authors may not have apprehended, what was actually at stake in this issue.

The stake was the control of the Pacific. We were determined to have as many of the captured islands as possible as our outright possession and to hold the others under a form of trusteeship that would not interfere too much with our strategic plans. Actually the provisions of trusteeship are so loose that the whole scheme of trusteeship will prove to be more of a dishonest pretension than the mandate system in the old League of Nations. The Russians know that we have these strategic plans in the Pacific for other reasons than our fear of Japan; for we intend to destroy the power of Japan, root and branch. Therefore the Russians are trying to prevent us from securing as absolute a hold on the Pacific bases as the formula of trusteeship, which we proposed, allows. The Russians are not very plausible proponents of the international idealism that their formula of trusteeship implied, for they will hold the whole of Eastern Europe under a tutelage, which will be qualified to only the slightest degree by the provisions of the San Francisco Charter. But it is actually idle to measure the relative virtues and pretensions of Russia and the Western powers in regard to this matter. The important fact about the whole struggle was that it revealed a lack of mutual trust between Russia and the West.

In the same way the struggle over the problem of how the Pan-American regional system should be related to the world system betrayed a lack of mutual trust. We were anxious to devise a system that would give the budding communist movements in South America as little support from Russia as possible. The Russians sought on the other hand to discredit this regional system in the name of the world system, despite the fact that they have a regional system of their own which threatens the world system. There is little to choose between our pretensions and those of the Russians in regard to this matter, though the Russians were much shrewder, even while they were less diplomatic than we, in advancing their claims. Our State

Department placed itself in a ridiculous position when it allowed Argentina's admission to the conference to become a symbol of our position. But these relative advantages and disadvantages pale into insignificance beside the more important fact that every action of the conference proved how little mutual confidence between Russia and the West really exists. The Russian attitude toward Poland certainly contributed as much as any of our mistakes to accentuate, rather than mitigate, this mutual mistrust.

The final outcome of the conference is that a system of world security has been devised on paper, which does not hide too successfully that each of the great powers is to control a part of the world. Even the " sphere of influence " solution has not been achieved with complete success. None of the great powers is quite certain that one of the other powers may not poach in the preserves assigned to the other.

Such are the power-political realities of the San Francisco settlement. They do not fill the apprehensive and yet hopeful soul with too much confidence in the future. They have in fact prompted something akin to despair among some thoughtful observers, though such despair is premature. There may still be a possibility of gradually working out better schemes of mutual accord.

In the light of these facts the religious interpretations of the conference have been unbelievably naïve. We have been favored from time to time by estimates from our Federal Council delegation of the achievements of the conference. In these estimates the " six pillars of peace " of the Federal Council's Commission have been used as a yardstick of the achievements of the conference almost as if they were some kind of ultimate standard, some new decalogue. The various provisions of the conference dealing with international law, ideals of international justice, etc., have been carefully measured against these ideal standards. Plus and minus marks were indicated with careful discrimination. But nothing was said about the power-political realities that underlay all these words. One blueprint was compared with another. But the fact that no foundation for an international security system had been laid was not fully comprehended. There was no desire on the part of our observers to fool us. They had merely been so preoccupied with the blueprints that they had not bothered to look too carefully at the actual bricks that had been laid at San Francisco.

47. CAN WE ORGANIZE THE WORLD?

A friend, Rev. Mr. Mordhorst of Detroit, asks why *Christianity and Crisis* does not give unequivocal support of the World Federalist Movement. It seems to him, as indeed it has seemed to many others, that the Christian church should take the lead in a movement that challenges the idea of unreserved national sovereignty in a day in which it is obviously necessary to stretch our political loyalties to global proportions.

This question deserves an answer. The movement for world government takes two forms; according to the one, it is assumed that the institution of world government would rob the Russians of their fear and would bridge the chasm between the communist and the free world. This project is simply refuted by the observation that no law or constitutional arrangement can supply the mutual trust that is the necessary basis of any community. The law in fact presupposes such mutual trust; and where it is lacking, no constitution can function. The chasm between the communist and the free world is so deep that it can obviously not be bridged by any constitutional arrangement.

That is why only a very few abstract idealists hold to this interpretation of world government. The majority believe that a world constitution would be an ideal instrument for solidifying the resources of the free world and rendering it safe against communist infiltration. In answer to this proposal it must be pointed out that even if we eliminate the communist-democratic chasm there is little " social tissue " to bind up the so-called free world together. The most obvious cement is the common fear of all nations. This common fear prompts them into all kinds of *ad hoc* arrangements such as NATO and the proposed Pacific Pact, which do in effect erode unqualified national sovereignty and which do in fact establish community between them.

The question is whether more unequivocal constitutional arrangements would hasten the building of world community. To this question one must give a reserved negative answer in the light of previous experience. The history of India gives us a tragic example of the impotence of constitutions. The very effort to arrive at a common constitution heightened the tension between India and Pakistan and insured that the Moslem and Hindu communities would found two, rather than one, nations. A contrasting example is equally instructive. The new state of Israel is composed of very religious and very consistently secular Zionists. There is a rumor that when it was proposed to have a constitution for the new state a wise man warned against the venture on the ground that each party would try to secure a maximum of security in the constitution and thus accentuate the differences between them. It was better, he declared, for the two parties to live together as best they could. This common life would allay some of the fears and would throw up some *ad hoc* forms of accommodation that would serve the future as a constitution. So it proved. Life is a better unifier than law. Law can only define and perfect what life has established.

In a day as tragic as our own it would be pleasant to believe that there is a simpler way than the tortuous process by which the nations are finding the road to community with one another. But the short cuts are illusory. Constitutional questions, before sufficient community is established, are divisive rather than unifying. How, for instance, would we decide how many votes Denmark, let us say, and the United States should have in a World Federalist senate? And what would the debate over that question contribute to the common defense against an immediate peril? In community building, as in other great human enterprises, the motto must be " precept upon precept," " line upon line." It is not a bad thing to spell out ultimate goals as well as immediate responsibilities. But we must be cognizant of the fact that some people have a habit of fleeing to ultimate ideals as a way of evading immediate responsibilities. For the moment, at least, the great moral issue for Americans is how a rich and powerful nation relates itself to a weak and impoverished world. Not in terms of ultimate constitutional arrangements, but in terms of immediate political policies. Some of the constitutional issues will be either irrelevant or sensible answers to them will be unattainable until we have accustomed ourselves to responsibility for the world community in our day-to-day decisions.

C. The "Enemy"

48. LOVE YOUR ENEMIES

In times of social and political conflict there are always Christians who obscure the very genius of the New Testament conception of love by their particular interpretation of one form of the love commandment, namely, " Love your enemies." They insist that it is not possible to love anyone with whom one is in conflict, and that it is important for this reason never to come in conflict with anyone.

These idealists agree with the cynics who regard the commandment to love our enemies as demanding a psychological and moral absurdity of us. Without fully realizing it, they have changed the injunction and have given it quite a different meaning. This new meaning could be expressed in the words: You must love all men, and since it is impossible to love an enemy, you must have no enemy.

A certain rather hysterical Christian idealist is at the present moment touring the country with the message that all people who are participating in the war will become so corrupted by hatred that they will be incapable of contributing to a decent peace. He is, therefore, calling upon the handful of nonparticipants to hold themselves in readiness to build a new world after the rest of us have ruined it.

If the idealists who place this interpretation upon the New Testament commandment were really correct, it would be necessary to sacrifice even the most cherished principles and to become traitor to even the most solemn responsibilities if anyone dared to oppose the principles or to challenge our discharge of the responsibilities. For to remain true to our trust would bring us into conflict with those who oppose us and conflict invariably betrays into hatred.

There must be something wrong with this theory. There is, in fact, a good deal of evidence to refute it. Wars and conflicts undoubtedly tempt many people to hatred, but this hatred is not nearly as universal as our idealists assume. And it is least general among those who are engaged in the actual horrors of belligerency. The old ladies back home may do a good deal of hating. But the soldiers upon the battlefield usually do not hate. They have a much

Christianity and Society, Autumn, 1942.

more impersonal attitude toward the conflict than is usually assumed. As one of the commanders of the British Army recently
wrote to the Moderator of the Church of Scotland, " Morale is not
strengthened by hatred but only by a moral purpose that transcends personal and individual consideration." The Moderator had
objected to a new type of school in the British Army that was encouraging hatred. The Army man expressed his agreement with the
objections of the church leader.

Not all soldiers remain free of hatred. But there have been men in
situations of conflict through all the ages who understood something of the difference between the evil that they oppose and the
hapless and tragic individuals who are for the moment the embodi-
ment of that evil. This distinction is possible even if the individuals, who are the instruments of the evil, have acquiesced in it. How
can we measure the degree of consent that a German soldier gives
the Nazi creed? Or how can we know his responsibility or lack of responsibility for the convictions that he may hold in a system of
government that does not allow individuals to form convictions
freely?

The source of confusion in regard to the love commandment is
partly a linguistic one. It is derived from the poverty of the English
language. The word " love " in English covers many shades of
meaning. It means everything from a purely physical desire of one
person for another to the sacrificial passion that ended upon the
cross.

The " Greeks had a word " for love which the New Testament did
not find adequate to express its highest conception. That word was
erōs. The connotations of that word linger most obviously in the
English adjective derived from it — the word " erotic." It is a word
that is rooted in the natural life of sex and which defines first sex-
ual, and ultimately other forms of attachment between people.
Plato did his best to spiritualize the concept, and his " intellectual
love " is something that quite transcends physical desires. But it
may be questioned whether it ever transcends the interests of the
ego.

At any rate, the New Testament used a Stoic word agapē and
filled it with new meaning when it sought to define the love of the
Kingdom of God. This love is something more than even the most
refined form of sympathy, for it does not depend upon the likes
and dislikes that men may have for each other. It is not determined

by interest or passion. It is not the love that we have for people because we share common ideas with them, or because we are intrigued by the tilt of their nose, or because we admire their intellectual brilliance, or because we take pity upon their weakness. The Swedish theologian, Professor Nygren, has sought to prove in his interesting work *Agape and Eros* that the classical and the Christian conception of love stand in opposition to each other. In this he may have overstated the case. For when Jesus compares parental affection (which certainly belongs in the category of EROS) with God's love, as he does in the words, "If ye then, being evil, know how to give good gifts unto your children, how much more will your heavenly father give good gifts to them that ask him?" he is not setting EROS and AGAPE in complete contradiction to each other.

There is, nevertheless, a distinction between them. The love that the gospel demands is justified and validated only transcendentally. We are asked to love our enemies that we may be children of our Father in Heaven. An attitude of spirit is enjoined without any prudential or selfish consideration. We are not told to love our enemies because in that case they will love us in return. The love that is asked of us does not move on the plane of emotion or desire.

Such a love is not easily achieved. In a sense no one ever perfectly achieves it. But it is, at least, no psychological absurdity. It does not demand that we should be emotionally attached to someone with whom we are in conflict. It does demand that we should desire the good of our enemy. If achieved, it purges us of hatred; for hatred always has an egoistic root. In so far as even the purest devotion to principle never completely excludes consideration of our own interests, there will, therefore, be an element of egotism in the defense of our cause and an element of hatred in our opposition to the enemy. But in so far as it is possible to defend a cause, not primarily because it is to our interest to do so, but because we regard the cause as objectively right, it is also possible to contend against the opponents of that cause without hatred.

The love that the New Testament defines as AGAPE is spiritually difficult; but it is psychologically possible. Emotional attachment between people upon the basis of any number of considerations is spiritually easier, but it is psychologically impossible to have such attachments across the chasm of any historic conflict.

It would be foolish for Christians to deny the difficulty of avoiding hatred in conflict. Already the literature that seeks to fasten a

congenital guilt upon the German race is tremendous. Human beings, who have a natural inclination to accept the most adverse evidence in estimating the virtues and vices of groups other than their
own, are bound to accentuate this error in times of conflict.

Nor is it easy to desire the good of an opponent when in the immediate instance we are doing him harm. There will always be
moralists who will laugh and jeer at the very attempt of combining
this ultimate attitude with the immediate tragic task in hand. If
they were wholly right, no officer of the law could ever arrest a
criminal, and no warden could ever jail him without hatred.
Though we have known of police officers who were filled with vindictive passion toward criminals, there certainly have been many
others who have genuinely desired the ultimate good of the hapless
men whom they were forced to harm in the immediate instance. International conflicts are, of course, never completely analogous to
these instances of domestic justice. For they offer no such vantage
point of disinterested judgment, from which blame and punishment
may be apportioned. But it would be ridiculous to assert that there
can be no moral and spiritual disinterestedness in international
affairs, simply because there is no political vantage point for
its expression. Morals do not depend upon politics as slavishly as
that.

Sometimes the idealists who insist most rigorously upon the impossibility of loving those with whom we are at war are not as
scrupulous as they might be in their conflict, short of war, with their
opponents. William Lloyd Garrison was certain that the Christian
ethic forbade the Civil War. But he hated the Southern slaveowners
with a personal hatred and failed to make any distinction between
the historic evil of slavery and the individuals who were caught in
the system. Guilty of a lack of AGAPE toward his opponents before the North and South were in overt conflict, he insisted that
there should be no overt conflict because it would not be possible to
maintain EROS during the war. He never knew to what degree his
self-righteous hatred of the South actually contributed to the inevitability of the conflict.

The hatred of an enemy who does not fight us but merely opposes
us is frequently combined with the pious avowal that we will not
fight because we do not want to hate anyone. The confusion may
be aggravated by the linguistic difficulties to which we have referred.
But its root lies deeper than the poverty of a language.

49. THE BOMBING OF GERMANY

The bombing of the great industrial region of the Ruhr valley has raised some interesting religious and moral problems in both Britain and America. When one estimates the destruction in Britain and then reflects that four to ten times as many bombs are raining on the Ruhr region, one is able to envisage the terrible destruction that is being wrought in Germany.

It was significant that while the newspapers, and sometimes the Broadcasting Corporation, seemed to gloat over the " revenge " that American and British planes now exacted for the destruction in Britain, common people both in Britain and America had the decency to feel and express sorrow over the necessity of this terrible measure of war. A simple old elevator operator in a London hotel touchingly observed to the writer, " I don't care what the newspapers say; I think the bombing of those cities is terrible, however necessary." A young student at Oxford, product of the Christian Student Movement, and preparing for service in the Royal Air Force declared: " I have written to the B.B.C. [radio] to protest against its gloating announcements. I will probably do some bombing myself; but I will take no satisfaction in the human misery it causes."

It is natural of course for those who are inclined to pacifism to declare that those of us who support this war prove the untenability of our position by this moral embarrassment and discomfiture. For the bombing of cities is a vivid revelation of the whole moral ambiguity of warfare. It is not possible to defeat a foe without causing innocent people to suffer with the guilty. It is not possible to engage in any act of collective opposition to collective evil without involving the innocent with the guilty. It is not possible to move in history without becoming tainted with guilt.

Even the most righteous political cause is tainted with antecedent, concomitant, and consequent guilt. Every " righteous " national or political cause is partly guilty of the evil against which it contends. That is its antecedent guilt. It involves itself in the evil of causing suffering to the innocent. That is the concomitant guilt of its enterprise. It will also be unable to remain untainted of subsequent guilt; for it will most certainly corrupt the virtue of its victory by egoistic and vindictive passions. There is no escape from guilt in history. This is the religious fact that Saint Paul understood so well and that is so frequently not understood by moralistic versions of the Christian faith.

Once bombing has been developed as an instrument of warfare, it is not possible to disavow its use without capitulating to the foe who refuses to disavow it. No man has the moral freedom to escape from these hard and cruel necessities of history. Yet it is possible to express the freedom of man over the necessities of history. We can do these things without rancor or self-righteousness. It has been reported by both American and British authorities that pilots of bombing planes, professing the Christian faith, have sometimes refused to take Communion before their perilous trips. This hesitancy does credit to their conscience. They ought on the other hand to be helped to understand that the Lord's Supper is not a sacrament for the righteous but for sinners; and that it mediates the mercy of God not only to those who repent of the sins they have done perversely but also to those who repent of the sins in which they are involved inexorably by reason of their service to a " just cause."

The Kingdom of God, of which the Sacrament is the symbol, is on the one hand the peace that comes to the soul when it turns from sin to righteousness. It is on the other hand the peace of divine forgiveness, mediated to the contrite sinner who knows that it is not in his power to live a sinless life on earth. ✓

50. THE GERMAN PROBLEM

Of the many tragic aspects of our age, none is greater than the failure of Germany. It is the failure of a great people, fallen to as low a state of moral and political corruption as we are likely to see for many centuries. Such insanity as the Germans developed would not, of course, have been possible if the rest of the world had not provided a static corruption as the soil out of which the dynamic evil of the German mania developed. Nevertheless the failure of Germany is truly tragic. It must be understood if it is not to arouse the victors to vindictive passions that will destroy every possibility of a creative peace. For hatred is always blind and confuses the counsels of individuals and nations.

We cannot understand Germany by counting Nazi and anti-Nazi noses and by debating the question whether there are more Nazis than anti-Nazis in Germany. We are fools if we think that all Germans are Nazis, and only a little less foolish if we imagine that the German tragedy can be explained merely as a Nazi conspiracy against a good Germany. The parent of a wayward son is not necessarily wayward. But that does not absolve the " good " parent of responsibility for the waywardness of the son. There is a " good " Germany; but this " other " Germany participates in the failure of the nation. Perhaps the first contribution that a profound Christian faith could make to an analysis of the German problem would be to deliver our culture from the vulgar " Pelagianism " that thinks of good and evil only in terms of an explicit obedience to, or defiance of, a moral code. The " good " Germany was tragically inept in politics and contributed to the rise of Hitlerism by this ineptness. No conscious perversity, such as the Nazi exhibited, characterized the good Germany. And there is no form of calculated punishment that will either cure Germany of its profoundest errors or serve as a deterrent for others.

The Germans have been politically inept for many reasons. In terms of social history they were inept because the middle class revolution that laid the foundation for democracy in the Anglo-Saxon world never achieved sufficient self-respect in Germany to break the power of the old aristocratic military tradition. It was not even able to do so when the collapse after the first World War produced a coalition of bourgeois and proletarian forces behind democracy. The older aristocratic tradition remained in power behind the scenes. Even today the Junkers may be more dangerous for the future peace of the world than the more corrupt and more fragile Nazi culture.

If we seek to explain this lack of spiritual power of the rising middle classes, and finally even of the working classes, we touch upon a whole maze of cultural and religious factors. The Germans have always had a too uncritical devotion to the state. Perhaps they learned this from Luther, who made the mistake of being more afraid of anarchy than of tyranny. The Germans were always better realists than the Anglo-Saxons. But their political realism was tainted with cynicism; and that was a more grievous error than the

sentimentality that colored Anglo-Saxon idealism. The stuff of political history is always morally ambiguous; but it may be better to
be blind to the " power " factors in politics, if that is the only way
men can be relatively devoted to standards of justice, than to fall
into the cynicism of making power self-justifying.

The Germans are philosophically minded. In both their religious
and philosophical history they have illumined some of the ultimate
issues of life more profoundly than any other people since the
Greeks. But, like the Greeks, they have been deficient in dealing
with the proximate issues of life, particularly with the all-important
issue of organizing the human community. Perhaps eminence in the
one field contributed to failure in the other, not only because the
best minds were drawn away from the problems of the community
but more particularly because a tolerable political harmony in any
community requires compromises and adjustments that the " systems " of abstract thinkers do not allow. Long before Hitler made
politics demoniacally religious all political life in Germany was too
religious. There was a separate *Weltanschauung* behind every political party.

To these unique German causes of failure we must in all fairness
add some other causes that modern Germany shared with the modern world. German liberalism in its naïve form was even more naïve
than Anglo-Saxon liberalism. When Hindenburg and von Papen
conspired to destroy the Weimar republic the German labor liberals futilely appealed to the supreme court and forgot that the supreme court, particularly in a chaotic world, follows the election
returns, or the power-political analogy of election returns. German
liberalism in its sophisticated form was even more sophisticated
than Western liberalism. It had lost all faith in standards and values
of any kind. It created the religio-cultural vacuum, into which the
seven devils of Hitlerism entered.

German Marxism in its social-democratic variety distilled the illusion of fatalistic inaction from Marxist determinism. German
Marxism in its communist variety separated Marxist cynicism from
its realism, and made the cause of revolution an end in itself, even
to the point where it was willing to co-operate with Nazis to bring
it about. Furthermore the two forms of Marxism divided the working class between them; and both helped to divide the industrial
poor from the agrarian poor. These aberrations Germany shared
with us. Only we were not far enough advanced in our social

thought to be deeply harmed by them. It may be well to remember that it is still possible for us to make some of these mistakes fifty years hence.

One could go on indefinitely measuring the various strands of error and futility that contributed to the rise of Hitlerism. Perhaps we have gone far enough to justify the suggestion that any imaginative approach to the failure of the German people must result in the conviction that the failure is too profound and elusive to be amenable to some simple form of calculated punishment, however exacting. We can save neither the German people nor ourselves by some nicely measured punitive justice. This tragedy can be comprehended in prayer and in tears; but it is not understood by either the soft or the hard sentimentalists.

The real problem about Germany is not how we can punish her but how we can finally relate her creatively to a community of nations. Perhaps the most serious part of this problem arises from the fact that she has automatically excluded herself from leadership in the organization of the European Continent, thus forcing essentially non-Continental world powers to organize the Continent, a difficult and desperate undertaking in which they may not succeed.

The final health of Germany depends upon the creation of a healthy Continent, just as a healthy Continent also requires an ultimately healthy and sane Germany, and as a tolerably healthy world community requires a decently reorganized European Continent. Our future destinies are thus mutually intermingled. The peril of vindictiveness lies primarily in the fact that it beguiles us from pursuing our mutual destiny. Any theory that assumes that we can solve the world's problem merely by fathoming the depth of evil in the German soul and seeking to suppress it betrays us into the evils into which self-righteousness is always betrayed. It does not understand that the evil against which we contend is only a different, and probably a more extravagant, form of the evil that is in our soul also.

Just as self-righteousness is the root of vindictiveness, so is contrition and the recognition of mutual guilt its cure. It is a question whether the recognition of the mutuality of guilt is possible in any other than profoundly religious terms. This is why the preaching of the gospel is so relevant to the reconciliation of nations. All conflict, and not only military conflict, makes for self-righteousness. We are better than the foe against whom we contend. There are at least many cases in which this is the case. But we are nevertheless profoundly involved in the sin of the foe. Sometimes we are guilty of milder forms of the evils that we oppose in the foe. One thinks of the pride of races and nations in the so-called democratic world as a potent source of international friction long after the Nazis are destroyed. Sometimes we are guilty of opposite errors. One thinks of the international anarchy of the democratic world that gave the tyranny of nazism its chance.

Yesterday we had to stand against the sentimentalists who declared that we had no right to resist Nazi tyranny because we were also guilty. They did not know that common guilt is a perennial fact in history, which does not annul our responsibility to strive for relative justice. Today we must resist the pharisees who imagine that our impending victory is the proof and the validation of our virtue. Yesterday the sentimentalists falsely regarded the humility that men ought to have in God's sight as a reason for being humble in the sight of the Nazis. Today the self-righteous Philistines will seek falsely to play the part of God and try to summon the defeated foe to a judgment in which they are themselves involved.

The recognition of the mutuality of guilt does not of course preclude the necessity and advisability of relative punishment for the relatively guilty. Here it will be important to make a sharp distinction between the profound guilt of the German people, which is too deep to be reached by our punishment, and the particular guilt of particular Nazi tyrants. It goes without saying that specific acts of tyranny and cruelty ought to be punished. It may be shocking to suggest that some of this punishment may well take place exactly in the hour of the Nazi collapse. The idea of international courts to try these criminals for the sake of establishing the sanctity of international law is largely illusory. An international court organized by victors may have the form, but will not have the substance, of such sanctity. It may make martyrs out of criminals. At any rate it may be better to have Germans destroy their criminals in hot blood than have the victors do it in cold blood. Either way has its hazards; and both ways will undoubtedly be tried. There is no reason for a zealous preference for one over the other.

It may be shocking to observe, but it is nevertheless true, that one reason for the severe punishment of these individual criminals is that it may act as a catharsis and draw off some of the vindictiveness

that Nazi cruelties have generated. Thus there would be less likelihood that vengeance will bedevil the peace.

As for the punishment of the German people as such, it must be
taken for granted that they must make restitution to the despoiled
peoples in so far as this is possible. This applies particularly of
course to the wealth that the Nazis have siphoned out of the whole
of Europe. No restitution will return its dead to life. But the possibilities here are limited. The last war proved the futility of long
reparation payments in terms of both economics and morals. Christian piety might well add counsel to the wisdom of the nations on
this point and remind them of the word of Scripture: " Vengeance
is mine, I will repay, saith the Lord." Which means that the processes of history under the providence of God visit such terrible punishment upon the evildoer that our power to add or subtract from
it seems puny indeed, and our effort to do so pretentious. The majesty of the German cities will have been reduced to rubble. The defeated nation will be politically, economically, morally, and spiritually bankrupt. It will face chaos and humiliation in every direction.
The war has punished the victors also. But no one would quarrel
at the justice of that fact, since they are also guilty of the evils that
we are seeking to overcome. If there is a difference in the proportion of guilt, as indeed there is, would anyone question that this is
not sufficiently measured by the difference between victory and
defeat?

No matter how we turn this problem or from what angle we approach it, it becomes apparent that the punishment of a guilty and
defeated nation is a very subordinate problem in reconstituting our
world. If we become obsessed with it, it will prevent us from ac-
complishing our real task.

Our real problem is to build a world community strong enough
to discourage the kind of aggression that the Nazis attempted. Our
real problem is to strengthen the bonds of mutual responsibility
between the nations in such a way that a future aggressor will not
be able to pit one peace-loving nation against another, or persuade
them to await the acts of the despoiler, each in turn, while all look
on in shivering and cowardly impotence. Our real task is to find political implements for the budding sense of mutual responsibility
that now exists. Our task is to find a working accord between the
hegemonous powers. If this is not done, one of them may well draw
Germany into its orbit, make it a partner in some future war, and

justify some future Vansittart in the thesis that Germany is congenitally corrupt.

Our problem is to extend the partnership between the hegemonous powers in such a way it will lead to the reorganization of the European and Asiatic continent. If for instance Europe is partitioned into spheres of influence between the great powers (a still possible and terrible method of briefly mitigating the conflict of interests between them), we will have another war, no matter what we do about Germany. In that case we may well find France in the position of championing the cause of the Continent against the hegemonous powers, and we might find a De Gaulle in the role of a slightly more decorous Hitler. Incidentally, the obsession of the tragic guilt of Germany has made us blind to the pathetic decay of France and oblivious to the fact that French tuberculosis may be as difficult to cure as German cancer.

In any event the primary task of the victorious nations is with themselves. They have the responsibility of organizing the world community. They have the power to do so. The future depends upon their willingness to use power responsibly and justly. If they fail, the German insanity may continue and be aggravated. If they succeed, Germany can be rehabilitated in the world community of nations.

It is important to remember that vengeance is an egoistic corruption of the sense of justice. It is concerned with what the enemy has done to us. Therefore it is inclined to forget the sin of the enemy against the community of mankind and against God and to obscure the like sin that we have committed. That is why it is important to remember that, whatever the validity of our relative judgments, the final judgment belongs to God, who sees into the secret of our hearts. " Therefore judge nothing before the time, until the Lord come who both will bring to light the hidden things of darkness and will make manifest the counsels of the heart; and then shall every man have his praise of God."

51. WHAT IS JUSTICE?

The war trials in Tokyo and Nuremberg continue, like some morning echo of last night's nightmare. In Tokyo they have just condemned six of the war leaders, including Tojo, to die. No one in Japan seemed concerned about the sentence of Tojo; but the audience in the chamber whispered, " Hard! hard! " on hearing the other sentences.

The "war criminals" who were guilty of various forms of cruelty no doubt deserved the punishment meted out to them. Those who were indicted and convicted of plotting an "aggressive war" stand in a different case. The whole idea of trying national leaders of a defeated nation on the charge of aggression is a project that only the pride of victors could have dictated. This does not mean that the accused may not have been guilty of plotting a warlike attack. But in the absence of a genuine international community, who is to determine what distinguishes an aggressive from a defensive war? If the victors set themselves up as judges, the vanquished will react with cynical contempt. They will regard the verdict as proving merely that the culprits lost the war. One can well imagine that wholly discredited war leaders in Japan will regain a certain measure of sympathy by achieving the position of national martyrs.

We have left some important dimensions of justice out of account in this whole procedure. We have forgotten that a court sentence must not merely be inherently just but must proceed from a tribunal that has a prestige for justice. That prestige is, of course, primarily derived from the guarantees of impartiality in the structure of the juridical institution. If the court rests upon a partial interest, its sentence will not be accepted as just, even if it should rise above the prejudices of the group which it represents.

Actually, the vanquished nations might have accepted a death sentence, executed on Tojo in hot blood in the hour of victory, as more just than this belated sentence, ground out years after the war's end. It would have belonged to the passions of the war. The present sentence pretends to belong to the measured wisdom of peace; but it cannot disguise the pride of the victors which dictates it. It is merely a special case of the old sin of man, his inclination to play the part of God.

Furthermore, the sentences reveal the inability of men and of nations to gauge the limits of justice in overcoming evil. Evil must of course be punished. But punitive justice has only a limited efficacy either in deterring from future crime or in changing the heart of the criminal. Forgiveness without punitive justice degenerates into sentimentality. But punitive justice without forgiveness becomes abortive. This is the more true in the relation of nations to each other because they cannot rise to a genuinely impartial justice. If they pretend to an impossible impartiality, they rob the justice of which they are capable of its redemptive power. Nations as such know nothing of a gospel of forgiveness. They are by nature self-righteous and vindictive. Yet one might have hoped that they could at least have touched the fringes of the mystery of the relation of forgiveness to punishment.

D. The Bomb

52. THE ATOMIC BOMB

Everybody recognizes that the atomic bomb has introduced a new dimension into the already complex realities of a technical society. Long before we had adjusted ourselves to the technical power, already in our possession, and brought it under the control of moral purpose and communal justice, we are confronted with this terrifying new dimension.

It is almost idle to speculate on the effect of atomic energy upon the peaceful industrial enterprise. We do not yet know how it will be harnessed to peacetime pursuits, how greatly it will multiply the productive capacity of the worker in industry, and to what degree it will therefore increase the perils of unemployment. The very fact that one thinks first of the perils of unemployment when one measures a new productive power proves how far society is from socially mastering the technical instruments already developed. We may be certain of only one thing in regard to the influence of atomic energy upon the social structure: it will hasten the general tendency toward socialization, whether for good or ill. It will do this for two reasons. One is that atomic energy has been developed by public funds; and the scientific labors, which have culminated in this achievement, have been co-operative and common. There is therefore slight possibility of the alienation of this public resource into private hands. The other reason is that the potentialities of this new energy are too great to permit any group of private persons to determine how it is to be used and how communal adjustments in the productive process, occasioned by the introduction of this new power, are to be made. The more new inventions introduce vast new potencies into an already complex industrial process, the more it becomes necessary for the community as such to determine how the power is to be used for the sake of gaining a maximum contribution for the general welfare and reducing the perils to a minimum.

The actual introduction of atomic energy into the military might of nations presents even more tremendous problems than those occasioned by its possible introduction into industrial power. First of all, it must be considered that atomic energy in military

Christianity and Society, Fall, 1945.

terms means destructive power. It is a weapon that can only be used, as it was used in the closing days of the war, for purposes of rather indiscriminate destruction. This proves that "total" war is not a Nazi invention. The Nazi only hastened and accentuated a historical logic implicit in a technical civilization. Technical society produces total war, because it enables men to harness the resources of a society for a certain end totally; and its instruments of destruction become more and more total. The thoughtful element in the democratic world has a very uneasy conscience about the use of the bomb against the Japanese. Critics have rightly pointed out that we reached the level of Nazi morality in justifying the use of the bomb on the ground that it shortened the war. That is exactly what the Nazis said about the destruction of Rotterdam and Warsaw. They claimed that a brief conflict aiming at total destruction was more merciful than a long-drawn-out war. In any case the use of the bomb was merely the culmination of our own strategy of total war, involving the use of ever more powerful obliteration bombing and incendiarism. Mr. Churchill reported honestly on how he and President Truman reached the decision to use the bomb after it had become apparent that, without it, the war against Japan might last many more months. It is a simple matter to condemn the statesmen who made the decision to use the bomb. The question is whether they were not driven by historic forces more powerful than any human decision. If we remember that the bomb was developed in competition with the Germans and under the lash of the fear that they might perfect it before we did, it becomes apparent that it was not possible to refuse to develop it. Once perfected, it was difficult to withhold it when its use held out the prospect of a quicker end of the war. We can criticize the statesman, however, for lack of imagination in impressing the enemy with the power of the bomb without the wholesale loss of life that attended our demonstration of its power. Suppose we had announced the perfection of the bomb to the enemy, threatened its ultimate use, and given some vivid demonstrations of its power in places where the loss of life would have been minimal. The moral advantage of such imagination would have been tremendous. As matters stand now, we have completely lost our moral position, particularly in the Orient. We speak rather glibly of the necessity and possibility of repentance on the part of Japan, without recognizing how difficult we have made repentance for a vanquished foe who feels that he was defeated by the use of an illegitimate form of destructiveness.

In regard to the future, it is almost idle to speculate what effect the bomb will have upon military strategy or the prospects of peace. It increases the general horror of war and thereby presumably adds something to the power of the will of nations to achieve an orderly world. But as soon as we look at the problem in terms of the detailed politics of international relations we have less assurance. For the moment the possession of this power of destruction increases the political power of the nations possessing it. Ultimately it may equalize military strength because it places a fairly cheap form of destructiveness in the hands of even weak nations, provided they have uranium deposits. For the moment, the possession of this destructive power establishes an even greater preponderance of power for the nations who hold the secret.

This fact might make for peace, though hardly for justice, provided that the great nations possessed this new power in common. But they do not. It is an Anglo-Saxon resource at the moment. The *London Sunday Observer* has noted that the unveiling of the bomb has given the Western powers an advantage over Russia, which will prevent Russia from challenging them as soon as it might have done under other circumstances. But suppose Russia asks to share in the secret, as the *London Daily Worker* has already suggested that she should? And suppose the secret is withheld and Russia then proceeds to elaborate this energy herself? For the secret behind the bomb is hardly a secret. The formulas are now sufficiently well known to permit anyone to develop them if they have the resources to do so.

It is, in other words, not probable that the introduction of this new energy will increase the unity among the hegemonous powers. It is much more likely that it will increase mutual apprehension among them. Thus there is no positive immediate gain for world peace in the introduction of this new destructive device.

The matter can be put more simply. The creation of a new dimension of military power could make the world more secure only if a stable universal government, which would have exclusive use of the power, could be presupposed. Lacking such a government and such a universal authority, a new power introduced into the military situation accentuates disunion and not order.

Ultimately, of course, the bomb may make for peace, because it proves that we must achieve an organized society in global terms or perish. But the prospect for the next decades, or indeed for the next century, is not reassuring.

53. THE HYDROGEN BOMB

Each age of mankind brings forth new perils and new possibilities. Yet they are always related to what we have known before. The age of atomic bombs, suddenly developing into a thousand times more lethal hydrogen bombs, is very different from the age of scythe and plowshare. It confronts us with the possibility of mutual mass annihilation. Yet we are no different from our fathers. Our present situation is a heightened and more vivid explication of the human situation.

One basic similarity between ourselves and our fathers is that our power over the course of human history is limited. We had imagined that the very technics that finally produced atomic destruction would make us the masters of history. But they merely produce an increased amount of power over nature that has a dubious role in the affairs of men. When we confront the problem of bringing the destructive possibilities of this power under moral control, the whole ambiguity of the human situation is more fully revealed.

Consider the facts. We had the knowledge to produce the more lethal bomb four years ago, but wisely did not exploit it. Then, when the news came that the Russians had the A-bomb, we were certain that they would be, as we were, on the way to achieving the more deadly H-bomb. There seemed, therefore, nothing to do but give orders to develop it. The fact that this was done without public debate represents a real threat to the democratic substance of our life. This merely accentuates the danger in which we have been ever since secret weapons have been developed. It is, at any rate, fairly certain that, had the President submitted the matter to Congress, the decision would have been identical with the one he made. Thus we have come into the tragic position of developing a form of destruction which, if used by our enemies against us, would mean our physical annihilation; and if used by us against our enemies, would mean our moral annihilation. What shall we do?

Christianity and Society, Spring, 1950.

The pacifists have a simple answer. Let us simply renounce the use of such a weapon, together with our enemies if possible, but alone if necessary. This answer assumes that it is possible to summon the human will to defy historical development with a resounding no. But where is this " human will " which could rise to such omnipotence? Unfortunately we do not have moral access to the Russian will. We have to limit ourselves to the will of America and of the Western world. Could we possibly, as a nation, risk annihilation or subjugation for the sake of saying no to this new development of destruction? Could we risk letting the Russians have the bomb while we are without it? The answer is that no responsible statesman will risk putting his nation in that position of defenselessness. Individuals may, but nations do not, thus risk their very existence. Would a gesture of defenselessness possibly soften the Russian heart? That is the other possibility implied in the pacifist solution. The answer is that we have no such assurance. Granted the Russian hope and belief that it has the possibility of bringing its peculiar redemption to the whole world, it is not likely to be impressed by any " moral " gesture from what it believes to be a decadent world. In other words, our will is neither powerful enough nor good enough to accomplish the miracle expected of us in the pacifist solution.

Yet we are never the prisoners of historical destiny, even though all pretensions of being its master have crumbled. What shall we do within the limits of our power? Perhaps, since the so-called Baruch plan has become obsolete through the loss of our monopoly in atomic destruction, the thing to do is to revise our proposals and make another effort to secure agreement with the Russians. This course of action is widely approved; and it probably ought to be tried. But it has little prospect of success. The Russians are almost certain to demand general disarmament as the price for any agreement in the field of atomic energy. That means that they believe it possible to dominate Europe politically if the military defenses against its encroachments are removed. We cannot pay that price because we cannot afford to deliver Europe over to communism.

Perhaps the most feasible possibility is that proposed by a group of eleven scientists who have suggested that we produce the H-bomb but make a solemn covenant never to use it first. This proposal has several merits. It would serve to allay some of the apprehensions that the world feels about our possible use of the bomb. It would also restrain those elements in our defense department who are placing undue reliance on the bomb and who may, if we are not careful, so develop our defenses that we could not win a war without using the bomb. It would also tend to counteract all those tendencies in our national life which make for the subordination of moral and political strategy to military strategy. We must not forget that, though we must be prepared to defend ourselves in case of war, it is more important to overcome communism by moral, economic, and political measures. In that case we would not have to fight the war for which the strategists are preparing our defenses. For this reason the proposals of Senator McMahon, looking toward a tremendous expansion of our aid to the Western world, are of great significance.

The refusal to use the bomb first is not of itself a sufficient strategy. But such a refusal would tend to encourage all the more positive strategies for preserving both peace and civilization. Yet the refusal to use the bomb first does have a further significance. We would be saying by such a policy that even a nation can reach the point where it can purchase its life too dearly. If we had to use this kind of destruction in order to save our lives, would we find life worth living? Even nations can reach a point where the words of our Lord, "Fear not them which are able to kill the body but rather fear them that are able to destroy both soul and body in hell," become relevant.

The point of moral transcendence over historical destiny is not as high as moral perfectionists imagine. But there is such a point, though the cynics and realists do not recognize it. We must discern that point clearly. A nation does not have the power to say that it would rather be annihilated than to produce a certain weapon. For, as the scientists have asserted, the production of that weapon may serve to guarantee that it will never be used. But to use such a weapon first represents a quite different moral hazard. It ought not to be impossible to nations to meet that hazard successfully.

PART
IV

---

*Love and Justice
and the Pacifist Issue*

54. A CRITIQUE OF PACIFISM

THE ATTITUDE OF THE AVERAGE MAN TOWARD HIS fellows is one of nicely balanced trust and mistrust, of confidence and fear. The relation of human groups to each other is usually characterized by the same kind of mixed attitude, though in group relations there is usually a little more fear and a little less trust, for the simple reason that groups have generally not been as ethical as individuals. Common sense would seem to justify such an attitude, for human nature is an intriguing amalgam of potential virtue and inchoate vice, in proportions sufficiently variable to prompt both trust and fear. The average man who has been taught by necessity to trust his fellow men, since an attitude of consistent mistrust would destroy all social life, nevertheless tempers this inclination by the shrewd observation that his virtue, carried to an extreme, may invite aggression and tempt his fellows to dishonesty.

This common-sense view of human relations is always under the necessity of maintaining itself against two forces that tend to disintegrate it. On the one hand, man easily becomes the victim of fear complexes that completely destroy his inclination to trust his fellow men. They usually follow upon some harrowing experience, some evidence of specific dishonesty or aggression, which for the moment outweighs all that man has learned about the general dependability of human nature. Sometimes, as in the case of some national groups in Europe since the war, such fear complexes are definitely pathological. On the other hand, the common-sense balance is threatened by the imagination of a minority, usually a religious minority, which maintains that trust is itself creative, that men tend to

The Atlantic Monthly, May, 1927.

become what we think they are, that they become trustworthy only as we trust them and lovable only as we love them. Whenever such religious imagination is developed to its highest potency, it not only essays to strengthen the forces of virtue by assuming them, but it definitely undertakes to overcome developed evil by failing to take cognizance of it. So Jesus counsels his followers to forgive, not seven times, but seventy times seven, and to turn the other cheek if they have been made the victims of aggression.

On the whole the common-sense attitude toward other men is not seriously imperiled by this force of religious imagination. Imagination is a virtue and achievement that is rare at best and that only occasionally rises to such a potency that it is able to create as well as to discover hidden virtue in other men. Even religion undertakes to cultivate that type of imagination only in rare moments of insight and power, and usually contents itself with maintaining the common-sense balance against the threat of unbalanced fears and hatreds. Yet there are times when mutual fears, resulting in mutual hatreds, reduce themselves to such an absurdity that large numbers of men are prompted to experiment with the attitude of trust. We are living in an age in which one element in every nation is still suffering from pathological fears created by the World War and another element in every national group is more than ordinarily anxious to adopt an attitude of trust because it has realized that the war was itself a spontaneous combustion resulting from excessive fears and hatreds. That is why the question of preparedness, of armament and disarmament, is so urgent in practically every Western nation.

Because of these influences of the war, large numbers of people espouse the cause of pacifism, of nonresistance and mutual trust, who realize only dimly what is involved in the adventure of trust. Many of them insist that if our nation or any other nation would be willing to make the venture of disarming itself, it could successfully challenge its neighbors to similar experiments in confidence. Still more believe that, while no nation can run the risk of making the venture alone, there is no reason why a simultaneous experiment in disarmament and mutual trust should not be initiated.

There is of course much to be said for this faith. If it accomplishes nothing else, it will at least help to re-establish the old common-sense balance of trust and mistrust which the war hatreds destroyed. But it is hardly sufficiently thoroughgoing to build the new world of which it dreams. Its weakness lies in the fact that it does not realize how consistent an ethical attitude toward other groups and individuals must be before it becomes in any sense a guaranty of security. Creative love must express itself not only in trust but in sacrifice. It may do for a Francis of Assisi to trust his fellow men and assume that even a bandit will finally do him no wrong; but it would be foolish for a village banker who holds a mortgage on most of the homes in the village to make a sudden venture in trust and decide to have his vaults open. He may have a legal and even a moral right to collect interest on his mortgages, yet it is not an insistence on rights, but a sacrifice of rights for the sake of fellowship, which finally creates that type of relationship in which there is security without recourse to force.

II

Applied specifically to our own and other nations, this means that the moral task that faces our generation is to persuade groups — groups of every kind, but particularly nations — to a measure of unselfishness as well as to a measure of trust toward their neighbors. That is a formidable task. Groups have never been unselfish in the slightest degree. L. P. Jacks has observed that all human groups tend to be predatory. Henry Adams, who shrewdly observed that the statesmen of England equivocated on the slavery issue during the Civil War until they could determine their course by considerations of expediency, came to the melancholy conviction: " Masses of men are always prompted by interest rather than conscience. Morality is a private, and a costly, luxury."

One reason why modern civilization finds itself in such moral chaos is that intergroup relationships are increasingly becoming more important than intragroup relationships without becoming as moral. It is difficult to introduce ethical attitudes into the relations between groups, partly because these relationships are comparatively recent and partly because the individual, even if he possesses a sensitive conscience, is not inclined to demand ethical actions of his group as long as his own attitude toward the group is ethical. There is an increasing tendency among modern men to imagine themselves ethical because they have delegated their vices to larger and larger groups. Yet the groups are not large enough to give moral unity to mankind, and the whole process may simply tend to make the next war an intercontinental war, a real world war instead of merely a Western world war.

Ethical individuals tend to condone unethical group actions partly because their individual attitude toward their group easily obscures the essentially selfish attitude of the group; but partly it is a strategy by which they are able to indulge their weaknesses without seeming to do so. We are proud, as white men, in our relation to other races because there is comparatively little opportunity to indulge our pride among white men. If we bully Mexico, that is partly to compensate ourselves for the lost opportunities of bullying individual neighbors.

Sometimes group selfishness is further aggravated by the inability of the individual citizen to see the consequences of national action in the attitudes of other nations who are geographically remote but in intimate economic contact with our own nation. America today has a standard of living in such flagrant disproportion to that of any other part of the world that it is arousing the envy of practically every nation. Dispassionate observers agree that America is falling into disfavor in every part of the world because the world is either envious of our luxury or afraid of our economic power. The envy may be unethical, but it is inevitable; and fear may not be justified by any malice in our hearts, but it is natural. A belligerently nationalistic paper recently criticized President Coolidge for insisting that we shall not arouse the mistrust of the world by increasing our armaments. The world hates us — so ran the argument of the journalistic critic — not for our armaments, but for our tariff and our immigration policy. The point would seem to be well taken. The feeling that the question of inter-Allied debts has created in European countries is but a symptom of a general attitude toward us, which is prompted by the fact that we live in a paradise that is protected by the two walls of the tariff and immigration restriction. Our immigration policy might be ethically defended by the reflection that as long as there is no universal birth control any effort to equalize the relation of national resources to population must prove abortive. Yet it is not this consideration which prompts our policy. We simply assume, as does every other nation, that it is our duty as well as our right to protect and preserve any advantages that our citizens may enjoy above those of other peoples.

Millions of Americans, not all of them thoroughgoing pacifists, of course, who are passionate in their espousal of world peace and disarmament, have never given the slightest consideration to these economic realities. They want America to trust the world and are sure that the world will in turn trust America. Their faith is too naïve. They do not realize that a nation cannot afford to trust anyone if it is not willing to go to the length of sharing its advantages. Love that expresses itself in trust without expressing itself in sacrifice is futile. It is not thoroughgoing enough to be creative or redemptive.

Since it is more difficult for groups than for individuals to moralize their actions, and since nations have long enjoyed complete moral autonomy, it would be foolish to expect any immediate or easy spiritualizing of national conduct; nor is it necessary to postpone every policy of international trust until nations have become completely ethical in their conduct. But it is obvious that it is at least as important to create an unselfish national attitude as to adopt policies of mutual trust. This fact is easily obscured, particularly in those nations which for the moment enjoy the highest privileges. There are Continental cynics and shrewd observers in other parts of the world who slyly suggest that pacifism is a virtue that only the two great Anglo-Saxon nations are able to enjoy. The implication is that England and America are the only two really solvent nations in the Western world, and that, since they have what they want and need, it is to their interest to preach peace. The hungry nations will meanwhile fail to react to this moral idealism. They will shrewdly and cynically observe that it is always the tendency of those who have to extol the virtue of peace and order and to place those who have not at a moral disadvantage.

It is quite impossible for the strong to be redemptive in their relation to the weak if they are not willing to share the weakness of the weak, or at least to equalize in some degree the disproportion of advantages.

III

It is for this reason that the " outlawry of war " idea so passionately espoused by many Americans takes so little root in Europe. The " outlawry of war " program is practically to adopt pacifism on a mutual and international scale, to persuade the nations of the earth to simultaneously disavow the use of force. Logically and legally the plan seems perfect. But it is weak psychologically. In a sense it is typically American; for America is sufficiently impregnable in her position to be emancipated from the fear complexes that disturb European, particularly Continental, nations, and she is sufficiently privileged to desire the use of force no more for purposes of aggression than for needs of defense. Meanwhile the insistence of many American peace idealists that America must not enter Europe and make its problems ours until Europe disavows the use of force merely tends to become an ethical sublimation of an essentially selfish national position. It gives moral sanction to a policy of isolation that has its real basis in quite other considerations. The real reason why we do not associate intimately with Europe is that we have many advantages that might be sacrificed in a too intimate fellowship. The general effect of the outlawry program is to beguile a nation that stands aloof to preserve the advantages of its strength into believing that it stands alone to preserve the advantages of its virtue.

In this connection it is to be noted that some of our statesmen and publicists who are most critical of European armaments and the alleged sanction of war in the Covenant of the League of Nations are the very ones who are most unyielding in the matter of inter-Allied debts. Senator Borah, who is in many respects the most honest and rugged statesman in Washington, and whose attitude in regard to Oriental and South American questions is probably the greatest single force for the moralizing of our national conduct, is singularly obtuse in regard to this European problem. For the peace of the world, it would be an immeasurable advantage if we could forget some of our moral scruples against Europe for the sake of entering into a more intimate fellowship with her, in which there might be some chance of mitigating the fears and hatreds that American wealth and strength are creating in impoverished Europe.

In a sense our advocates of national preparedness represent the sober common sense of the nation against the moral obfuscation of many peace enthusiasts. A strong and privileged nation, strong enough to be emancipated from the fear of any immediate attack, and privileged enough to need nothing that the force of arms might be able to secure, may indulge the peace ideal for the moment. But ultimately both its strength and its privilege will incite enmity and aggression. Except it uses its strength more wisely than seems probable from past history, and shares its privileges more unselfishly than any nation has yet been inclined to, it is bound to array the world against it. That is the prospect that America faces.

Those of us who are pacifists ought to realize more clearly than we do that spiritual attitudes can never guarantee us security in the possession of material advantages. There is much to be said for the position that a civilization and a culture may not only be protected without the use of force, but that they can be maintained uncorruptibly in no other way. But it requires an army to preserve a higher standard of living than the rest of the world enjoys. An essentially selfish nation cannot afford to be trusting. Its selfishness destroys the redemptive and morally creative power of its trust.

Many individual idealists are taking the justified position that the best way to bring unethical groups under ethical control is to disassociate themselves clearly from the unethical conduct of the group, at whatever cost. Too few of them have realized that if such action is to be morally redemptive, it must disassociate the individual not only from the policy of using physical force but from the policy of insisting on material advantages that destroy human fellowship and make the use of force necessary.

55. PACIFISM AND THE USE OF FORCE

When defining pacifism and discussing its relation to the social problems of modern society, it is important to begin by disclaiming the right to express anyone's opinion except one's own. Pacifists are no more divided than other groups who try to apply general principles and ideals to the specific facts of the common life; but it is inevitable that they should hold with varying degrees of consistency to the common principles that bind them into a group. In a general way pacifists may be defined as social idealists who are profoundly critical and skeptical of the use of physical force in the solution of social problems. At the extreme left in the pacifist group are the apostles of thoroughgoing nonresistance, who refuse to avail themselves of the use of physical force in any and every situation. At the right are the more circumspect social analysts who disavow the use of force in at least one important social situation,

The World Tomorrow, May, 1928.

as, for instance, armed international conflict. What really unites this group in spite of its varying shades of conviction is the common belief that the use of force is an evil. The consistent exponents of nonresistance would regard it as an unnecessary evil in all situations. Those who are less consistent regard it as an evil in all situations but as a necessary evil in some situations.

The writer abhors consistency as a matter of general principle because history seems to prove that absolute consistency usually betrays into some kind of absurdity. He must begin, therefore, by stating two positions that represent the two poles of his thought. One is that the use of physical violence in international life has impressed itself upon his mind as an unmitigated and unjustified evil. The other is that some form of social compulsion seems necessary and justified on occasion in all but the most ideal human societies. Between these two positions a line must be drawn somewhere, to distinguish between the use of force as a necessary and as an unnecessary evil. Different men of equal intelligence and sincerity will draw that line in different places. Perhaps some, while claiming to be critical of the use of force, will find it practically necessary in so many situations that they may hardly be counted among the pacifists. It is necessary, therefore, to draw an arbitrary line and count only those among the pacifists who express their critical attitude toward the use of force by disavowing it completely in at least one important situation. Perhaps it ought to be added that a true pacifist will prove the sincerity of his conviction by seeking the diminution of force and by experimenting with other methods of social co-operation in every social situation.

Armed international conflict stands in a category of its own because history has proved its worthlessness as a method of solving social problems so vividly that it has become practically impossible to justify it on any moral grounds. It is morally so impotent and so perilous chiefly for two reasons. One is that force in an international dispute is used by the parties to a dispute, and it therefore aggravates rather than solves the evils and misunderstandings that led to the dispute. If there is any possibility of force being redemptive, it is an absolute prerequisite that it be exerted by an agency that is impartial and unbiased with reference to the controversy. The other reason is that the use of force in international conflict inevitably issues in the destruction of life and, what is more, in the destruction of the lives of many who have had no share in the dispute and who are innocent of the evils that a war may be designed to eliminate.

If international conflict is outlawed on these two grounds, it would follow that the use of force by some society of nations would fall in a different category. If force is under the control of an impartial tribunal, it has a better chance of being redemptive, or at least of not being totally destructive of morals, than if it is merely the means of conflict. However, it must be observed that it is so much more difficult to create an impartial society and an impartial tribunal with reference to disputes between large groups, national and economic, than with reference to controversies between individuals that it is much more necessary to seek the total abolition of force in overcoming group conflict than in settling the difficulties of individuals within a group. A "league to enforce peace" between nations has much less chance of succeeding than has a government to enforce peace between individuals, simply because the total number of groups that make up the league is relatively so small in comparison with the number that may be engaged in a controversy that it is practically impossible to guarantee the impartiality of the groups that enforce the decision of a tribunal. Added to this is the fact that a league of nations is no more able to punish a recalcitrant nation without destroying the lives of innocent people than is a single nation. Economic pressure rather than military force may reduce this moral hazard to a certain extent and it may therefore have a higher moral justification than the latter; but it does not entirely remove the difficulty and must therefore be regarded as a dangerous expedient. Though it is a dangerous expedient, it does not follow that it is an expedient that may never be justified on moral grounds.

Pacifists assume too easily, it seems to me, that all controversies are due to misunderstandings that might be solved by a greater degree of imagination. When the strong exploit the weak they produce a conflict that is not the result of ignorance but of the brutality of human nature. It may be that the strong can be convinced in time that it is not to their ultimate interest to destroy the weak. But they can hardly gain this conviction if the weak do not offer resistance in some form to oppression. It may be that this resistance need not express itself physically at all. It may express itself in the use of the "soul force" advocated by Gandhi. But even as thoroughgoing a spiritual idealist as Gandhi has realized that the forgiving love of the oppressed lacks redemptive force if the strong are not made to realize that alternatives to a policy of love are within reach of the oppressed. Oppressed classes, races, and nations, like the industrial worker, the Negroes, India, and China, are therefore under the necessity of doing more than appeal to the imagination and the sense of justice of their oppressors. Where there is a great inequality of physical advantage and physical power it is difficult to establish moral relations. Weakness invites aggression. Even the most intelligent and moral individuals are more inclined to unethical conduct with those who are unable to offer resistance to injustice than with those who can. It must be admitted that an inert China did not succeed in inviting the attention of the world to its maladies, while a rebellious China did. Even the social idealists in the Western world who were not totally oblivious to the evils of Western imperialism in the Orient before the nationalist movement assumed large proportions had their conscience quickened by it.

It is obviously possible to resist injustice without using physical force and certainly without using violence. In a world in which conscience and imagination have been highly sensitized, the oppressed may seek relief against their oppressors and punish them for their misdeeds by indicting them before the bar of public opinion. But it seems that the world in which we live is not so spiritual that it is always possible to prompt the wrongdoer to contrition merely by appealing to his conscience and to that of the society in which he lives. It may be necessary to deprive him of some concrete advantage or inflict some obvious hurt upon him to bring him to his senses. In other words, Gandhi's boycott in India and the Chinese boycott against the English in Hong Kong and the strike of the industrial worker would seem to be necessary strategies in the kind of world in which we live. It is possible to justify the use of such force without condoning violence of any kind. The distinction between violence and such other uses of force as economic boycotts is not only in degree of destruction that results from them but in the degree of redemptive force that they possess. Parents frequently find it necessary to aid the defective imagination of a child by creating painful consequences by artificial means for acts that would result in painful consequences of their own accord in the long run. But the character of the child might be ruined before it had the opportunity to test the actual consequences. On the other hand, if such punishment is administered violently, it will confuse rather than clarify the moral judgment of the child. When oppressed groups resort to violence they also confuse the moral judgment of the society from which they seek justice. They give society the pretext for identifying social maladjustments with social peace and for maintaining the former in the effort to preserve the latter. In the same way the effort of society to maintain a social equilibrium by the undue use of force, particularly by the violent use of force, inevitably confuses rather than clarifies the moral judgments of its minorities and easily prompts them to violence and destruction.

If force is used, therefore, for the sake of gaining moral and social ends, it is necessary to guard its use very carefully. Every society, every individual as well, is easily tempted to overestimate the importance of force in the creation of social solidarities. Many people live under the illusion that a nation is integrated by force and that order is maintained in its life by police power. The fact is that societies are created by attitudes of mutual respect and trust; and standards of conduct within a society are created by mutual consent. Every society seems under the necessity of maintaining its integrity against and forcing its standards upon a certain antisocial minority by the use of force. It is this antisocial minority which justifies, or at least seems to justify, the use of a certain minimum amount of force. It is because every society tends to overemphasize the place of force in its social strategy that absolutists have considerable justification for the thesis that force ought to be completely abolished; for the social efficacy of force is very definitely limited, and most societies have been too uncritical to discover these limitations.

The first obvious limitation is that force can be used only upon a very insignificant minority. If the great majority of a people do not choose to observe a law, it is not possible to enforce it, be it even the most ruthless police action. If a government does not rest upon the consent of the governed, every effort to maintain it by ruthlessness must ultimately result in complete disintegration, as for instance in the Russian Revolution. If a political policy does not achieve the uncoerced acceptance of a vast majority of the population, every effort to enforce it finally proves abortive. Even when the minority that opposes a government or a governmental policy is numerically small and insignificant, its coercion is fraught with moral and social peril. A so-called antisocial minority is, for one thing, never as completely antisocial as the society that tries to coerce it imagines. A part of the minority is usually made up of social idealists who resist the moral compromises upon which the life of every society is inevitably based, not because they are too high for its attainment but because they are too low for its ideals. It has been the tragic mistake of almost every society to number its prophets among its transgressors. Thus the same coercion by which it sought to avoid social disintegration has operated to produce social stagnation. The same force that preserved its standards also destroyed the social forces by which those standards might have been gradually perfected. A high degree of imagination, which few societies have achieved, is required to distinguish between the creative and the disintegrating forces in its life. It may be observed in passing that while it is in the interest of social progress to dissuade societies from undue reliance upon coercion it will probably always be necessary for creative minorities to pay a certain price in martyrdom for their achievements. All social organisms are conservative and are bound to resist not only those who try to draw them backward but those who try to pull them forward.

Even after the distinction between creative and disintegrating forces in the social minority has been made, there is no clear case for the use of force upon the remaining, really " criminal " minority. Some force may be necessary in dealing with the criminal, but every undue reliance upon force obscures the defects in the life of society itself, which have helped to create the criminal. A wayward child is just as much the product of a faulty pedagogy as of innate human defects. It is dangerous to follow Clarence Darrow's moral nihilism and insist that every individual is merely the product of his environment and therefore without blame; but it is obvious enough that much antisocial conduct is definitely due to maladjustments in society. That is what Jesus meant by suggesting that he who is without guilt should throw the first stone. Of the cases of criminality that remain after those for which society is responsible have been subtracted a certain proportion must be attributed to purely pathological causes. A wise society will deal with these without passion and will use force only to put their unfortunate authors in social quarantine.

What is left after all these subtractions have been made represents the real criminal minority. While physical restraint and coercion are probably necessary in dealing with this group, it is obvious that even here force has its limitations. Imagination and understanding may restore a goodly portion of this group to useful membership in society, while the uncritical use of force will merely aggravate its defects. We must arrive, then, at the conclusion that the use of force is dangerous in all social situations, harmful in most of them, and redemptive only in a very few.

The validity of the pacifist position rests in a general way upon the assumption that men are intelligent and moral and that a generous attitude toward them will ultimately, if not always immediately, discover, develop, and challenge what is best in them. This is a large assumption which every specific instance will not justify. The strategy of love therefore involves some risks. These risks are not as great as they are sometimes made to appear for the simple reason that love does not only discover but it creates moral purpose. The cynic who discounts the moral potentialities of human nature seems always to verify his critical appraisal of human nature for the reason that his very skepticism lowers the moral potentialities of the individuals and groups with which he deals. On the other hand, the faith that assumes generosity in the fellow man is also verified because it tends to create what it assumes. If a nation assumes that there is no protection against the potential peril of a neighbor but the force of arms, its assumption is all too easily justified, for suspicion creates suspicion, fear creates fear, and hatred creates hatred. It is interesting to note in this connection how in the relations of France and Germany since the war every victory or seeming victory of the nationalists in Germany has given strength to the chauvinists of France, and vice versa, while every advantage for the forces of one nation that believe in trust has resulted in an almost immediate advantage for the trustworthy elements in the other. Hence the contest between the apostles of force and the apostles of love can never be decided purely on the basis of scientific evidence. The character of the evidence is determined to a great degree by the assumptions upon which social relations are initiated. This is the fact that gives the champions of the strategy of love the right to venture far beyond the policy that a cool and calculating sanity would dictate. It may not be true that love never fails; but it is true that love creates its own victories, and they are always greater than would seem possible from the standpoint of a merely critical observer.

56. WHY I LEAVE THE F. O. R.

Historically the Fellowship of Reconciliation is an organization of pacifists, born during the war, and holding to the Quaker position on war beyond the confines of the Quaker fellowship. In a sense the Fellowship has been a kind of Quaker conventicle inside of the traditional church. Gradually the effort to present a Christian testimony against war forced an increasingly large number of F. O. R. members to oppose the capitalistic social system as a breeder of war and injustice. As long as they could believe that the injustice of capitalism could be abolished by moral suasion there seemed to be no particular conflict between their pacifism and their socialism. They held to the generally accepted position of Christian socialists who believed that the peculiar contribution of religion to the social struggle must be an insistence upon nonviolent or even noncoercive methods of social change. In the recent poll of the membership it was revealed that 21 per cent of the membership still believed that the Fellowship should endeavor through "methods of love" to bring about a new social order "without identifying itself with either the underprivileged or the privileged class."

This position probably mirrors quite accurately the conviction of a very considerable portion of the liberal Protestant Church, which has not yet recognized that it is practically impossible to be completely neutral in a social struggle and that the effort at neutrality is morally more dangerous in a class conflict than in an international war because it works to the advantage of entrenched interests against advancing forces.

NEUTRALITY IN THE CLASS STRUGGLE

Another 22 per cent of the Fellowship believe in "identifying itself with the just aims of the workers" but "without the use of any form of coercion." Taking these two groups together we find that almost half of the Fellowship disavows any form of coercion. Since this type of ethical perfectionism is not related with any ascetic withdrawal from the world, which might give it consistency, it may be assumed that it is a good revelation of the failure of liberal Protestantism to recognize the coercive character of political and economic life. To refuse the use of any coercive methods means that it is not recognized that everyone is using them all the time, that we all live in and benefit or suffer from a political and economic order that maintains its cohesion partially by the use of various forms of political and economic coercion.

THE DISMISSAL OF MR. MATTHEWS

Another group in the Fellowship (47 per cent to be exact) believes in the use of some form of coercion short of violence. One part of the group believes in " assisting the organization of the workers and in leading them in strikes for a living wage " and also in organizing them into a political party that will use " nonviolent political and economic coercive measures " and a smaller number in this group go as far as willingness to support the workers in an armed conflict but without themselves participating in the attendant violence in any way.

If the two groups that abjure any form of coercion and those which will not participate in any type of violent coercion are taken together, they represent about 90 per cent of the Fellowship. This is quite natural and logical in an organization of pacifists. It is idle, therefore, to make it appear that the action of the council, which dismissed J. B. Matthews from his position as secretary, was in any sense irregular or unfair. It was the only logical step for the Fellowship to take. Furthermore, though I share, roughly speaking, the political position of Mr. Matthews, I do not agree with the publicity that those who are supporting him have released since the dismissal.

I am not a good enough Marxian to declare that convictions are determined purely by class interests and that every pacifist is therefore a conscious or unconscious tool of capitalism. I think it is quite probable that there are wealthy Quakers who abhor all violence without recognizing to what degree they are the beneficiaries of an essentially violent system. In fact, I have known Philadelphia Quakers to give hearty approval to Mr. Hoover's treatment of the bonus army. At the same time I am not willing to attribute to men like Nevin Sayre, John Haynes Holmes, and Kirby Page, who represent the middle section of the Fellowship and who believe in the use of nonviolent coercion as a means of attaining social justice, the

" class interests " that have been ascribed to them by those who oppose them.

The pacifist position, whether in its pure form of nonresistance or in the more qualified form of nonviolent resistance, has always been held by a minority in the Christian church. It may be plausibly argued that such pacifism will benefit entrenched interests more than it will help the proponents of a higher social justice when the day of crisis comes. But to suggest that it is dictated by class interests not only does injustice to these courageous champions of justice, but it presses the economic interpretation of history to precisely that point where it becomes absurd. Anyone who recognizes the terrible tension between the Christian ideal of love and the hard realities of life is certainly bound to respect the effort of those who, recognizing the horrors of violence, make nonviolence an absolute in their social ethic.

WE ARE NOT PACIFIST!

While respecting this position of the pure and the qualified pacifists, I am bound to admit that I cannot share their position. For this reason I am forced to associate myself with 20 per cent of the Fellowship who are pacifists only in the sense that they will refuse to participate in an international armed conflict. Perhaps it would clear the issue if we admitted that we were not pacifists at all. We probably all recognize the terrible possibilities of violence. We regard an international armed conflict as so suicidal that we are certain that we will not participate in it.

In the case of the social struggle that is being waged between the privileged and the disinherited classes in every Western nation, some of us, at least, know that there are possibilities that modern civilization will drift into barbarism with the disintegration of the capitalistic system. We believe that not only fascism but communism has the perils of barbarism in it. The peril of the latter arises not so much from its preaching of violence as from its preaching of hatred. Hatred is very blinding; and those who are blind cannot be good enough statesmen to become the instruments of a new unity amid the complexities of Western civilization. We would certainly have as much sense of responsibility toward the avoidance of barbaric civil strife as any other intelligent and responsible person.

The reason we cannot, in spite of our scruples, maintain our connection with the majority of the Fellowship is because we regard all problems of social morality in pragmatic rather than absolute terms. The only absolute law that we recognize is the law of love, and that is an ideal that transcends all law. The purely Marxian section of this 10 per cent minority would probably not recognize the validity of the ideal of love at all. They would think of the social struggle simply as a contest between two classes in which the one class is fated to play the role of creating a classless society. Those of us who are Christian Marxians would renounce some of the utopianism implied in this belief. We believe rather that the world of nature and history is a world in which egoism, collective and individual, will never be completely overcome and in which the law of love will remain both an ideal for which men must strive and a criterion that will convict every new social structure of imperfection.

A PRAGMATIC PROBLEM

We realize that the problem of social justice is a pragmatic and even a technical one. Modern capitalism breeds injustice because of the disproportions of economic power that it tolerates and upon which it is based. We expect no basic economic justice without a destruction of the present disproportion of power and we do not expect the latter without a social struggle. Once we have accepted the fact of the reality of the social struggle we do not feel that we can stop where the middle portion of the Fellowship has stopped. We are unable to stop there because we can find no stable absolute in the shifting situation of the social struggle where everything must be finally decided in pragmatic terms.

If we should agree with one portion of this middle section that we will use nonviolent coercion in behalf of the disinherited but will discourage any coercion that may issue in violence, we feel that we would give an undue moral advantage to that portion of the community which is always using nonviolent coercion against the disinherited. This is precisely what the liberal church is constantly tempted to do. It is furthermore usually oblivious to the fact that nonviolence may be covert violence. Children do starve and old people freeze to death in the poverty of our cities, a poverty for which everyone who has more than the bare necessities of life must feel some responsibility.

We cannot agree with another group of these qualified pacifists who would participate in an armed social conflict but who would not personally participate in its violence, contenting themselves with noncombatant services, because we have come to believe that such an attitude represents an abortive effort to maintain personal purity while holding an organic relation to a social movement that is bound to result in some degree of violence in the day of crisis.

Is This Division Academic?

The outsider may think that those careful definitions of just what degree of violence or nonviolence one accepts in a social struggle represent academic hairsplitting. I quite admit that this discussion as to just what any of us would do in the day of crisis is very unrealistic in many ways. As a Marxian and as a Christian it reveals to me the futility of finding a moral absolute in the relativities of politics. If anyone should suggest that those of us who have thus renounced the pacifist position ought not any longer to regard ourselves as Christian, I would answer that it is only a Christianity that suffers from modern liberal illusions that has ever believed that the law of love could be made an absolute guide of conduct in social morality and politics. As a Marxian and as a Christian I recognize the tragic character of man's social life, and the inevitability of conflict in it arising from the inability of man ever to bring his egoism completely under the dominion of conscience.

As a Marxian I will try to guide that conflict to a goal that guarantees a basic economic justice and creates a society that makes modern technical civilization sufferable. As a Christian I will know that even the justice of a socialist commonwealth will reveal the imperfections of natural man and will not destroy the contest of wills and interests which will express itself in every society. As a Christian I will achieve at least enough contrition before the absolute demands that God makes upon me and that I never completely fulfill to be able to deal with those who oppose me with a measure of forgiveness. Christianity means more than any moral attitude that can express itself in social politics. But it must at least mean that the social struggle is fought without hatred. Nonhatred is a much more important sign and symbol of Christian faith than nonviolence.

The Choice of the Radical

To make the matter short, the Fellowship controversy has revealed that there are radical Christians who can no longer express themselves in pacifist terms. For some of them pacifism was the last remnant of Christianity in their radicalism. With pacifism dissipated they are inclined to disavow their Christian faith or to be quiescent about it. Others of us have merely discovered the profundity of the Christian faith when we ceased to interpret it in merely moralistic demands.

I think we ought to leave the Fellowship of Reconciliation with as good grace as possible. Perhaps we could even prove that there are some of the fruits of the spirit within us by leaving without rancor and without impugning ignoble motives to our comrades to whom we are bound in many cases by inseparable ties of common purpose and affection. In so far as we are radical Christians we must find a more solid ground for the combination of radicalism and Christianity than the creed of pacifism supplied. But we will always maintain our respect for the purity of purpose that animates the men who conceived the Fellowship of Reconciliation and will carry it on in spite of discouragement in these critical days. Perhaps the day will come when we will be grateful for their counsels.

Recognizing, as liberal Christianity does not, that the world of politics is full of demonic forces, we have chosen on the whole to support the devil of vengeance against the devil of hypocrisy. In the day in which we live, a dying social system commits the hypocrisy of hiding its injustices behind the forms of justice, and the victims of injustice express their politics in terms of resentment against this injustice. As Marxians we support this resentment against the hypocrisy. As Christians we know that there is a devil in the spirit of vengeance as well as in the spirit of hypocrisy. For that reason we respect those who try to have no traffic with devils at all. We cannot follow them because we believe that consistency would demand flight to the monastery if all the devils of man's collective life were to be avoided. But our traffic with devils may lead to corruption, and the day may come when we will be grateful for those who try to restrain all demons rather than choose between them.

57. PACIFISM AGAINST THE WALL

The Italian-Ethiopian dispute has brought the problem of the compatibility between consistent pacifism and support of the League of Nations to a sharp focus. Since the war, pacifist sentiment has increased to a remarkable degree, particularly in England and the United States. From the traditionally pacifist Christian sects, such as the Quakers, it has spread to the Christian churches in general. To a certain degree it has also expressed itself in purely secular terms. Usually this postwar pacifism was compounded with devotion to the principle of collective security embodied in the League of Nations. The present dispute between the League and Italy raises the question whether it is possible to combine the pacifist disavowal of every form of armed conflict with the obligations of international government implied in the organization of a League of Nations. Pacifists have evaded this issue to the present moment by assuming that moral pressure and economic sanctions would constitute a sufficient force with which to discipline a recalcitrant nation. Italy's threat to use military force in the event of a League oil embargo upon her (a threat that has for the moment been successful in preventing the embargo) proves rather conclusively that nonviolent sanctions cannot be applied without running some risk of issuing in violence. If any international government should therefore specifically limit its use of force to nonmilitary measures, it would insure the futility of such measures. The recalcitrant nation need only declare that it will counter economic sanctions with military measures to scare the international body into impotence. Mussolini's defiance of the League has thus brought the whole problem of the relation of pacifism to collective security into sharp focus.

To understand the confusion of contemporary pacifism on the question of sanctions, it is necessary to point out that various elements have entered into modern pacifist convictions. The ingredients of the modern compound of pacifism are chiefly three: religious absolutism as expressed in the Sermon on the Mount; the general presupposition of modern liberalism — that rational persuasion is gradually and progressively displacing coercion as the method of arbitrating all forms of social dispute; and finally a moral nausea over the brutalities and futilities of the World War.

The American Scholar, Spring, 1936.

Religious absolutism in its pure form is either apocalyptic or ascetic. In either case it is not compatible with political responsibility. When apocalyptic, as in the thought of Jesus, it sets the absolute principles of the coming Kingdom of God, principles of uncompromising love and nonresistance, in sharp juxtaposition to the relativities of the economic and political order and assumes no responsibilities for the latter. When ascetic, as in the case of Francis of Assisi or Tolstoi, it sharpens individual ideals of the spirit in contrast to the whole range of physical necessities, from the individual will-to-survive to a nation's will-to-power. It does not deny that the actual world is one of conflict between egoistic impulses or that the business of politics is to reduce this conflict to some kind of equilibrium of balanced egoistic forces. It merely insists that such equilibriums are not free of the " sin " of egoism or the peril of conflict. Every equilibrium of contending social forces is only subdued conflict, which may break out into actual conflict, and every actual conflict may result in violence. In its pure form religious pacifism is therefore a realistic reminder of the fact that the " peace of the world " is never more than an armistice.

Since the dawn of modern liberalism, particularly in America, this religious pacifism has been mixed with the political presuppositions of rational liberalism. The basic presupposition of liberalism is that the forces of rationality are gradually increasing in human society and that we may therefore confidently look forward to the day when all social disputes will be arbitrated by a mutual regard for the rights and interests of opposing parties in a conflict situation. This assumption of liberalism implies a very optimistic view of the goodness of human nature, an interpretation of human history in terms of the idea of progress, and a belief that collective behavior differs from individual conduct only in a certain tardiness in reaching the ideals of the latter. These articles of the liberal credo have prompted a great deal of pacifism that justifies itself in pragmatic terms and therefore specifically disavows the political irresponsibility of religious absolutism. It claims that it has actually found a superior social technique for the establishment of peace and justice and therefore seeks to commend its program as a politically wise one. Usually this pacifism defines its position in terms that permit nonviolent resistance and coercion and excludes only violent forms of resistance and coercion. It never fully faces the fact that it is impossible to draw a sharp line between violence and nonviolence and that every possible economic sanction (boycott and embargo, for instance) may result in the destruction of both life and property. In modern religious liberalism this type of pacifism is usually identified with the position of Jesus though there is nothing in the teachings of Jesus that justifies a distinction between violent and nonviolent forms of resistance. The perfectionist ethics of the Christian Gospels teach complete nonresistance and therefore establish a contrast not between violence and nonviolence but between any prudential and pragmatic effort to establish justice and maintain peace by resistance, coercion, and the balance of power, and the millennial and anarchistic ideal of a completely uncoerced and voluntary social peace and co-operation. Sometimes the modern religious liberal seeks to combine the pragmatic considerations of a liberal ethic with the absolutistic motifs of a purely religious ethic. Thus in the writings of John Haynes Holmes, one of the outstanding pacifists of our generation, pacifism is alternately commended as the best method of achieving social justice and as absolutely right whatever its social consequences. This inconsistency runs through practically all modern religious pacifism.

The third element in modern pacifism is moral nausea and disillusionment over the futilities and brutalities of the World War. This brings into the pacifist fold a large number of people who have no clear notions about the implications of their position — which is essentially negative. They are not certain how war is to be prevented or how social justice is to be achieved. They merely hold the understandable conviction that armed conflict is in any case a method that destroys the ostensible ends it intends to serve. In this group must be counted the radicals who regard war as the consequence of capitalism and refuse to participate in it because they want to disassociate themselves from capitalistic imperialism and nationalism. Their position, however, is really not pacifistic at all. They have merely decided that conflict between nations is futile and tends to aggravate the social injustices of our civilization. They are equally certain that a class conflict may establish a new type of society in which international conflict will be abolished. But since this group usually does not regard itself as pacifistic and sometimes specifically disavows pacifist principles, it deserves the criticisms leveled at liberal pacifists only when, as in the case of radical student organizations, it adopts the " Oxford pledge " as its own. This pledge, which promises to abstain from military defense of the nation under all circumstances, has meaning and sincerity only if it expresses religious absolutism. Among those signing it have been some radical students who would be quite ready to engage in military service provided, for instance, their nation supported Soviet Russia in a war with Japan.

The recent crisis in Europe has prompted a great deal of searching of hearts in pacifist circles and has drawn a clear line of cleavage between the pacifists in whom motives of religious perfectionism are dominant and those who hold to a more pragmatic justification of nonviolence. The former are inclined to condemn sanctions because they may lead to war. In England this group, headed by George Lansbury, former leader of the Labor Party, Lord Ponsonby, its leader in the House of Lords, and "Dick" Shepherd, former Dean of Canterbury and influential in religious circles, have formed a new pacifist organization that specifically disavows economic as well as military sanctions. From a pacifist standpoint this position is logical enough, particularly since the present crisis has made it apparent that no form of political and social coercion can be guaranteed never to result in violence. This English group is noteworthy chiefly for the prominent statesmen enrolled under its banner. Yet it seems rather strange that even a saint in politics, of the type of George Lansbury, should not realize that the logic of his position is really incompatible with government itself. If one is to take such a position consistently, one must either believe that it is possible to have government without coercion (accept the ideals of anarchism in short) or be indifferent toward the problems of government.

A larger number of pacifists have taken the position that they will support political coercion provided the power of coercion is wielded by an international and impartial organization and provided nonviolent means of coercion are used. Thus Kirby Page, one of the most influential exponents of pacifism in this country, heartily advocates economic sanctions against Italy and took the same position with reference to Japan in the Manchurian crisis. The difficulty with this position is that it does not give any guidance to a statesman who, in using nonmilitary sanctions, is faced with the threat of military reprisals. If he should commit himself in advance to the position of his pacifist supporters, he would insure the futility of his venture, for the recalcitrant nation is bound to threaten reprisals as soon as economic sanctions really imperil the victory of its arms. Such threats might be made insincerely, but the " bluff " in them could be revealed only by risking war. It is interesting to note that the Hoare-Laval proposals, condemned by all supporters of the League as treason against it, were made partly because it was feared that an oil embargo against Italy might lead to war. The British Foreign Secretary feared such a war, not because of pacifist scruples, but because the promise of co-operation by France in the event of war was too reluctant to give him security. He seems also to have been prompted by the consideration that a possible Italian-French-English military entente might be more effective in stopping a resurgent Germany than the system of collective security under the League that Anthony Eden sought to construct. In any event the threat of the use of armed force, dangerous as it is, is still a necessary weapon, even for a League of Nations.

The serious embarrassment of League proponents who are also pacifists is illustrated by a recent article in the English weekly *The New Statesman and Nation*. The article by C. E. M. Joad justifies pacifist support of the League on the ground that since the world has refused to accept the pacifist solution of disarmament the pacifist is forced to espouse a " second-best " policy. He need not, however, be personally responsible for this second-best policy of sanctions because it is not his own policy.

" The use of force is after all not his policy; and it is only because he has been unable to convert the world to his policy that the use of force by the League has come to· seem the least evil of the various courses that are practicable. But the pacifist has no *personal* obligation to take part in a course that he advocates only under duress. . . . His " best " is disarmament. Meanwhile, because of the hardness of men's hearts and the thickness of their heads, he is driven to support sanctions as the best that is offered under the circumstances and as a means to the absolute best."

This argument is a perfect illustration of the naïve individualism of modern liberalism. The necessity of coercion in social life is attributed to the failure of other people to arrive at the same degree of enlightenment enjoyed by the pacifist. It does not occur to him that the necessity of coercion in politics may flow from defects of the human imagination and the human heart that even the most enlightened individuals betray. Can Mr. Joad be really so certain that a higher degree of intelligence will really free human society from the brutal conflicts of power that have characterized all human history? Perhaps the growth of human intelligence will accentuate as well as mitigate this conflict. After all, the "enlightened" nations have a stronger imperial will and are more effective in expressing it than the more vegetative backward nations. Mr. Joad's effort to escape the pacifist dilemma reveals how implicit the idea of progress is in all liberal approaches to the political problem. It may be that human history is a much more tragic enterprise than these liberal optimists assume.

An analysis of pacifist scruples about the League and sanctions would be incomplete without reference to the radical position of such men as Sir Stafford Cripps, leader of the Socialist League in the British Labor Party. His position, shared by most Socialists in America, is that the League is too much the instrument of capitalistic imperialism to be an effective instrument of peace. It merely supports the satiated imperialistic nations against the hungry ones, Italy, Germany, and Japan, whose special crime is that they came too tardily upon the division of spoils in the game of imperialism. This position is not pacifistic in any exact sense of the word. It betrays no scruples against the use of force in government. It merely regards the League of Nations as a pretense in international government rather than as a reality. And it can hardly be denied that many facts support this criticism. The League of Nations did not act in the Japanese-Manchurian dispute because the imperial interests of France and Britain were not threatened by Japanese aggression. Nor did it act energetically against Italy until British interests in Africa were threatened. Even now it fails to act without equivocation because the interests of France and Britain are only partially compatible on this particular issue.

The real fact is that the League of Nations is, in the present moment, the combined force of French and British diplomacy plus the moral prestige of the common opinion of the small nations of Europe. The force of the small nations, as a balance wheel of imperial politics, is the only really significant gain achieved through the World War. But how solid this gain is may well be regarded as a question upon which no clear or convincing answer can be given. Certainly the facts do not justify League enthusiasts who speak of the League as if it were an impartial international government, above suspicion or reproach. The facts do not warrant the kind of loyalty to the League that the religious forces of Britain marshaled for the Tory party in the last election because of its assumed support of the League. Nor is it at all certain that the League of Na-

tions is a sufficiently authentic instrument of international government to warrant America's entry into it at the present juncture. It
is more important at the present moment that our neutrality laws
should be so designed as to prevent the sabotaging of League sanctions. That is more important than entrance into the League on the
one hand, and on the other than the kind of neutrality that assumes
no responsibility for the disciplining of recalcitrant nations.

While it is important therefore not to overestimate the virtues,
achievements, or possibilities of the League, it is equally unrealistic
to abstain from every possible support of its policies on the ground
that its course is dictated or influenced by the imperial politics of
Britain or France. One need not regard either British or French
diplomacy as morally pure to be willing to use it to prevent a European conflagration. Moral purists who advance this consideration
might well be challenged to point to any possible or conceivable
force in politics of such purity as their criticism of the League suggests as possible. The fact is that politics is always confronted with
the task of beguiling conflicting egoistic wills into some kind of
harmony or equilibrium. The anarchy of nations happens to be
greater than the anarchy within nations, and for this reason the
self-interest of the component parts of an international community
is more apparent than in domestic politics. But that is all the more
reason why it is inadvisable to make moral demands of too absolute
a nature upon the diplomacy of nations. If the League as now constituted gives any promise of holding Italy, Germany, and Japan
in check, it is worth supporting even though the radical knows full
well that it cannot guarantee permanent peace. The alternative is
that each one of these nations, freed of the fear of any international
force opposed to them, will break loose, destroy Soviet Russia (by
simultaneous attacks on the part of Germany and Japan) and establish a triumphant fascistic nationalism in both Europe and Asia.
Such a resolution of the present covert anarchy would be decidedly
worse than the present uneasy armistice in both Europe and Asia.
The armistice has no real virtues of peace in it and cannot last in
the long run. But it is better to try to maintain it than to allow overt
anarchy to break out. While there is peace there is always a possibility that the imperialistic policies of the dominant nations in
Europe will be altered through internal pressure. That is a more
hopeful alternative than to permit anarchy to break loose in the
hope that the next war will destroy capitalistic imperialism and es-

tablish a socialistic peace in the world. The greater probability is that the next war, particularly if it should result in the success of German and Japanese arms, will lead to unalloyed fascism and to a general disintegration of the civilization and the culture of the world.

Absolutistic scruples against the League of Nations and sanctions, whether they are pacifist or radical, thus tend to increase the anarchy that they abhor. That is unfortunately the unvarying consequence of moral absolutism in politics. The political order must be satisfied with relative peace and relative justice. Refusal to participate in its relativities, because they represent imperfect approximations of the ideal of human brotherhood, are bound to lead to a further disintegration of its always tentative peace and its always imperfect justice.

58. AN OPEN LETTER
(TO RICHARD ROBERTS)

I am sorry that I could not answer your open letter in our last issue of *Christianity and Society*, but time and space prevented. I am the more anxious to answer it because it is the first communication I have received from a pacifist that has not been ill-tempered. I do not accuse all pacifists of ill-temper, for I have personal friends among pacifists who debate their convictions with me personally in the spirit of love. But the correspondents have been uniformly abusive and have revealed how much more difficult it is to obey the " law of love " than their official creed recognizes.

You say that the charge of " self-righteousness " is a boomerang and convicts the one who uses it of not being " too sure of the position that he is defending." Maybe you are right. I have never known a controversy between human beings in which the contestants are not more certain of the righteousness of their cause than they have a right to be. All human controversies are controversies between self-righteous sinners. But this does not absolve us of the necessity of seeking for the truth between contrasting claims, just as the sin-

Christianity and Society, Summer, 1940.

fulness of all nations does not obviate the necessity of making discriminate judgments between their positions.

I accuse pacifists of self-righteousness because most modern pacifists have only a slight inkling of the real contradiction between life itself and the law of love. They seem to think that you can obey the law of love if you only set your mind to it. If any of us declare that all historical existence is involved in a self-love that contradicts the law of love, they accuse us of defeatism and apostasy. One of the most prominent pacifists in this nation runs up and down the country accusing me and my kind of " moral breakdown " and "moral bankruptcy." My view of what human character and historical existence is like may be wrong; but I have arrived at it by as honest an analysis of human behavior, including my own, as I am capable of. There is a type of Christian pacifism that does not rest upon illusions about the goodness of man. But I can find little of that type of pacifism around about me. Most of the pacifism I know is deficient in the " tragic sense of life " and corrupts its perfectionism by offering its refusal to participate in conflict as a political alternative to the contest of power that is the very character of the political order.

You ask: " Why should any incident in history impose a moratorium upon the business of human redemption? Am I to soft-pedal the incarnation of God in Jesus Christ at every international crisis? " This question neatly poses the issue between us. Fully analyzed, the question reveals the theological gulf between pacifism and nonpacifist Christianity. I do not believe that war is merely an " incident " in history but is a final revelation of the very character of human history. I do not believe that we ought to "soft-pedal the incarnation at every international crisis." I believe that an international crisis merely reveals in its most vivid form what human history is like, and I accuse pacifists of not being aware of its character until it is thus vividly revealed. At that moment they seek to escape history and its relative responsibilities by a supreme act of renunciation. I do not believe that the incarnation is " redemption " from history as conflict. Since I believe that sinful egoism expresses itself on every level of moral and spiritual achievement and is not absent from the highest levels of Christian life, I cannot regard redemption as freedom from sin. The redemption in Christ is rather the revelation of a divine mercy that alone is able to overcome the contradictions of human history from which even the best of us cannot extricate ourselves. I believe, with the Protestant Reformation, that any claim that we have overcome this contradiction and that Christ has become our possession merely leads to a new form of egoism, namely, pharisaic pride. In other words I take the Reformation doctrine of " justification by faith " seriously and I observe that the spiritual ground upon which our modern pacifism has grown is a sectarian perfectionism that hasn't the slightest idea of what the Reformation meant by its doctrine of " justification by faith." In terms of theological history our modern Protestant perfectionism is more deeply engulfed in illusions about human nature than the Catholic pretensions of perfection, against which the Reformation was a protest.

In its most consistent form Reformation Christianity is inclined to substitute the concept " *Christus pro nobis* " completely for the idea of " *Christus in nobis* " and thus to deny any possibility of making Christ the norm of our life. This is an error. But it is no greater error than that which is committed by both Catholic and sectarian perfectionism that believes that divine grace actually lifts man out of the sinful contradictions of history and establishes him above the sins of the world. The real situation is that the final possibility of love in history is forgiveness; and this forgiveness of the foe is possible only to the contrite sinner who knows himself to be involved in the sins of history. Every form of Christian righteousness that rests upon a too simple doctrine of redemption must degenerate into a self-righteousness in which the "man in Christ " looks with scorn and judgment upon the man who is presumably not in Christ. In this connection the analogy between Christ's strictures against the Pharisees and the Reformation criticism of Catholic self-righteousness is instructive.

You, of course, in distinction to many pacifists, are quite conscious of the persistence of sin in life. You say that you try to " follow Him and fail all the way. But this does not entitle me to make a virtue or a sort of philosophy out of my failure." You are afraid that those who follow our position may not realize that " the relativist attitude is itself sin in spite of what seems to be its inevitability at the moment." Of course you are quite right. Relativism easily degenerates into opportunism, and opportunism into unprincipled conduct. You are quite right in declaring that " it is my business to keep alive the tension within me between the very relative good that I at best achieve and the ideal good that I profess." But you forget that it is also the business of a Christian to preserve some relative decency and justice in society against the tyranny and injustice into which society may fall. He cannot do this without supporting relative standards of justice against the threats of anarchy and injustice. You are willing to slightly favor the Allies against Hitler, but you are not willing to allow such a discrimination to result in an action in favor of one side against the other. To allow such an action is to involve yourself in sin. Your difficulty is that you want to try to live in history without sinning. There is no such possibility in history. The danger of admitting this is, of course, that we make sin normative when we declare it to be inevitable. We must see the sinfulness of war, but we must also see the sin of egoism in which all life is involved and of which war is the final expression. Furthermore, we must be able to see the difference between the relative virtue of a decent scheme of justice and the real peril of tyranny. All modern pacifism regards the Kingdom of God as a simple alternative to the contests of power, which lie at the foundation of the political order and which we may beguile into some decent balance of power if we understand their true nature. If we do not understand their true nature, our effort to set up the Kingdom of God on earth ends in a perverse preference for tyranny, simply because the peace of tyranny means, at least, the absence of war.

In this connection I call your attention to the fact that many of your pacifist brothers are so anxious to prove the sensitivity of their moral and political judgments that they are leaning over backwards and end in the perverse judgment that Hitlerism is really preferable to British imperialism because it is "more honest," or because bombing cities is morally preferable to a blockade. Meanwhile all that is still decent in Europe is under the grave peril of coming under complete Nazi domination and corruption.

A civilization that fights tyrannical barbarism must know at what points its sins approach the barbarism of its foes. But it must also know at what points it is the custodian of values that transcend the sins of its "imperialism." Otherwise its uneasy conscience will betray it into the hands of those who have no moral scruples at all. It is a good thing to know what to do with an uneasy conscience. On the one hand an uneasy conscience must bring forth fruits meet for repentance. On the other hand the Christian must know that he can find no vantage point in history where his conscience can become easy, except as it is made easy by the knowledge of divine forgiveness. If he does not know this, he must either resign himself to historical futility or he must nerve himself to action by the self-righteous illusion that he has achieved the vantage point of sinlessness from which it is possible to act.

Just one more point. You say: " I would give a good deal to be able to accept your doctrine. It would make life easier for me; there's the sense of alienation of my people, the coolness of friends, the suspicion of disloyalty, the spite of intolerance and the like, which hurt me deeply." I quite appreciate the courage that is required to maintain the pacifist position in a country at war. But how relative these matters are! If you were only in this country, in which liberal Christian orthodoxy has combined with nationalistic fears and a dread of becoming involved in war which amounts to almost a psychosis, you would find your position very popular, and it might be necessary to come to the help of some of the rest of us who are accused of not being Christian at all. I do not say that your pacifism has anything in common with the very relative political judgments that dominate our national scene and the national self-righteousness that mistakes the uncovenanted mercy of three thousand miles of ocean for the superior genius of America in comparison with the warlike tribes of Europe. I only say that, whatever the merits or demerits of our position, it can hardly be prompted by the desire to conform to the world. Our world for the moment has compounded Christian perfectionism and nationalistic viewpoints into a new kind of Christian patriotism, which denounces nonconformists in both theological and political terms. So we are both uneasy in our nonconformity, though I admit that the perils and strains of war in a belligerent nation make nonconformity more dangerous there than in a nation still at peace. But if the present mood of America continues we will have to raise the cry from Macedonia to some of you Christian pacifists in belligerent nations, asking you to give proof by such a spirit of understanding as you reveal in your letter that you do not count us among the damned because we hold convictions that are contrary to the orthodoxy of our nation though they are also contrary to the heterodoxy of your nation. On the whole I have found Christians in the British Empire less inclined to identify their cause with the Kingdom of God than American Christians are inclined to identify neutrality with the Sermon on the Mount.

59. TO PREVENT THE TRIUMPH OF AN INTOLERABLE TYRANNY

The editor of *The Christian Century* has invited representatives of various shades of opinion to state what their attitude and conviction would be in the event of the involvement of this nation in the World War. The invitation of the editor begins with the following statement: " The cumulative steps taken by our Government during the past year, culminating in the adoption of conscription, have brought the nation to a point where America's participation as a belligerent in the war is an imminent possibility."

It is indicative of the deep chasm that separates some of us in the Christian church today that I cannot even accept this statement as presenting a true picture of the situation in which we stand. It implies that we have been brought to the edge of war primarily by contrivance of the Administration. I should have thought that when a storm is raging in the seven seas of the earth one could hardly hold any pilot responsible for not steering the ship of state in such a way as to avoid the storm. Living in an age of war and revolution, no possible statesmanship could have avoided at least the danger of involvement. But perhaps I am plunging into the argument too hurriedly by this introduction.

No Rush Toward War

I will therefore begin again with the simple statement that if our nation should be involved in the world conflict, I will have no hesitancy in supporting the war effort of the nation. I am assuming, in making such an unqualified statement, that the nation will not be drawn into the war if there is a decent and honorable way of remaining out of it. The suspicion in which the isolationists hold the international policy of the Administration will of course prompt them to challenge this assumption. But I believe that contemporary history refutes the idea that nations are drawn into war too precipitately. It proves, on the contrary, that it is the general inclination, of democratic nations at least, to hesitate so long before taking this fateful plunge that the dictator nations gain a fateful advantage over them by having the opportunity of overwhelming them singly, instead of being forced to meet their common resistance. More than a half dozen nations of Europe mourn the loss of their liberties today, who might have preserved them if extreme caution had not enervated their resolution of self-defense.

I shall seek to justify my determination to support the nation in war by a political and a religious analysis of the moral problems involved, since every moral problem is political on the side of its application and religious on the side of the basic presuppositions from which the moral judgment flows.

On the political side I view the situation that confronts us as follows: Germany, on the pretext of righting the wrongs of Versailles, is engaged in a desperate effort to establish her mastery over the whole Continent of Europe. She may succeed. Nothing but the resistance of Great Britain now stands in her way. One nation after the other has collapsed before the might of her arms or before a diplomacy that knows how to exploit all the weaknesses and internal divisions of her adversaries. These imperial ambitions of Germany are in quality and extent perilous to all the nations outside Europe.

Peril to All Civilized Values

In quality they represent a peril to every established value of a civilization that all Western nations share and of which we are all the custodians. In extent the German ambitions must immediately reach beyond Europe, because Europe is not economically self-sufficient and a German-dominated slave economy would immediately stand in fateful competition with us and would use all means, fair and foul, to make us the subservient accomplices of its economic and political penetration. It is not necessary to fear an immediate invasion of our shores to regard the imperial expansion of Germany with apprehension. I have never shared the naïve belief that all war could be avoided if only you could persuade nations not to cross each other's borders. I am perfectly certain that if an enemy of mine did not invade the sanctity of my home but posted sentries at my gate and pointed a gun into my windows and, by virtue of such threats, presumed to dictate my comings and goings or even dared to levy tribute on my trade, he would be no less an enemy of my liberties than if he invaded my home.

Far from believing that we can permit anything to happen in Europe while we enjoy peace and democracy upon an island of security in a tyrannically organized world, I am convinced that if Britain should fall and Germany should be triumphant, we could do nothing but spend all our energies in the next decades in arming against all possible perils and attacks and in contriving to outwit a resourceful and ingenious foe. This is what we would do at best. There is a worse alternative. We might accept the advice of Colonel Lindbergh and other appeasers of his type and become the accomplices of such a victor. I fear there are many of us for whom nothing succeeds like success and who would be easily persuaded that after all nothing must interfere with the ultimate sanctity of a commercial society: trade.

SIGNS OF MORAL CONFUSION

On the point of the quality rather than extent of the German ambitions I must confess that I have found nothing so difficult to understand as the constant appeals of *The Christian Century* to the President to be more perfectly neutral in this conflict so as not to involve America in it by favoring one side. I regard such advice as the typical fruit of the moral confusion that issues from moral perfectionism, whenever moral perfectionism seeks to construct political systems.

A FURY FED BY PAGANISM

We have allowed ourselves to forget as much as possible that this resurgent Germany not only shares imperial ambitions with all strong nations, but that its fury is fed by a pagan religion of tribal self-glorification; that it intends to root out the Christian religion; that it defies all the universal standards of justice that ages of a Christian and humanistic culture have woven into the fabric of our civilization; that it threatens the Jewish race with annihilation and visits a maniacal fury upon these unhappy people that goes far beyond the ordinary race prejudice that is the common sin of all nations and races; that it explicitly declares its intention of subjecting the other races of Europe into slavery to the " master " race; that it intends to keep them in subjection by establishing a monopoly of military violence and of technical skill so that they will be subordinate in peace and in war; that it is already engaged in Poland and Czechoslovakia in destroying the very fabric of national existence by wholesale expulsion of nationals from their homeland and the forced colonization of Germans in their place; that, in short, it is engaged in the terrible effort to establish an empire upon the very negation of justice rather than upon that minimal justice which even ancient empires achieved.

If anyone believes that the peace of such a tyranny is morally more tolerable than war, I can only admire and pity the resolute dogmatism that makes such convictions possible.

Since some of us who express convictions of the kind I have outlined have been accused of being swayed in our opinions by ties of family and friendship that bind us to Great Britain, I would like to add the personal word that I am an American of pure German stock, that I gained most of these convictions in many visits to Hitler's Germany, that I share them with pure Germans such as Thomas Mann and many others, and that far from being swayed by any ties with Britain I thought Britain was much too slow in understanding or challenging the peril that Nazi imperialism presented to both our common civilization and the vital interests of Britain, just as I believe that we have been too tardy in understanding this peril.

Challenge to Conscience

It will appear from the above analysis that my primary difficulty in recent months has been, not the fear of becoming involved in war, but an uneasy conscience about living in security while other men are dying for principles in which I very much believe. The question whether or not we should declare war is therefore not primarily one of morals but of strategy in the sense that I believe we ought to do whatever has to be done to prevent the triumph of this intolerable tyranny.

This assertion brings us immediately to the deeper issues involved in the religious presuppositions of our moral judgments. As I understand those who regard such a position as I have stated with abhorrence to believe, to quote a recent letter in *The Christian Century,* that we are " crucifying the Lord afresh," they hold that the avoidance of conflict is in some sense the realization of the Christian law of love. They judge men's virtue by the degree of their noninvolvement in conflict. Thus *The Christian Century,* in the months just preceding the invasion of the Low Countries, spoke of the little neutral nations as the " custodians " of European civilization. The nations at conflict had forfeited civilization since, in the view of *The Christian Century*, it is not possible to preserve civilization in conflict because war is the negation of civilization. I find it a little amusing to prefer Latvia to Great Britain as to the quality of its civilization because the one was at war and the other one was not, more particularly so since Latvia, and many similar small neutral nations, rather suddenly lost both their virtue and their lives by being gobbled up.

PERFECTIONISM AND HISTORICAL REALITY

The fact is that this whole pitiless perfectionism, which has informed a large part of liberal Protestantism in America, is wrong not only about this war and the contemporary international situation. It is wrong about the whole nature of historical reality. It worries about some of us " crucifying the Lord afresh " by being involved in war and does not recognize that the selfishness of the best of us is constantly involved in the sin of crucifying the Lord afresh. It thinks there is some simple method of extricating ourselves from conflict, when as a matter of fact all justice that the world has ever known has been established through tension between various vitalities, forces, and interests in society. All such tension is covert conflict and all covert conflict may on occasion, and must on occasion, become overt.

The premium placed by some of our liberal Protestants upon neutrality, upon noninvolvement in war, is not merely an error in the present situation. It is a perennial source of error in judging all history. It has sought to make a success story out of the story of the cross, and has admonished men to be resolute in sacrificing their lives and interests because in that way they would not have to sacrifice their lives and interests, for their goodness would shame their enemy into goodness so that he would cease to imperil them. They do not understand that the perfect love of Christ comes into the world, but that it does not maintain itself there; that the cross therefore stands at the edge of history and not squarely in history; that it reveals what history ought to be but not what history is or can be; and that Christian faith has quite rightly seen in this cross a revelation of the nature of the divine and eternal as well as of the ultimate historical possibility and impossibility.

Christ reveals the mercy of God, and the gospel declares that everyone is in need of that mercy, that without it we are undone. Why? Because all of us continue to be, even in our highest moral achievements, in contradiction to God and therefore require his mercy. This is to say that Christ is not our simple possibility. In one sense he is not our possibility at all but a revelation of the resources of divine mercy, which knows how to overcome the sinful contradiction of human history to its true pattern. Most of our liberal Protestantism has neatly disavowed all the profounder elements of the gospel, which reveal the tragic character of history, and has made the gospel identical with the truism that all men ought to be good and with the falsehood that goodness pays. The end of pure goodness, of perfect love, is the cross.

There is, of course, a place in Christian thought and life for the kind of goodness that knows martyrdom to be its end and that declares that rather than be involved in the claims and counterclaims of politics, in the struggle for justice with its ambiguous means and its dubious and speculative ends (there is always a risk that the struggle for justice will result not in justice but in anarchy), it would prefer to be defrauded and to die. There is a place for such perfectionism as a symbol of the Kingdom of God, lest we accept the tragic sin in which the struggle for justice involves us as ultimately normative.

There is a place for that kind of perfectionist pacifism, but we have precious little of it in America because most of our pacifism springs from an unholy compound of gospel perfectionism and bourgeois utopianism, the latter having had its rise in eighteenth-century rationalism. This kind of pacifism is not content with martyrdom and with political irresponsibility. It is always fashioning political alternatives to the tragic business of resisting tyranny and establishing justice by coercion. However it twists and turns, this alternative is revealed upon close inspection to be nothing more than capitulation to tyranny. Now capitulation to tyranny in the name of nonresistant perfection may be very noble for the individual. But it becomes rather ignoble when the idealist suggests that others besides himself shall be sold into slavery and shall groan under the tyrant's heel.

CONNIVANCE WITH TYRANNY

Our American Christian isolationists have had the greatest difficulty in obscuring the fact (which they consciously deny) that in terms of practical politics their policies lead to the acceptance of, or connivance with, tyranny. They profess to be horrified by criticisms that are made of Colonel Lindbergh. Does he not desire peace and ought the apostles of peace be thus vilified? they ask. But they neglect to point out that his peace policy means connivance with tyranny in very precise terms. In the *Nofrontier News Service,* a pacifist organ, we read in the issue of October 22 that it, the news service, is "able to state categorically" that rumors of a certain peace move "are true"; that in this peace move the Germans offered Britain, among other things, the opportunity to "take over all the French colonies" and "to control the United States economic sphere"; that negotiations over these proposals were "brought to a halt by the understanding arrived at between England and the United States including the destroyer-naval base swap." The news service makes this information public because "the American people have a right to know of the responsibility their Government has taken upon itself in causing the war to be carried on in an ever-widening sphere." I am not as certain as this news service that the rumor it reports is true. But that is irrelevant. I find it very shocking that it should assume so naïvely that any kind of peace, involving even the most dishonorable sacrifice of the interests of other nations, is preferable to carrying on the war.

No matter how they twist and turn, the protagonists of a political, rather than a religious, pacifism end with the acceptance and justification of, and connivance with, tyranny. They proclaim that slavery is better than war. I beg leave to doubt it and to challenge the whole system of sentimentalized Christianity that prompts good men to arrive at this perverse conclusion. This system must be challenged, not only in this tragic hour of the world's history, lest we deliver the last ramparts of civilization into the hands of the new barbarians. It must be challenged in peace and in war because its analysis of human nature and human history is fundamentally false.

60. THE CHRISTIAN FAITH
AND THE WORLD CRISIS

It is our purpose to devote this modest journal to an exposition of our Christian faith in its relation to world events. This first article will therefore seek to offer a general introduction to the faith that is in us. We believe that many current interpretations have obscured important elements in that faith and have thereby confused the Christian conscience. This confusion has been brought into sharp relief by the world crisis; but it existed before the crisis, and it may well continue after the crisis is over. We therefore regard our task as one that transcends the urgent problems of the hour, though we do not deny that these problems are the immediate occasion for our enterprise.

At the present moment a basic difference of conviction with regard to what Christianity is, and what it demands, runs through the whole of American Protestantism and cuts across all the traditional denominational distinctions. There is, on the one hand, a school of Christian thought that believes that war could be eliminated if only Christians and other men of good will refused resolutely enough to have anything to do with conflict. Another school of thought, while conceding that war is one of the most vivid revelations of sin in human history, does not find the disavowal of war so simple a matter. The proponents of the latter position believe that there are historic situations in which refusal to defend the inheritance of civilization, however imperfect, against tyranny and aggression may result in consequences even worse than war.

This journal intends to express and, if possible, to clarify this second viewpoint. We do not believe that the Christian faith as expressed in the New Testament and as interpreted in historic Christianity, both Catholic and Protestant, implies the confidence that evil and injustice in history can be overcome by such simple methods as are currently equated with Christianity. We believe that modern Christian perfectionism is tinctured with utopianism derived from a secular culture. In our opinion this utopianism contributed to the tardiness of the democracies in defending themselves against the perils of a new barbarism, and (in America at

Christianity and Crisis, first issue of the journal, February 10, 1941.

least) it is easily compounded with an irresponsible and selfish nationalism.

POLEMIC AND IRENIC PURPOSE

We intend this journal to be both polemic and irenic, as far as human frailty will permit the combination of these two qualities. It will be polemic in the sense that we shall combat what seem to us false interpretations of our faith, and consequent false analyses of our world and of our duties in it. It will be irenic in the sense that we will seek to appreciate the extent to which perfectionist and pacifist interpretations of Christianity are derived from genuine and important elements in our common faith.

Perfectionists are right in their conviction that our civilization stands under the judgment of God; no one can have an easy conscience about the social and political anarchy out of which the horrible tyranny that now threatens us arose. But they are wrong in assuming that we have no right or duty to defend a civilization, despite its imperfections, against worse alternatives. They are right in insisting that love is the ultimate law of life. But they have failed to realize to what degree the sinfulness of all men, even the best, makes justice between competing interests and conflicting wills a perennial necessity of history.

The perfectionists rightly recognize that it may be very noble for an individual to sacrifice his life or interests rather than participate in the claims and counterclaims of the struggle for justice (of which war may always be the ultima ratio). They are wrong in making no distinction between an individual act of self-abnegation and a political policy of submission to injustice, whereby lives and interests other than our own are defrauded or destroyed. They seek erroneously to build a political platform upon individual perfection. Medieval perfectionism, whatever its limitations, wisely avoided these errors. It excluded even the family from the possible consequences of an individual's absolute ethic, and it was profoundly aware of the impossibility of making its rigorous standards universal.

We believe that there are many Christians whose moral inclinations might persuade them to take the same view of current problems as our own, except for the fact that they are inhibited by religious presuppositions that they regard as more " purely " Christian than those represented by the consensus of the church through all the ages. Therefore we will begin with an analysis of these religious presuppositions.

RELIGIOUS ISSUES

Christians are agreed that the God who is revealed in Christ is source and end of our existence and that therefore his character and will are the norm and standard of our conduct. It is only in recent decades, however, that it has been believed that the " gentleness " of Jesus was a sufficient and final revelation of the character of God, that this character was one of pure love and mercy, and that this revelation stood in contradiction to an alleged portrayal of a God of wrath in the Old Testament.

Both the Old and the New Testament take the wrath of God as well as the mercy of God seriously. The divine mercy, apprehended by Christian faith in the life and death of Christ, is not some simple kindness that is indifferent to good and evil. The whole point of the Christian doctrine of atonement is that God cannot be merciful without fulfilling within himself, and on man's behalf, the requirements of divine justice. However difficult it may be to give a fully rational account of what Christ's atoning death upon the cross means to Christian faith, this mystery, never fully comprehended by and yet not wholly incomprehensible to faith, speaks to us of a mercy that transcends but also satisfies the demands of justice.

The Biblical answer to the problem of evil in human history is a radical answer, precisely because human evil is recognized as a much more stubborn fact than is realized in some modern versions of the Christian faith. These versions do not take the problem of justice in history seriously, because they have obscured what the Bible has to say about the relation of justice to mercy in the very heart of God. Every sensitive Christian must feel a sense of unworthiness when he is compelled by historic destiny to act as an instrument of God's justice. Recognition of the common guilt that makes him and his enemy kin must persuade him to imitate the mercy of God, even while he seeks to fulfill the demands of justice. But he will seek to elude such responsibilities only if he believes, as many modern Christians do, that he might, if he tried a little harder, achieve an individual or collective vantage point of guiltlessness from which to proceed against evildoers. There is no such vantage point.

ETHICAL ISSUES

Christians are agreed that Christ must be the norm of our human life as well as the revelation of the character of God. But many modern versions of Christianity have forgotten to what degree the perfect love of Christ was recognized both in the Bible and in the Christian ages as finally transcending all historic possibilities. The same Saint Paul who admonishes us to grow into the stature of Christ insists again and again that we are " saved by faith " and not " by works "; which is to say that our final peace is not the moral peace of having become what Christ defines as our true nature, but is the religious peace of knowing that a divine mercy accepts our loyalty to Christ despite our continued betrayal of him.

It cannot be denied that these emphases are full of pitfalls for the faithful. On the one side there is always the possibility that we will not take Christ as our norm seriously enough, and that we will rest prematurely in the divine mercy. On the other hand, an abstract perfectionism is tempted to obscure the most obvious facts about human nature and to fall into the fury of self-righteousness. The Protestant Reformation was in part a protest against what seemed to the Reformers a too optimistic Catholic doctrine of human perfection through the infusion of divine grace. Yet modern Protestant interpretations of the same issue make the Catholic doctrine wise and prudent by comparison.

Once it is recognized that the stubbornness of human selfishness makes the achievement of justice in human society no easy matter, it ought to be possible to see that war is but a vivid revelation of certain perennial aspects of human history. Life is never related to life in terms of a perfect and loving conformity of will with will. Where there is sin and selfishness there must also be a struggle for justice; and this justice is always partially an achievement of our love for the other, and partially a result of our yielding to his demands and pressures. The intermediate norm of justice is particularly important in the institutional and collective relationships of mankind. But even in individual and personal relations the ultimate level of sacrificial self-giving is not reached without an intermediate level of justice. On this level the first consideration is not that life should be related to life through the disinterested concern of each for the other, but that life should be prevented from exploiting, enslaving, or taking advantage of other life. Sometimes this struggle takes very tragic forms.

It is important for Christians to remember that every structure of justice, as embodied in political and economic institutions: (*a*) contains elements of injustice that stand in contradiction to the law of love; (*b*) that it contains higher possibilities of justice that must be realized in terms of institutions and structures; and (*c*) that it must be supplemented by the graces of individual and personal generosity and mercy. Yet when the mind is not confused by utopian illusions it is not difficult to recognize genuine achievements of justice and to feel under obligation to defend them against the threats of tyranny and the negation of justice.

Love must be regarded as the final flower and fruit of justice. When it is substituted for justice it degenerates into sentimentality and may become the accomplice of tyranny.

INTERNATIONAL ISSUES

Looking at the tragic contemporary scene within this frame of reference, we feel that American Christianity is all too prone to disavow its responsibilities for the preservation of our civilization against the perils of totalitarian aggression. We are well aware of the sins of all the nations, including our own, that have contributed to the chaos of our era. We know to what degree totalitarianism represents false answers to our own unsolved problems, political, economic and spiritual.

Yet we believe the task of defending the rich inheritance of our civilization to be an imperative one, however much we might desire that our social system were more worthy of defense. We believe that the possibility of correcting its faults and extending its gains may be annulled for centuries if this external peril is not resolutely faced. We do not find it particularly impressive to celebrate one's sensitive conscience by enlarging upon all the well-known evils of our Western world and equating them with the evils of the totalitarian systems. It is just as important for Christians to be discriminating in their judgments as for them to recognize the element of sin in all human endeavors. We think it dangerous to allow religious sensitivity to obscure the fact that Nazi tyranny intends to annihilate the Jewish race, to subject the nations of Europe to the dominion of a " master " race, to extirpate the Christian religion, to annul the liberties and legal standards that are the priceless heritage of ages of Christian and humanistic culture, to make truth the prostitute of political power, to seek world dominion through its satraps and allies, and generally to destroy the very fabric of our Western civilization.

Our own national tardiness in becoming fully alive to this peril has been compounded of national selfishness and religious confusion. In recent months American opinion has begun to respond to the actualities of the situation and to sense the fateful destiny that unites us with all free peoples, whether momentarily overrun by the aggressor or still offering heroic resistance. How far our assistance is to be carried is a matter of policy and strategy. It could be a matter of principle only if it were conceded that an absolute line could be drawn in terms of Christian principle between " measures short of war " and war itself. But those who think such a line can be drawn have nevertheless opposed measures short of war. They rightly have pointed out that such measures cannot be guaranteed against the risk of total involvement.

The measures now being taken for the support of the democracies are a logical expression of the unique conditions of America's relation to the world. They do justice on the one hand to our responsibilities for a common civilization that transcends the hemispheres, and on the other hand to the fact that we are not as immediately imperiled as other nations. Whether our freedom from immediate peril will enable us to persevere in the reservations that we still maintain cannot be decided in the abstract. The exigencies of the future must determine the issue.

We cannot, of course, be certain that a defeat of the Nazis will usher in a new order of international justice in Europe and the world. We do know what a Nazi victory would mean; and our first task must therefore be to prevent it. It cannot be our only task. The problem of organizing the technical civilization of the Western world upon a new basis of economic and international justice, so that the anarchy and decay that have characterized our life in the past three decades will be arrested, and our technical capacities will be made fruitful rather than suicidal, is one that must engage our best resources. We must give some thought and attention to this great issue even while we are forced to ward off a horrible alternative.

We believe that the Christian faith can and must make its own contribution to this issue. The task of building a new world, as well as the tragic duty of saving the present world from tyranny, will require resources of understanding and resolution that are inherent in the Christian faith. The profoundest insights of the Christian faith cannot be expressed by the simple counsel that men ought to be more loving, and that if they became so, the problem both of war and of international organization would solve itself.

Yet there are times when hopes for the future, as well as contrition over past misdeeds, must be subordinated to the urgent, immediate task. In this instance, the immediate task is the defeat of Nazi tyranny. If this task does not engage us, both our repentance and our hope become luxuries in which we indulge while other men save us from an intolerable fate, or while our inaction betrays into disaster a cause to which we owe allegiance.

61. PACIFISM AND "AMERICA FIRST"

A recent development in the antiwar and isolationist movement may, if fully analyzed, throw some interesting light upon the whole religious history of America in the past decades. This development is the increasingly intimate relation between pacifist groups and the " America First " movement.

At a recent Lindbergh meeting, Dr. John Haynes Holmes offered the invocation and another nationally known pacifist clergyman is reported to have sent a letter of endorsement. The " Ministers No War " committee, which is alleged to be receiving support from the " America First " committee, has now sponsored a new movement, the " Churchmen's Campaign for Peace Through Mediation." According to the chairman, Dr. Albert W. Palmer, this movement will be patterned closely after that carried on by Senator Burton K. Wheeler and Colonel Charles A. Lindbergh and the "America First " committee. Furthermore, many pacifist clergymen have openly joined the " America First " committee, although this committee believes in the strongest possible military and naval defense of our hemisphere.

This increasingly intimate relation between those who are supposedly religious absolutists and a political movement that has no trace of religious idealism or perfectionism in its program must be understood in the light of the criticisms leveled by the religious perfectionists against those of us who believe that our Christian faith is not incompatible with our conviction that tyranny must be resisted. We are told that God may have winked at the times of man's ignorance, but since the discovery of the "historical Jesus" and his "way of love" it is no longer possible for Christians to be identified with any political movement except one that is based upon the program of "perfect love." The mail of every interventionist Christian leader is filled with letters accusing him of "crucifying the Lord afresh," of being a "traitor to the gospel," and of "being unworthy of his Christian calling."

The presupposition of all this criticism is, of course, that there is a "gospel" political program, based upon the Sermon on the Mount, and that anyone who engages in the rather dreadful but necessary business of resisting aggression and defying tyranny is untrue to his Christian faith. Many of the critics admonish the victims of their criticisms to "love" Hitler; and manage in the same breath to pour such maledictions upon those in the household of faith with whom they disagree that one is tempted to suggest that "love" which they would lavish upon Hitler might appropriately be extended to fellow Christians who happen to have a different interpretation of the meaning of the Christian faith than those critics.

It has always been apparent that most of these criticisms proceed from a type of religious liberalism that has only the scantest understanding of political realities and an almost equally limited understanding of the final demands of the Christian ethic, which transcends all historic existence and is yet never irrelevant to any historic action. If either politics or the final demands that God makes upon the human conscience were clearly understood, it would have been apparent, long before a tragic war situation clarified the point, that there is no political program that stands in a direct relation to the ethic of the Sermon on the Mount, and that the only personal ethic that stands in such a relation is one that prompts the earnest believer to choose martyrdom rather than resistance to evil (a course of action that only a few perfectionists have ever followed consistently with reference to their own interests). So great is the confusion of the champions and protagonists of "love" in politics and life about the relation of the absolute demands of God upon our conscience and the relative evil of all our actions that many of them work themselves into a perfect fury in criticizing their foes, not recognizing that the identification of our relative political and moral perspectives with the absolute will of God is sin in its quintessential form. Those of us who are nonresisters in politics are in fact constantly confronted with the difficult spiritual task of trying to be nonresisters toward unjust accusations of those who profess nonresistance as a creed. One must exempt from this charge, of course, the genuine religious perfectionists who do not mix politics with their creed of perfection and who give proof of that " broken spirit and contrite heart " which ideally still preserve the " unity in Christ " between those who have different political convictions.

Since it is precisely the political school, rather than the more purely religious type of pacifism, that is most cruel and self-righteous in condemning its foes, it is important to analyze the political creed with which it identifies itself increasingly. Is there anything of the Sermon on the Mount in this political creed? Is there any touch of gospel perfection in it? To answer that question let us look at the latest pronouncements of Mr. Lindbergh and Senator Wheeler, made at a recent " America First " rally.

Mr. Lindbergh declares himself " ready to fight anybody and everybody who attempts to interfere with our hemisphere " and he believes that we can " rely upon our own strength, our own ability, and our own courage to preserve this nation and to defeat anyone who is rash enough to attack us." If there is anything in the gospel that outlaws all wars except those with hemispheric defense as their purpose, we have not been properly instructed in the Scripture. Admitting that hemispheric defense is a highly relative political objective, why should it be more Christian to believe that the hemisphere can be defended by military might alone than to believe, as many of us do, that a Nazi victory will make the defense of South America practically impossible?

National Self-interest

One of the main planks in the " America First " platform is that we must rely purely upon our own resources. Mr. Lindbergh declares that we " can compete in commerce or in war with any combination of foreign powers " and Senator Wheeler asserts that " no nation dependent upon another is or can be an independent nation." One wonders whether, by that standard, there has ever been an independent nation, for certainly there have been few nations in the history of the world who could match the combined might of all other nations. The idea that America can stand alone and preserve all the virtues of its present civilization, even if forced to defend its heritage against a totalitarian world, belongs in the category of military and political strategy. We know of no religion that throws any light upon such strategic questions. In so far as there are moral implications in this problem of strategy, we should have thought that a policy that emphasizes that we are "members one of another" would be a little nearer to a gospel ethic than one that rests upon American pride.

An ironic aspect of this strange alliance between Christian idealists and the protagonists of national self-interest in its narrowest terms was made apparent in the President's address to the nation on May 27. The President was careful to justify his course of defense purely to our hemisphere. Of course, he did try to extend the concept of hemispheric defense so that it would include more than the repulsion of an actual invasion and would anticipate strategic movements that might make invasion by the enemy easier. But he did not dare go beyond that in the hope of finding a formula that would broaden the basis of unity for this sadly divided nation.

Nevertheless, the emphasis was so strongly upon our own interests and our own defense that one wonders what "Christian idealists" think of this limitation upon national policy, forced upon the Government by their intimate allies, the proponents of "America First." Does it sound very "Christian" to them? If it does, what becomes of their criticism of other nations and empires who are accused of lacking Christian principles because they act only when their own interests are involved?

We understand, of course, better than the Christian idealists, that geography sets certain limits to moral principles in politics, and that no degree of moral imagination can make a European nation out of one that must have its eyes upon two oceans and that enjoys the comparative security of its own continent. Nevertheless, one would expect Christians to have a certain sense of uneasiness about these geographic limitations rather than to revel in them.

POLITICAL AND SPIRITUAL DEFEATISM

Mr. Lindbergh has reiterated in his recent address, what he has constantly asserted, that one reason he is opposed to America's entry into the war is because the Allies had lost the war before they began it. " I knew," he said, " that Britain and France were not in a position to win and I did not want them to lose." Here again is a strategic issue. Does such defeatism on a strategic question have more gospel warrant than a more hopeful view? Since unwillingness to join issue with a ruthless opponent inevitably invites further and further encroachments, must we be driven to the conclusion that it is " unchristian " to challenge an enemy because one's own previous Governments were foolish enough to allow that enemy to gain air superiority?

Another basic tenet of " America First " is, in the words of Mr. Lindbergh, that " democracy is not likely to survive such a conflict," and in the words of Senator Wheeler that " if we enter the conflict, we will become in that moment a regimented nation — and from such a state democracy could hardly be restored." It must be observed that some members of " America First " mean by " democracy," in the words of Archibald MacLeish, "the chance to make ten millions in the market." But even supposing their devotion to essential democracy to be genuine, are we to regard the political dictum that the inevitable restrictions of liberty in time of war lead to the permanent destruction of democracy to be a particularly " Christian " judgment? It is a judgment frequently made by all kinds of libertarians who equate democracy with the right of everyone to do as he pleases. Granting that the burdens of war subject a national social system to great strains that might, if the social system is very unhealthy, lead to its destruction, is it more " Christian " to believe that one cannot oppose tyranny without becoming transmuted into a tyranny than to believe that submission to tyranny presents a nation with a more intolerable fate? Must one, in order to be a Christian, really believe that democratic values are more imperiled in Britain than in France and that, whatever the outcome of the war, Britain would have a more tolerable democracy if she had followed one Munich with a dozen more Munichs?

If this is really a " Christian " judgment, then Christianity dooms us to slavery. For to say that democracy cannot resist tyranny without becoming totalitarian is to seal the doom of democracy. Any democratic civilization that believed such a dictum would have to yield to every demand of the dictators, and would invite the dictators to make constantly fresh demands, in the certain knowledge that the democratic civilization that they were bent upon destroying was inhibited by fears and scruples from offering effective resistance.

What strange strategic and political philosophies have achieved the aura of sanctity under the ministration of our religious perfectionists! What curious doctrines may be preached in the name of the "gospel" while those of us who believe that we owe an obligation to protect our own and other peoples' liberties, by resistance if necessary, are consigned to the outer hell reserved for apostates!

IDEA OF A NEGOTIATED PEACE

The final dictum that brings "America First," the "Ministers No War" committee, and the religious "Churchmen's Campaign for Peace Through Mediation" closer together than any other, is the idea that a negotiated peace is possible at the present time and that it represents a real alternative to what is admittedly a dark future for all of us as we assume the task of continued resistance. Here Senator Wheeler and Stanley Jones speak the same language and utter the same ideas. Senator Wheeler declares: "You, Mr. President, could appeal to the world for peace. You could appeal not to Hitler, not to Mussolini or to Churchill, but to the people of Germany, Italy, and Japan. You could demand that the warmakers, the Hitlers of Germany, the Churchills of England, and the Knoxes and Stimsons step down and out. I believe you could bring about the peace of the world, if you would." This curious appeal reaches the limits of unrealistic politics. How are Hitler and Mussolini to be overthrown without a military defeat? Does Senator Wheeler know of anyone who is making a similar appeal in Germany? Does he know how the people of Germany can be reached by such an appeal?

This idea of a peace through mediation has become the particular vehicle of "religious idealism" in this final hour of America's decision. Some of its proponents distinguished themselves at the outbreak of the war by asking the President to set up a perpetual peace conference consisting of Italy (at that time not in the war) and of the small nations of Europe who have since been swallowed up. This was heralded as a possible "diplomacy in the grand style." Must one really believe such political nonsense in order to be a "Christian"? And must one now believe that a totalitarian tyranny that is within an ace of victory (at least in its own estimation), which controls practically the whole Continent of Europe, which has good prospects of controlling South America as well, and which regards the political confusion expressed in these very fantasies as one of its assets, would be ready to offer a "decent" peace? Must one really be a sophomore in matters of politics and strategy in order to be a Christian?

CONFUSION IN RELIGIOUS PERFECTIONISM

The fact is, that every one of the propositions, political, strategic, and moral that Christians are asked to accept as a more " idealistic " solution of the world's problems than that which the rest of us, who know of no way of defeating tyranny without resisting it, can offer, is a revelation of the spiritual and moral confusion that has characterized so much of our Protestant Christianity in recent decades. A religious perfectionism that shuns the realities of politics in one moment and embraces the sorriest political relativities in the next is the natural fruit of decades of sentimentality in which religious absolutes were regarded as easily achieved goals of political justice. It is the fruit of a " religious idealism " that never gauged the tragic factors of human sin in human history adequately. It was an idealism ostensibly devoted to the " truth," but yet unwilling to face the truth about man. It met every attempt to face the human situation realistically with the admonition that we must not " discourage " man. If he were to learn what depths of evil there are in his soul and to what depths of malignancy his common life might sink, he might not continue to be " idealistic." As a consequence this whole culture is unable to gauge the peril that it faces. It may well be that our civilization will not survive. It has been too filled with sentimental and utopian illusions to know what a precious and precarious thing any achievement of human justice is, how easily it can be destroyed by the vicissitudes of history, and how readily it may succumb to the decay that it has itself nourished.

If it does not survive, it would be a quite appropriate though terrible fate if its final destruction should have been hastened by the fantasies of religious idealists who had, in the words of Karl Barth, " mistaken humility before the foe for humility before God "; who had involved themselves in American pride in their effort to state the gospel truth that all men are sinners (having failed to include America in this sweeping judgment) ; and who had imagined that the peace that Vichy enjoys was somehow closer to the peace of the Kingdom of God than the horrible realities of war. One might dismiss all these confusions as the mistakes of good people who are ignorant of the realities of politics and strategy. But the fact is that every mistake points to, and is derived from, a basically false analysis of human history and human nature.

We are living in a tragic era in which no alternatives are pleasant and every possible policy presents hazards and uncertainties. In such a situation it is important to remember that equally sincere men will choose courses that will seem abhorrent one to the other. In this situation there can be " unity in Christ " only on the highest level of religious experience, at which point we know both ourselves and our foes, whether they be Nazis or those who would come to terms with them, to be equally in need of divine mercy.

If, however, political utopianism is substituted for this ultimate reconciliation in Christ, and if those who do not believe in this kind of utopianism are cast into outer darkness and accused of apostasy, then the apostles of reconciliation become the bearers of a moral fury that knows nothing of reconciliation because it knows nothing of the universality of human sin. Seeking to establish a sinless position in politics, it ends by involving itself in a political program that regards capitulation to tyranny or illusions in regard to the realities of the struggle as more sinless or more Christian than the alternative policy.

It is necessary for us who do not agree with this program not only to express our opinion that it represents bad politics, but also that it is derived from bad religion. The political confusions in it arise from religious illusions. This is the final fruit of a theological movement that thinks that the Kingdom of God is a simple extension of human history and that men may progress from the one to the other at any time if they have become sufficiently courageous, pure, and selfless. All such illusions finally end in disaster. Communist utopianism ends in the sorry realities of Stalinism, and this liberal-Christian utopianism ends by giving the dubious politics of " America First " the sanctity of the Sermon on the Mount.

62. HISTORY (GOD) HAS OVERTAKEN US

For years we argued whether or not we should go to war. The implicit assumption of all these arguments was that we had the complete power to make this decision. Then history descended upon us

Christianity and Society, Winter, 1941.

and took the decision out of our hands. We might have known that it would be like this. History is not as completely under the control of human decisions as either the interventionists or pacifists assumed.

The interventionists wanted us to go to war by a clear moral decision. The isolationists thought we could stay out if only we willed to do so resolutely enough. The isolationists underestimated the element of " fate " in history, the fact that the decisions of others frequently take the initiative out of our hands. The interventionists overestimated our power of will. They (or let us say we) argued that our moral obligation to the community of free nations required our participation. Or they contended that our own national self-interest required that we act. They were right on both counts. They did not recognize the " defect of our will," or understand that over all human actions, and possibly over collective actions particularly, there hangs the terrible truth of the confession, " The will indeed is present with me but how to perform that which is good I know not." This is to say that ideally we ought to resist injustice done to others as much as we resist it when done to ourselves. But we do not. The force of self-interest alone finally makes the will strong enough to meet its obligations to others.

In collective life our inability to act is further increased by the fact that we cannot consider our own peril if it is not immediate or obvious. Our self-interest is, therefore, not wise enough to come to the support of our sense of obligation to others until we stand in immediate peril. However important the national unity, achieved under Japanese attack, may be from a political standpoint, it cannot be denied that there is something pathetic about it from the moral standpoint. Only it must be understood that it is a pathos that all human actions betray, and that collective actions only reveal more vividly. We could not agree upon the peril in which we stood as a national community until the peril was upon us; that is the stupidity of collective man. And we could not agree upon our responsibilities to the victims of aggression until we had been joined to them, not by moral act but by historical fate.

The cynics might draw the conclusion from this fact that man, particularly collective man, acts only from motives of self-interest. But that would be an erroneous interpretation of the human situation. Man is not totally depraved. Complete egoism would be total depravity. Man has a dim sense of awareness of his obligations to his fellows and a weak desire to fulfill those obligations. But the desire is not strong enough to produce action until self-interest and social interest reach some kind of coincidence. It is interesting to note that already the Wheelers and the Tafts and all that ilk, who yesterday insisted that Britain had nothing but national and imperial motives, today make virtue of the fact that it is our duty to " beat hell out of " our foes when their militarism challenges our liberties and not those of another nation only. Tomorrow they will be proving that we are fighting, not merely out of motives of self-interest, but to " preserve civilization."

They will be right about that too, as they were wrong about Britain when they contended that the admixture of national egoism completely excluded every other-regarding motive in British national policy. They will be right about us as they were wrong about Britain, because it is no more possible for us to act from motives of pure self-interest than it is to act from motives of pure social interest.

It is this fact that makes such nonsense of all purely moral interpretations of human action, and that tempts pure moralists to be either pharisees who have persuaded themselves that they are purely moral, or to be irresponsible, hoping for the day when they can act purely, and when they can find a political cause that will stand for international order without an admixture of self-interest or national prejudice.

The political life of man must drive pure moralists either to despair or to the fury of self-righteousness and sentimentality. It can be understood only from a profoundly religious standpoint. These two elements of cynicism and sentimentality have indeed been present in our whole modern culture. Our universities are filled with political scientists who either take adolescent delight in proving to their students that all nations are moved by self-interest alone, thus prompting them to an immoral cynicism, or who take an equally adolescent satisfaction in inventing schemes, either educational or political, that will make nations " unselfish."

We cannot contemplate our political life decently without a proper and grateful understanding of the " grace " of God. For the grace of God is on the one hand the providential working in history by which God makes the wrath of man to praise him, and transmutes good out of evil. In the immediate situation, that means that he persuades sinful men to consider the miseries and necessities of their fellow men by throwing them into like miseries and necessities. Of course, if there were no moral content in our life at all, if we were consistently selfish, even this experience would not make it possible for us to build communities and achieve just relations between ourselves and others, either individually or collectively. There is, therefore, no point where the grace of God destroys the moral content of our life by overriding the evil in us. Even now, while we have been thrown into the community of nations, it will be a matter with which our conscience must wrestle, whether or no we will remain in that community after the immediate peril is past. Without some moral response on our part, even the tragic experience of today will not avail us tomorrow. We might withdraw again from our international responsibilities at the end of this war in a mood of self-righteousness and irresponsibility, as we did after the World War.

The other element in divine " grace " is the element of forgiveness. If we cannot believe that God has resources to negate and to wipe out the corruption of egotism that all our actions betray, if we do not know that we are " justified " not by our goodness but by the goodness of God, we remain in the awful predicament of either trying to find a vantage point in history from which we can act " purely," or persuading ourselves that we have found such a vantage point and declaring a " holy war " from it. It is significant that the chief organ of Christian isolationism revealed how little it understood the ultimate meaning of the Christian faith by recent editorials in which it sought to persuade British Christians that they did not exhaust the full resources of their faith if they did not proclaim a " holy war."

Of course, there can be no acceptance of grace without repentance. If we do not understand how sinful even good nations are, we will have no gratitude toward a merciful providence that makes us do good against our will and gives us a chance to serve mankind, even though we want to serve ourselves. But, also, there can be no repentance without faith; for in that case the realization of the awful realities of man's collective life drives us to despair.

Despair is the fate of the realists who know something about sin, but nothing about redemption. Self-righteousness and irresponsibility is the fate of the idealists who know something about the good possibilities of life, but know nothing of our sinful corruption of it. They are, therefore, always looking for the other person or nation who has corrupted it. Thus they add the fury of moral pride to the sin of selfishness and bedevil the understanding of our common history by criticizing the British from the vantage point of the pure Americans, or the Jews from the vantage point of the good Christians, or the bad Continentals from the vantage point of the good Anglo-Saxons.

Let us hope that the catastrophes of these days will not only make us more resolute in achieving such justice and international community as sinful men may establish by the grace of God, but more humble and, therefore, more merciful in judging both our allies and our foes.

63. THE QUAKER WAY

In our dealings with Russia it is fairly clear that the peace of the world must be preserved for some decades to come by the preponderance of power in the West. It must be understood, however, that the power of which we are speaking is not merely military power. It is in fact not primarily military power. The Russians are challenging us primarily by moral and political means and our defense must be primarily moral and economic. If we can preserve and extend the moral health of the noncommunist world, we will preserve the preponderance of power. In an actual conflict military might is, of course, the ultima ratio. But the power by which conflict is avoided is primarily nonmilitary.

This method of preserving peace must not, of course, exclude continued contact with Russia. We must preserve the bridge between ourselves and Russia at almost any cost. But there are approaches to the present issue that make it appear that it might be easy to dissolve the Russian intransigence, if only we tried hard enough. Take for instance the Quaker proposals, recently published by the Yale University Press, entitled *The United Nations and the Soviet Union, Some Quaker Proposals for Peace*. In this document, which is a good deal more realistic than most pacifist approaches to the problems of our era, the chasm between ourselves and the Russians is nevertheless constantly underestimated by suggestions that it could be bridged if only we tried hard enough. Thus we read: " In the light of Quaker experience in dealing with human beings of many different nationalities and in all parts of the world, we believe that an extension of opportunities for personal relations between the Russians and Americans could benefit both peoples. Neither has a monopoly on either virtue or vice." There is first of all a certain pharisaism in that phrase "in the light of Quaker experience." The Quaker experience has indeed been rich. But even we who are, in their estimate, second-rate Christians know that such personal contacts are valuable. We also know that neither people has a monopoly on either virtue or vice. The Russian people are, in fact, wonderful people. But this sentence makes it appear that the primary difficulty lies in misunderstandings between the peoples, which is not a fact. Furthermore, it implies that we could establish such personal contacts if we tried resolutely enough. Former Ambassador Bedell Smith has just reported that he never ceased offering the Russians exchange scholarships, exchange professorships, and that he tried every other strategy for breaking the moral isolation of the people. But all has been to no avail. The Russian dictatorship cannot afford these interchanges. It keeps up a constant barrage of propaganda that makes the noncommunist world appear to be perishing in a mire of misery, and therefore it cannot afford to let the Russian people discover the truth. Bedell Smith tells us how difficult it was for the dictatorship to erase from the minds of the soldiers their sense of contrast between what the propaganda had said about the Western world and what they actually found.

We are told furthermore that both nations "claim their Governments to be democratic," although the Soviet definition of democracy has tended to emphasize "government for the people" whereas the United States has placed emphasis upon "government by the people." This idea that only a semantic difficulty separates us also has been tried recently by a U.N.E.S.C.O. project for the definition of "fundamental concepts." The truth in such statements is obvious enough. But they are also pious frauds if they are meant to imply that a little more semantic accuracy or a little more common experience will teach one side to add "for the people" and the other side "by the people."

That is the kind of debate which is actually going on between socialist Europe and capitalist America; we hope for the enlightenment of both sides. But the Russians are having no part in the debate. They seal off every organ of communication that would make an exchange of interpretations possible. Furthermore, a definition of Russian " democracy " that does not give a hint of the tragedy involved in the cynical corruption of the original Marxist democratic dream is misleading. It would even be misleading if it were assumed that the corruption were merely a Stalinist aberration and if it did not reveal that the degeneration from the democratic dream to the tyrannical realities is derived from serious miscalculations in the Marxist interpretations of the human situation. It is precisely because Russian communism legitimatizes a corrupt politics by utopian illusions that it is so dangerous to the world and so blinding to its devotees.

The Quaker proposals go on blandly to offer all kinds of advice on specific issues without revealing how difficult it is to follow the advice. Thus we are told: " United States policy should have as its objective the conclusion of a general peace treaty with a unified Germany, the inclusion of Germany in the United Nations and its related agencies, and the establishment of all possible safeguards to insure that Germany's strategic position between the East and West will not result in increased tensions between the two power blocs." As if this bland solution of the vexing problem did not obscure the depth of the whole tragic situation in which we are involved! The Russians will not let go of their part of Germany if they do not get in return the dominance over the whole of Germany. That is why they refused a unified military control of Germany at the end of the war. Nor could we let go of our part of Germany if we thought that it might be subject to communist infiltration. After Russia's breaking of every agreement intended to guarantee a noncommunist but united front government in Poland, Rumania, and Hungary, we must obviously be wary of any similar agreements. This proposed solution therefore throws no light whatever upon what we have to do in the German question, any more than the general advice helps to solve the total question.

It is natural enough in tragic times that people should be tempted to seek for ways out of a great dilemma that reveal their inability to measure the proportions of the dilemma. But we hope that it will not be regarded as particularly " Christian " to close one eye because the reality that breaks upon the sight of both eyes is too terrible to contemplate.

64. IS THERE ANOTHER WAY?

There are many parts of the Quaker approach to world problems with which I personally agree and that are in full accord with the foreign policy platform of Americans for Democratic Action. Among them are:

One — Insistence that the contest with communism, particularly in Asia and Africa, is conducted against the background of previous " imperialism " by the white nations and that our cause is gravely imperiled by residual resentments against " colonialism " and against the white man's arrogance toward the colored people. Any policy that corrects and expiates past evils is both morally and politically correct and better than undue reliance on military force. As A.D.A.'s 1955 platform declares:

" We need a policy not of massive retaliation but of massive renovation. We need a clearer view of the new place of Asia and Africa in world affairs, a more concrete and positive policy of opposition to surviving colonialism and racism. Only within such a context can programs of economic aid effectively contribute to the development of common self-interest between ourselves and the other peoples of the world and provide us with the power needed to force a worldwide retreat of communist totalitarianism."

Two — Our negative attitude toward our problems with communism, our preoccupation with its evils and our frantic ferreting out of " subversives " with little discrimination between genuine disloyalty and mere dissent, has lowered our prestige in the world and not aided us in the real contest. Happily the worst aspects of the psychosis known as " McCarthyism " seem to be overcome in the present more sober mood of the nation. A.D.A., however, like the Quaker approach, continues pledged " to inalienable rights of every American — freedom of speech, of thought, of inquiry, and of dissent. . . . We believe that the impairment of these liberties on any level, be it national, state, or local, violates the principles of democracy and saps the strength of a democratic society in its struggle against totalitarianism."

Three — Any undue reliance on military weapons in general, and atomic weapons in particular, and the concomitant neglect of all

Comment on a Quaker publication: " Speak Truth to Power," *The Progressive*, October, 1955.

political, economic, and moral policies that strengthen the unity
and health of the noncommunist world, is a grave error against
which all democratic forces must marshal all their strength.

We cannot, however, allow our knowledge of the limits of military
forces in the world community to persuade us to adopt the pacifist
disavowal of force as an end in itself. Force is merely the ultima ratio of political life. It cannot be disavowed even though every effort
must be made to keep it in its proper place.

Thus, holding that "American policy toward the Soviet bloc
must remain based on the assumption that Soviet policy is hostile to
all sources of power not amenable to its control" and that "military
weakness invites aggression," A.D.A. favors the building of our
armed strength. It maintains that "security without provocation
must be our policy toward the Soviet bloc, but that we should be
prepared to negotiate . . . whenever there is reasonable indication
that the Soviet group is willing to join in a bona fide effort to dis-
mantle some or all of the barriers that now divide their world and
ours."

Our points of agreement with the Quaker proposals, particularly
on policies that do not raise the ultimate issue of the disavowal of
force, cannot obscure the basic distinction between pacifist and nonpacifist policies. This distinction would seem to be on the absolute
disavowal of force by the pacifists.

But the difference between pacifism and nonpacifism actually is
more profound than the question of the use of force or "violence."
The document makes this profounder distinction quite clear. The
Quaker attitude toward political questions puts "power" and
"love" in contradiction to each other. This contradiction leaves
out the whole problem of the attainment of justice. Justice may be
the servant of love, and power may be the servant of justice. Every
historic form of justice has been attained by some equilibrium of
power. Force in the narrow sense may be an element in the arsenal
of power, but power is wider than force. It includes all the vitalities
of life by which men seek to accomplish their ends.

Power is not evil. It may be put in the service of good ends.
When the ends of men or nations conflict, the conflict may, of
course, issue in violence. All sensible people will seek to avoid these
violent conflicts whether on the national or international level. But
only if one adopts the principle that it is better to suffer injustice
than to resort to force can one wholly disavow the use of force. It is

possible, though not always advisable, for individuals to suffer injustice rather than let the dispute come to an ultimate issue. But statesmen, responsible for values beyond their own life, do not have this option. They must seek for justice by an accommodation of interests and they must protect precious values by force if necessary. Even the terrors of a possible atomic conflict cannot disengage them from such responsibilities, though it must naturally make them very hesitant to use a form of force that might spell mutual annihilation.

Every emphasis on the new dimension of destructiveness in war does not seriously alter the problem of the statesman's responsibility. It may persuade him, in the words of President Eisenhower, that " in an atomic age there is no alternative to peace," but it cannot persuade him to accept injustice or submission as the price of peace, particularly when the alternative is not between peace and war but between submission and the risk of war. We want our statesmen to be careful about that risk. But no nation will choose present submission as the alternative for a future risk. That is why pacifism remains an irrelevance even in an atomic age. But this need not prompt us to disrespect for the Quaker witness. That witness is most impressive in the Quaker works of mercy, and least impressive in all the problems of the political order where power must be placed in the service of justice, and where on occasion force may be legitimate in the arsenal of power and justice.

INDEX

LaVergne, TN USA
11 January 2011
211871LV00001B/215/A